The Union Prison
at Fort Delaware

The Union Prison at Fort Delaware

A Perfect Hell on Earth

BRIAN TEMPLE

McFarland & Company, Inc., Publishers

Jefferson, North Carolina, and London

To Martha, who knows
the value of dreams

Library of Congress Cataloguing-in-Publication Data

Temple, Brian, 1955–
The Union prison at Fort Delaware :
a perfect hell on earth / Brian Temple.
p.   cm.
Includes bibliographical references and index.

ISBN 0-7864-1480-4 (Illustrated case binding : 50# alkaline paper)

1. Fort Delaware (Del.)   2. United States — History — Civil War, 1861–1865 —
Prisoners and prisons.   3. Prisoners of war — Delaware — Fort Delaware —
History — 19th century.   4. Prisoners of war — Delaware — Fort Delaware —
Social conditions — 19th century.   I. Title.

E616.D3T46   2003   973.7'72 — dc21   2003001311

British Library cataloguing data are available

Cover illustration ©2002 Art Today

Manufactured in the United States of America

*McFarland & Company, Inc., Publishers
Box 611, Jefferson, North Carolina 28640
www.mcfarlandpub.com*

Contents

Preface

When I was eight years old, my Cub Scout pack went to Fort Mott, which is located along the New Jersey side of the Delaware River. As we stood on top of the dungeons, I looked out and saw a fortress sitting on an island in the middle of the river. I asked my Cub Scout leader what it was. "Oh," she said, "that's Pea Patch Island. It used to be a Civil War prison." That was the only answer she gave me.

As I went through school during the 1960s and early 1970s, there was never any mention of the Civil War prison that was less than ten miles away. No one I knew could even tell me how to get to it other than vague directions like "Go across the Delaware River and head south." That was all I knew about Fort Delaware, or the island it sat on, for many years.

One day, I took my wife and infant daughter to Fort Mott. I had just begun my writing career and was thinking out loud about what I could write next. My wife looked across the river and asked, "What's that over there?" I gave her the same answer I had received in Cub Scouts. Martha, who has the ability to get quickly to the heart of the matter, said, "Why don't you write about that?"

It was one of those moments when the lightbulb comes on over your head. I now had a goal not just for writing, but also for myself. I wanted to find out all about Pea Patch Island and its importance in the Civil War.

It was clear from the beginning of my research that relatively little had been published on Fort Delaware. Recent books had no information on Pea Patch Island or the fort; in fact, they barely mentioned prisoners or prison camps other than Andersonville. I was more intrigued than frustrated by the lack of information.

Fortunately, there was help available. The Fort Delaware Society was formed in 1950 to preserve the fort and to educate the public on its history. Their library is located in Delaware City. The librarian, Martha Bennett, gave graciously of her time and information. Every time I visited the society's library, Martha always had some new letter, diary, picture, or artifact to share with me. Without her help and the support of the Fort Delaware Society, I could not have written this book.

The Gloucester County (N.J.) Library was also very helpful in locating diaries and books on the fort. I used their interlibrary loan system so much that I became known as "that guy who gets all the Civil War books."

The Pennsville (N.J.) Public Library and the Salem County (N.J.) Historical Society were also a big help through their books and newspaper clippings, which gave me insight on how people who lived nearby were affected by the fort. Finally, the library at my alma mater, Rowan University, was almost as great a treasure trove of information as the Fort Delaware Society Library. I had plenty of information to study between the books, newspaper clippings, and diaries; their copy of the *Official Records of the Civil War*; and their excellent Stewart Collection.

Things have changed since I started researching this book. I can stand on the same spot where I first looked at Fort Delaware and also see a pier where, between April and September, a boat leaves on its scheduled trip to Delaware City and Fort Delaware. And to the question "What's that over there?" I can now give my children — and, I hope, my readers — a better answer.

Introduction

The Civil War was an event that scarred and shaped America like few have in its history. Arguments over states' rights and slavery pushed the country into a war that many thought would not last more than a few weeks. Instead, it was a conflict that lasted four years and the repercussions of that war lingered long after the last battle had been fought. What is sometimes forgotten is that there was an aftermath to these battles and the aftermath created a new series of battlegrounds. They were places where soldiers from both sides struggled and sometimes died. The battles fought there were not for honor and country, but for survival. The names of these battlegrounds are not as famous as Shiloh or Gettysburg, but the men who struggled there had no easier a time than the men on the battlefields. These places were the prison camps that were set up to house the prisoners of war.

Prison camps were first set up to merely hold prisoners until they could be exchanged. At the beginning of the war, that time would be only a few days or weeks. This system broke down due to the sheer number of prisoners both sides generated. When this happened, overcrowding took place in camps that were designed to hold a small number of prisoners. The overcrowding created unsanitary conditions in the prisons. Food shortages also became a part of the list of problems and the outcome was a dangerous situation for many of the men held in captivity. The stories told about the camps created dread in the heart of anyone on either side who had been captured.

The soldiers had every right to be afraid. During the course of the war, of the 194,743 Union soldiers held as prisoners in the South, approximately 30,218 died, which is 15.5 percent of all the Union troops held captive. On the other hand, of the 214,865 prisoners in Northern hands, approximately 25,976 died in Northern camps, which is 12 percent of the Confederate soldiers held.

This book is about one of those camps, situated on a small island in the middle of the Delaware River. The story of Fort Delaware does not begin with the Civil War. It reaches back to the creation of America, and its development was as complex as the war in which it saw its greatest service.

❧ 1 ❧

Construction of
Fort Delaware

In the late 18th century, America was still in its infancy, trying to find its own way like a child taking its first steps without any help. Unlike a child, the parent in this case was a former mother country that did not want the newly formed United States of America to walk on its own. Resentment had grown in England toward America because the new country was able to create a prosperous commercial trade in the years following the end of the Revolutionary War.[1] England and France were at war at this time and the British were not so inclined to respect the neutrality President Washington proclaimed in 1793. Any American ship that sailed was under the threat of attack from the dominant British fleets and there were concerns that the British could easily sail into any American bay or river and wreak havoc up and down the coastline. To counter that threat, plans were drawn up to create defensive positions around the country. Major Pierre L'Enfant, who was designing the new capital of Washington D.C., was assigned to inspect the Delaware River and Bay to see if and where new fortifications should be placed. He submitted his report to the Secretary of War on May 16, 1794. In it, he wrote that he believed a fort should be placed on Pea Patch Island, situated on the Delaware River opposite Eagle and Reedy Points near the entrance of the Delaware Bay. Major L'Enfant's opinion was that a fort should be erected there not for its commercial value, but because of its military importance. Placing a fort at this location would not only protect the entire Delaware coastline, but also serve as protection for the city of Philadelphia, the new nation's temporary capital city.[2] The report was not acted upon at that time, but it was filed away for future reference.[3]

Pea Patch Island received its name from a colonial legend that claimed that a ship filled with peas ran aground on a sandbar. The peas took root, dirt and sediment from the river collected around them, and eventually created the island.[4] Whether or not the story was true, the island was enlarged due to the dirt deposited by dredges being used to keep the channel in the river clear for ship traffic. The size of the island during colonial times was about 80 acres. The average level was 3 feet, 4 inches above sea level and 9 feet, 8 inches at its highest.[5] The island's greatest claims to fame during this time period were that it was a fishing resort and a popular place to shoot crows, of which there were many.[6] It remained as it was until the outbreak of the War of 1812. At that time, a British blockade squadron under the command of Admiral Sir John P. Beresford positioned itself at the entrance to the Delaware Bay. In early 1813, Admiral Beresford sailed his squadron into Delaware Bay and demanded from the town of Lewes, Delaware, "twenty live bullocks with a proportionate amount of vegetables and hay" to defray the strain of feeding his men. The people of Lewes refused and the town was fired upon. Fortunately for the towns-people, very little damage was done. Beresford then proceeded to work his way up the bay, attacking the settlements along the coast. This exercise in looting and torching towns came to an end when a flotilla, consisting of nineteen gunboats, sixteen armed barges, and two block sloops, made the British turn around.[7]

This incursion was all that was needed to get the government moving on protecting the Delaware Bay and River. The federal government contacted the Delaware legislature on its desire to have the island ceded over to it for the purpose of erecting fortifications on the land. The legislature voted on the proposal and it was passed.[8] These actions were met with approval by the people of Philadelphia. At that time, the only protection they had was Fort Mifflin, which was too close to the city and was not in good condition. A fort positioned at the base of the Delaware River would compel any foreign army to leave its ships far to the south of the city and march towards their objective. This would give the American army additional time to block the advance of the enemy before they could reach Philadelphia.[9]

On May 22, 1813, an engineer was requested by Brigadier General Joseph Bloomfield, the commander of the 4th Military District, to build the authorized fort on the island, as well as to help shore up the defenses at nearby Fort Mifflin and Philadelphia. Lieutenant Sylvanus Thayer, an engineer and deputy commissary of ordinance in New York, was sent to the island to begin work on drawing up plans for a fort. He submitted his plans to the War Department and no action was taken for another year. It took another assault, this time the two pronged attack by the British at New Orleans and up the Chesapeake Bay, to spur the government to act. Captain Samuel Babcock was sent from Baltimore to assess the situation and begin construction of fortifications at Pea Patch Island and at Red Bank on the New Jersey shore opposite Fort Mifflin, north of the island. The War Department also contacted the Committee of Safety of the Corporation of the City of Philadelphia to inform them of Captain Babcock's mission.[10] Committees, like the one in Philadelphia, sprang up in cities along the coastline during the war because they had a lack of trust in the federal government to protect them. The committees were made up of a cross-section of the most successful bankers, lawyers, and merchants in their cities. They would demand that any federal troops and engineers near them be placed at their disposal and the War Department had to pay for the cost of bringing out the local militia. The Philadelphia committee pushed hard to have the Army engineers build an elaborate system of defense along the Delaware River and to place a fort on Pea Patch Island.[11] Captain Babcock explained to them that the committee would be expected to defray the cost of the increased defenses. Babcock soon wrote back to Secretary of War Armstrong that the committee thought that the money they would put out was a loan and they expected to be repaid. He also stated that he was ready to begin the project as soon as the issue of payment was settled.

While Captain Babcock was waiting for the money problem to be resolved, the British advanced through the Chesapeake Bay, up the Potomac River, and torched Washington D.C.. Another force also went up the Patapsco River to try to attack Baltimore. Captain Babcock was immediately recalled to Baltimore to help in its defense. In September 1814, it was decided that the sinking of ships in the Delaware River to use as barriers, placing a ship with heavy guns near those ships, building an artillery battery of six 24-pound guns opposite Fort Mifflin, and Fort Mifflin itself should be enough to defend Philadelphia.[12]

After the War of 1812, the American government decided once again that a fort on Pea Patch Island was in the national interest. Captain Babcock was again sent to begin construction of fortifications. Money was appropriated and the project was started in 1818.[13] The foundation was created by driving pine logs of about thirty feet in length into the soft earth of the island. Then a layer of logs was laid flat on top of the foundation. Walls thirty feet high by about thirty feet in width were then placed into position.[14] The fort was finished in 1825[15] and the first complaint about the unhealthiness of the site was documented in the summer of 1826. The commander at the time protested that the fort was "one of, if not the most, sickly station in the whole nation." He also stated that the heat during July and August made it difficult to keep men stationed there. The adjutant general replied to Major A.C.W. Fanning, the commander, that he was authorized to take his troops down the river to make camp near Cape May, N.J. "for the duration of the sickly season." Cape May was and is a summer resort.[16]

The construction of the fort may have been finished, but it was not a sturdy building. Large cracks soon developed in the foundation and the fort was destroyed by fire in February 1831. The commander, Major Benjamin K. Pierce, brother of the future President Franklin Pierce, not only had to supervise the withdrawal of his men across an ice-filled river, but also had to transport the body of his wife who had died the day before.[17] Major Pierce took his men to the arsenal at New Castle, Delaware, and there Companies A and B of the 4th Artillery stayed until their barracks on the island were repaired.[18]

On April 18, 1833, General Order #32, written by Major General Macomb, declared that the fort would be called Fort Delaware. In the same year, Captain of the Engineers Richard Delafield was assigned to assume command of the rebuilding of the fort. Captain Delafield requested $10,000 so that the old buildings could be torn down and temporary quarters and workshops put up. A work force of one hundred men was brought onto Pea Patch Island to take down the remains of the old fort and to make protective works around the island to protect it from tidal damage.

On July 2, 1833, a lawyer came to the fort and demanded a list of the island's citizens. Mr. Belin, Captain Delafield's civilian assistant, refused to give him what he wanted. The lawyer then threatened to return in a few days with a "writ of ejectment." This was the beginning of a protracted legal battle for Pea Patch Island.[19] Dr. Henry Gale had bought the island in 1813 and created a fishery on it, which he maintained until he was removed by the United States government after Delaware gave the island to the nation. Dr. Gale's argument was that the island was within the boundaries of the State of New Jersey, not Delaware.[20] If the island was within New Jersey's boundaries, then the ceding the land by the State of Delaware to the federal government was an illegal action.[21] The battle for the ownership of the island raged on for years, but work continued at the fort. Large orders for bricks and stones were ordered in July and September of 1836 so that the foundation could be finished. Timber was also ordered in October of that year. Construction eventually came to a halt in 1838 to wait for the ownership controversy to end, with only 1095 piles in place of the 6594 needed to build the base of the fort.

Delaware was awarded ownership of Pea Patch Island in 1848[22] and it was then that the federal government finally became determined to finish the project. The year before, Congress had put aside 1 million dollars to turn Fort Delaware into the largest and most modern fortification in the United States. It was supposed to be larger than Fort Sumter at Charleston, S.C., which at the time was the largest fort in the country.[23] After the legal roadblocks were removed, Brevet Major John Sanders was ordered to the island to begin construction.[24] Sanders was an engineer who had studied at West Point, where he graduated second in his class in June 1834.[25] He directed improvements on the Ohio River above Louisville, Ky., from 1836 to 1841 and served with distinction in the Mexican War. He contracted diabetes at that time and suffered from ill health during his tenure at Fort Delaware.

Once he arrived at the fort, Major Sanders had an inventory taken of the equipment available for use. He had this done because of the length of time it had been since there had been any kind of construction activity going on at the island.[26] Another reason was because the island had been covered by a high tide two years earlier and he was concerned about the condition of the equipment.[27] The inventory showed that four steam engines needed extensive overhauling, boilers needed to be replaced, and timber and six scows were rotted beyond repair. The good news was that 42,000 feet of pile timber, 1.3 million bricks, and 19,000 tons of stone were mostly usable. The problem was that most of this equipment had to be moved because it was in the way of the new plan for excavation.

An embankment was built around the island for 1⅓ miles to protect the island from the river. Some stones were bought for that purpose, but most of them were taken from the debris of Major Babcock's old building. The new fort had a pentagon shape which was laid out over six acres.[28] Sanders used a steam pile driver of his own invention to drive the pilings into the island. Pea Patch Island had been formed in the center of an S-shaped bend of the river by alluvial deposits in the mostly still water. This action was due to the tide flooding and ebbing in turn on one bank and the other. The aggregate deposit was about 45 feet thick and rested on a coarse sand.[29] This made it essential to create a firm platform to build the fort on, otherwise it would suffer the same fate as the last attempt to build a fort on the island. One pile was driven into the ground for every 10½ square feet of surface, some as deep as seventy feet. The piles were then leveled off with whipsaws. This was done by digging up the ground around the pile head to make the cutting easier. The lower tier of grillage was fastened to the pile heads with oak treenails 18 inches long and 2½ inches in diameter. The upper tier was made up of one foot square timbers notched and spiked at 3½ foot intervals to the lower level, then dirt was rammed around the pile heads and grillage timbers. Then 4 inch thick planks were spiked to the lower timbers, which finished the grillage platform that the masonry of the fort was built upon.

Piles were driven into the island beginning on May 1, 1849. The excavation for the fort was flooded so that the logs could be floated into position, as well as making it possible to move the scow-mounted pile drivers into place. White oak and yellow pine logs 45 feet long were used for pilings. Sanders noted that the piles driven in years before had risen several inches off the ground. It was decided that every pile previously driven had to be redone, which took 18 months.[30] The expense for the pilings alone used up the million dollars Congress had put aside for the fort, so an extra million was appropriated to continue the work.[31] The last planks of the grillage were spiked on May 14, 1852. The wooden platform covered almost 4 acres and was supported by more than 6000 spikes. In 1853, the foundation was pumped out and the platform was prepared for the stone masons.

Over 200 people lived on Pea Patch Island, including Major Sanders, during the construction. There was no commuting to the mainland. The only access to the island was by either rowing or sailing boats. It was a mile in either direction to Delaware or New Jersey in frequently turbulent water. In the winter, high winds and floating ice made travel across the river impossible. Because of this type of isolation, public health was a concern, especially since the War Department issued regulations in 1850 prohibiting the provision of medical assistance to Army personnel by civilians at government expense. Sanders requested a change in this policy and twenty days later, Dr. Hamilton of Delaware City became the post medical officer. However, it took two years to get the four bed hospital started. Quarters provided by the post commander were stocked by supplies donated by the mechanics and laborers on the island, who were organized in the Fort Delaware Employees Mutual and Sick Fund.[32]

On July 3, 1851, Bvt. Capt. George B. McClellan reported for duty at the fort.[33]

He had been assigned by the Army Corps of Engineers in June to leave his previous post at West Point to help with the construction. It was a typical assignment for an officer of his rank, but it was nothing like the posts that he had requested to be sent to. McClellan, however, actually grew to like his new assignment. The construction was not done in a hurried pace and this gave the future general plenty of time to devote to other interests. He was able to read, study, and learn to speak German. Pea Patch Island was also a great place to hunt and fish. This fact was not lost on the new officer on the island. As he wrote in a letter to home, McClellan said that "I have gone on the principle of making myself perfectly acquainted with my duties before I go to amusing myself." He also said in the same letter that "I shall soon be able to work it so as to fish & shoot without interfering with my work." He did not stay at Fort Delaware very long because he was reassigned to Washington, D.C., by the winter of the same year to prepare the bayonet manual he had written for publication.[34]

The working day on the Fort Delaware project was ten hours long.[35] Some slaves were used, since Delaware was a slave state, and their masters received forty cents a day for their work,[36] but the majority of the workers were skilled laborers. These men were not just local men. German, English, and Irish immigrants also came to the island to get work because of the money being offered. Laborers were paid a dollar a day; mechanics got $2.00 to $2.50 a day; and clerks and draftsmen received $80.00 to $90.00 per month. The money was good because Sanders wanted to have the best laborers, so there was an air of prosperity around the general area at the time. He paid top dollar and kept people working even in the winter. In that season, stone cutters did piece work, carpenters built new shops, smiths made wheelbarrows and repaired machinery. Laborers worked through the winter and spring of 1854–1855 to build up the parade grounds. They used horse and ox carts to haul mud out of the river that was excavated at low tide; they also utilized the mounds of dirt that Captain Delafield's men dug up to create the ditches on the island.

Everyone was paid monthly in gold and silver pieces. At first, Major Sanders drew a check for the monthly payroll and exchanged it at the Delaware City Bank. However, by June 1855, the payroll had grown to $10,500 for a work force of 297 men. Nine denominations of coin from 3½ cent pieces to double eagles,[37] which were $20.00 gold pieces,[38] were too much for the small bank, so from then on, the payroll came from the Philadelphia Mint and was delivered directly to the work site by a courier from the Adams Express Company for two dollars a thousand. The base rates for the workers existed until 1856, when Major Sanders asked the government to declare that the official work day be limited to ten hours a day with time and a half for overtime.

In his annual report of 1855, Sanders informed the government that he thought that Fort Delaware would be ready by the fall of 1858.[39] The major was slightly off on his estimation as to when the construction of the fort would be completed. In 1856, Secretary of State Jefferson Davis asked Congress to give the Fort Delaware project another $750,000 so that the fort could be finished by 1859. The money was granted and work on the fort continued.[40]

The duties of Major Sanders as commandant of Fort Delaware included much more than just building the fort. He was the community leader, guardian, first officer of the post, and the paymaster. Looking out for the welfare of the people on the island also extended to those not under his command. On June 28, 1858, the major authorized the creation of a school for the children on the island. Miss Louisa Gribble was hired to be their teacher. Tuition was required to be paid by the parents.

The summer of 1858 also was the time that the ill health that lingered with the commandant during his tenure on the island finally caught up with him. On July 29, 1858, Brevet-Major John Sanders died on Pea Patch Island of carbunculous boils terminating in erysipelas. He left behind a wife and seven children. In 1860-61, Mrs. Sanders asked Congress for a pension. Her request was not granted until February 24, 1876, when she was given $30 a month, starting at the approval date, not retroactive to March 1, 1861.

Lt. William Price Craighill was appointed acting commander after Major Sanders' death. He held that position until Captain John Newton arrived to assume command in October 1858. At that point, the estimated time of arrival for the guns, garrison and supplies for the troops was June 30, 1860. An emergency operation could be set up, if necessary, to hold 1½ to 2 regiments with 156 guns of large caliber, 91 in the bomb proof casements and 65 firing over the top of the wall if the government was willing to put out the money and a month's notice.

Construction of the fort was completed in 1859, except for whatever was needed to be built to receive armament.[41] The fort was pentagon-shaped, the outside walls were covered with granite and the inside walls were made out of brick casements with arched brick walls. There were three rows of windows which were long and thin; the gun embrasures were much wider. Most of the openings for the big guns were on the two sides facing downriver toward Delaware Bay. There were also gun openings on the New Jersey side and the north wall, but not on the Delaware side. The enlisted mens' barracks were situated in a building there. The kitchen and mess for the men were on the first floor and they slept on the other two levels. There were also officers' barracks built facing the parade ground on the north wall with the administration building. The offices of the fort were on the first level and the officers and their families lived on the next two floors. There was also a smaller building which ran along the Jersey side.[42] The walls were anywhere between 7 feet and 30 feet thick and 32 feet tall. The entire 6 acre fort was surrounded by a moat 30 feet wide and 12 feet deep. The moat was designed as a defensive weapon, as well as a means of removing sewage from the fort. Waste was thrown into the moat and cleaned out at low tide by a gate system that flushed everything into the river. There was only one entrance, or sally port, that had a drawbridge that could be raised in case of attack. Fort Delaware was considered to be the ultimate in engineering, capable of defending Philadelphia from any attack. All it needed was weapons and the troops to use them.[43]

⚜ 2 ⚜

From One Extreme
to Another

Fort Delaware was considered the best and most up-to-date fortification in the United States at the end of 1860, ranking as high as Fort Sumter at Charleston. However, the comparison did not end there. Neither fort was occupied by a strong garrison at the time, just workmen doing detail work.[1] That situation changed for Fort Sumter when it was occupied on December 26, 1860, by Federal troops who were stationed at nearby Fort Moultrie. This occurred only because Major Robert Anderson believed that moving his troops there without orders was a good thing because Sumter was a better defensive position for his men to hold in the face of the secession movement in South Carolina. Major Anderson also believed that holding Fort Sumter would prevent bloodshed.[2] The fort on Pea Patch Island was also positioned in a slave state and, as such, a possible target for Southern supporters to seize as other forts had been taken throughout the South. In fact, there was talk from Southern sympathizers who lived in nearby Delaware City and in the rest of the state of requesting that the state militia do just that. The Northern supporters in Delaware were also vocal in their desire that regular troops be sent to occupy the fort and have it fully armed.[3]

It was a time when paranoia had a grip on Delaware. Citizens were arming themselves and creating organized companies of men complete with weapons. One firm in Wilmington had sold 1,500 pistols. Militia companies were formed in the cities of Wilmington, Odessa, Milford, Dover, and Newark, which were all supporters of secession. Dr. A.H. Grimshaw, the postmaster of Wilmington and a strong Republican supporter, wrote to a friend expressing his fears. Grimshaw was worried that the former sheriff of New Castle had a company of men and a cannon and that New Castle was only five miles from Fort Delaware. He thought that the sheriff's brother, Benjamin Ogle, the head carpenter at Fort Delaware, was "a secessionist and a traitor." Grimshaw was worried that Ogle was allowed to stay at the fort when it only had a small guard to man it. The secessionists in Maryland were only twelve miles away and could invade the island by boat. Ten men had already deserted the fort and Grimshaw wondered who talked them into doing it. He was also concerned that the son of the captain of a boat that worked the river was a secessionist. It was rumored that the father would surrender the boat if confronted by secessionists. Grimshaw wanted weapons to form a company and he also sent the same letter and request to Secretary of War Stanton. Grimshaw received an answer on April 17 telling him that Ogle was removed from the island, but any request for weapons had to go through the Delaware governor.[4] The situation was settled when Federal troops finally did arrive in February 1861 under the command of Captain Augustus A. Gibson. However, he only had 20 men with him.[5]

The flag of the United States was lowered on Fort Sumter on April 14, 1861. The very next day, President Lincoln announced a proclamation requesting 75,000 men from militias across the country to put a stop to the secessionists.[6] The answer to this order from the Upper South was crucial for the survival of the United States. If the eight states that made up the Upper South — Virginia, Maryland, Delaware, Kentucky, Arkansas, North Carolina, Tennessee, and Missouri — all went with the Confederacy, it would tip the balance of power to the South.[7] As for Delaware, there was no real danger of the state leaving the Union. The Delaware legislature had listened to a speech by Judge Henry Dickinson, commissioner from Mississippi, urging the state to join the Confederacy, but the address did not have the desired effect because on January 3, 1861, the legislature voted unanimously to show "unqualified disapproval" for secession. However, there were many Southern sympathizers in Delaware and there were real fears of armed violence between the Union and Rebel supporters. This belief was supported by the actions of Delaware citizens after the war broke out. Whole towns were divided, with men, women, boys, and girls all taking opposing sides. Some communities had one half of their population not speaking to the other half. Their answer to the President's proclamation was to not send any troops to Washington; they stated that they did not comply because they did not have a militia.[8] All of these actions made the federal government concerned about the situation and how it would impact on Fort Delaware. They were afraid that the fort might be sabotaged, so plans were made up to destroy the upper sections of the barracks and officers' quarters. These plans were eventually put aside.[9]

There were also concerns in Salem, N.J., across the river from the fort, about sabotage. About a week after Fort Sumter was taken over by the Confederacy, Charles Perrin Smith, special adviser to Governor Charles S. Olden of New Jersey, alerted the military authorities to the lack of security at Fort Delaware. He mentioned that to prove the ineffectiveness of the soldiers at the fort, R. C. Johnson and Jonathan Ingham of Salem rowed out to the island to see if they would be spotted by anyone.

They landed in the evening and no one in the fort noticed them. They walked around the island and tried to attract attention, but without success. No one saw them and they returned to Salem.[10] Soon after this incident was reported, 50 regular troops and the Commonwealth Artillery from Philadelphia reported for duty, boosting the number of troops to 150 men. However, the soldiers had to wait another month before the first of their cannons arrived.[11]

At this point, work was started on temporary wooden barracks on the parade grounds designed to hold 350 men and 15 officers. In Captain Newton's report of June 30, 1861, he stated that 47 guns had been mounted: 20 flank howitzers, 8 eight-inch columbiads placed on the second floor, and 5 ten-inch and 14 eight-inch columbiads in the barbette.[12] The columbiads were cannons that could fire a 128 pound shell a distance of 5,000 yards.[13] This kind of firepower made sailing past the fort a dangerous idea for any unfriendly ship. There were temporary quarters enough for the garrison. The bakery was done, but the shot furnaces for the 42-pounders had not begun. The medical facilities only had a civilian doctor and a small cooperative hospital. The Surgeon General put medical operations on a war footing and the last of Fort Delaware's civilian doctors, George W. Webster, was discharged in December of 1861.[14]

Even though the country was now at war, security at Fort Delaware was still not airtight. Daily excursion boats brought visitors from Philadelphia and Wilmington[15] to tour the fort. It was a great morale boost for people to be able to go to see how well protected they were from any Rebel ships that might sail up the Delaware. These visitors could go anywhere on the island and did so until the late summer of 1861. The visits were stopped at that time because it was discovered that several of the fort's big guns had been spiked by visiting Southern sympathizers.[16] This was also around the time that 50 regular army artillery soldiers and eighty volunteers, who had banded together to form an artillery group called the Independent Battery A, came to Fort Delaware to boost the number of Union soldiers to 250 men.[17]

There was not much in the way of excitement on Pea Patch Island during the first year of the war. Many of the soldiers did not want to be at Fort Delaware. One soldier wrote home in February 1862 stating that he laughed at those soldiers "for I am contented as a woodsawyer and if I was discharged tomorrow I would go and join another company. It is a lazy life a soldiering and suits me for I don't like to work anyhow." The soldiers drilled with the cannons twice a day and stayed inside in the winter because it was too cold. Some of them also liked to get drunk on pay day and when that happened, they were put into cells to sleep it off.[18]

The fear of boredom was temporally pushed aside by a letter from General McClellan dated March 9, 1862. In it, McClellan warned the commanding officers of Fort Delaware, Fort Mifflin, New York Harbor, Newport, R.I., New London, Ct., Boston Harbor, and Portland, Me., to be on the lookout for the Confederate ironclad ship the *Merrimac*. It had destroyed two frigates near Fort Monroe. He was concerned that the *Merrimac* might go to sea and try to pass any of the above places.

McClellan wanted all of them to be battle ready in case the *Merrimac* happened to try to run by them. As it happened, the *Merrimac* met the Union iron-clad ship the *Monitor* the same day that McClellan wrote the letter. The *Merrimac* was defeated and the danger of it passed as quickly as it had come.[19] Boredom once again became a way of life on the island for the Union soldiers until the Battle of Kernstown changed everything.

The Battle of Kernstown on March 23, 1862, was important for several reasons. First, the reason for the battle was that General Jackson's troops were ordered to stop the transfer of Federal soldiers from the Shenandoah Valley to General McClellan's command. Jackson led his 4,200 men against what he thought was a smaller force. Instead, they attacked a 9,000 man division. The outcome was that the Rebel forces were soundly defeated. However, they succeeded in their assignment because Jackson's attack made President Lincoln believe that if Jackson would attack, then he must have had a sizable force of his own. Lincoln canceled the transfer order, as well as ordering 35,000 men from General Irwin McDowell's corps to stay in northern Virginia to protect Washington, D.C. It had the effect of hampering General McClellan's plans for an offensive against the Confederate forces in the Virginia Peninsula.[20] This battle also had a strong impact on the men stationed at Fort Delaware. The Rebel soldiers captured during this battle were the first prisoners of war sent to Pea Patch Island.[21]

The original purpose of Fort Delaware was to be the watchdog of the Delaware River, to protect Philadelphia from any kind of attack. However, as the war went on, the Federal government came to the conclusion that the Confederate navy was not strong enough to send a force up the Delaware to do any kind of harm to Philadelphia.[22] This made the fort almost useless unless it was used as a holding place for prisoners. The Federal and Rebel governments realized that the war was not going to end quickly as they had first assumed and both sides had a desperate need for facilities to keep prisoners in. Fort Delaware, sitting on a low-lying island, was considered a perfect spot for a prison camp. The guidelines for running such a camp were already in place. According to Article 37 of U.S. Army Regulations, prisoners were to be disarmed, sent to the rear, and their name, rank, and corps written down. A prisoner's private property was to be treated with the respect due to his rank. Every prisoner was to be fed and the wounded cared for in the same way their own wounded were. Exchanges of prisoners and the parole of officers were to be arranged by the order of the government. The Confederacy also had its own rules concerning prisoners. On May 21, 1861, the Confederate Congress passed an act that stated that all prisoners would be provided for and would be fed the same as the Confederate soldiers on the field.[23]

Tradition in combat was that after a battle, anyone who was captured was held prisoner until an exchange could be arranged or they could be paroled. Being on parole meant that a prisoner could be released on his own recognizance. He would return home and promise not to return to combat until he received word that he had been exchanged. Once exchanged, he was free to return to his military duties.

Fort Delaware would serve the war effort by being one of the holding areas for Confederate prisoners until their exchanges could be arranged.

Exchanges themselves proved to be difficult from a political perspective. President Lincoln did not want to initiate an exchange program because the system had always been done between two countries. Lincoln felt that to set up exchanges meant that he was admitting that the Confederacy was actually a separate country, not a part of the United States which was in rebellion. The Confederacy realized this as well and pushed for a formal exchange system. In spite of his feelings on the subject, Lincoln did arrange for a type of exchange for prisoners. It was agreed that the federal government was dealing with an army, not a separate government. The exchange cartel went into existence on July 22, 1862, and lasted for ten months. Before the cartel was set up, commanders on the battlefield had arranged their own exchanges. They thought that it was easier to exchange the prisoners right there on the battlefield so that they would not have to use their supplies for prisoners when they sometimes barely had enough to take care of their own troops. If one side did not have enough prisoners for an even exchange, the remaining prisoners were placed on parole. Captured officers were placed on parole, as directed by General Winfield Scott in July of 1861, based on the following oath: "We and each of us for himself severally pledge our words of honor as officers and gentlemen that we will not again take up arms against the United States nor serve in any military capacity whatsoever against them until regularly discharged according to the usages of war from this obligation." This was during a time when an officer's word was his bond. To break it was to be disgraced as a gentleman and immediately shunned by one's peers.[24]

The prisoner exchange cartel created between the North and the South stated that prisoners would be exchanged private for private, captain for captain, etc. However, the cartel also allowed of exchanges for soldiers and sailors of different ranks within the following guidelines: an admiral or a general who was a commander in chief could be exchanged for 60 seamen or privates, a flag officer or major general for 40 seamen or privates, a commodore or brigadier general for 20 seamen or privates, a navy captain or colonel for 15 seamen or privates, a commander or lieutenant-colonel for 10 seamen or privates, a lieutenant-commander or major for 8 seamen or privates, a lieutenant, master, or master's mate in the navy or a captain, lieutenant, or ensign in the army for 4 seamen or privates, midshipmen, warrant-officers in the navy, merchant vessel masters, and commanders of privateers for 3 seamen or privates, and second captains, lieutenants or merchant vessel mates, privateers, and navy petty officers in the navy or all noncommissioned officers in the army or marines for 2 seamen or privates.[25] Both sides agreed that the exchanges would occur within 10 days of capture.[26]

When Captain Gibson first got word that his fort was expected to hold prisoners. he contacted Washington, D.C., and protested the decision. He stated that he was preparing the fort to be war-ready and he did not have the time, the room, or the troops necessary to take care of prisoners. He was informed to do the best he could and make room for prisoners. When the first prisoners arrived, the Union troops were moved out of their barracks on the 2nd floor and placed on the 3rd floor. This did not create enough space, so fifty prisoners were placed in the lower level where gunpowder was supposed to go.[27] They went down a damp tunnel to get to the former storage area.[28] There was no light except for one oil lantern in each room. Ventilation came from air passages that ran from the dungeons to the top of the building. These ventilation passages were too small to permit even the smallest of men to use as a means of escape.[29]

Even before the first prisoners arrived on Pea Patch Island, the federal government was working on plans on how to accommodate captured Rebels. In a letter dated March 17, 1862, Col. William Hoffman wrote to General M. C. Meigs, Quartermaster-General of the U. S. Army, describing his ideas on the housing of prisoners. He wanted to do it as economically as possible. In the letter, he states that :

> A building to quarter 165 men should be 140 feet long and 24 feet —. This will allow of one long room with bunks on each side, affording a space of 7½ by 16½ for 12 men and a room at each end of 12 feet by 24 for a kitchen, all of rough boards without battening, without ceiling and without shingles. There will be seven half windows on a side. The cost of such a building according to my estimate will be full $592.25. Two such buildings which are only equal to one building of the plan submitted will cost $1,185, while one on the proposed plan will cost $1, —. The two occupy sixteen feet more than double the ground occupied for the two-story house, and to quarter the same number of men is in the inclosure the buildings must be very much crowded together. At all the camps established last summer when the huts were covered with boards they have been obliged after suffering much inconvenience from leaks to put on shingle roofs, and if the huts are to be occupied in winter they will have to be ceiled with rough boards overhead as in the plan proposed, and the final cost will thus far exceed that of the — — — — — erecting. To put on shingles will cost $179 and to — — rough ceiling will cost $50.00; the contractors estimate one building with shingle roof without ceiling at $800. If the shed huts are to be built shall it be done by the present contractors, by a new contract or by the quartermaster? The buildings I propose to erect for the major and surgeon, the hospital and additional barracks for the guard cannot well cost less and be suitable for the purpose. You will see by the description of them that they are roughly closed in and I have made very careful calculations to be sure that there is a very small margin for profits. Nothing has yet been done and I will wait for your instructions.[30]

In early April, Captain Gibson received some direction from Major General Dix concerning the treatment of prisoners. The soldiers held at Fort Delaware were permitted to receive letters, clothing, and gifts as long as they were proper and examined before they were given to the prisoners. However, visitors were not permitted unless they had a pass from headquarters in Baltimore. Letters could be sent by the prisoners, but they too had to be checked out before being sent. A letter would either be returned to the prisoner or destroyed if it contained anything that could be considered either treasonous or had "improper reflections upon the United States Government" in it. The same standards also applied to letters received by the prisoners.[31]

The 248 prisoners that arrived from the Battle of Kernstown were just the beginning for the garrison on Pea Patch Island. Soon after these prisoners arrived at the fort, a Captain Joseph Drake was transferred there from Fortress Monroe.[32] Gibson did not have to hold these first prisoners for very long. On June 11, 1862, he was ordered by the War Department to release on parole the men from General Jackson's army and send the list to headquarters.[33]

With the influx of prisoners, the duties of the soldiers at Fort Delaware changed. They only drilled once a day with a short knapsack and had guard duty three times a week. Problems with the health of the prisoners also began. In a letter dated June 12, 1862, one Union soldier wrote: "The rebels are dieing fast, two has died this morning and we wheeled a great lot of medicine into the hospital today enough to kill a thousand of them." There were also concerns among the Union soldiers that there were not enough soldiers to guard all of the prisoners coming into the fort. The prison population was growing on a regular basis with no let up in sight and the guards were afraid that unless they received reinforcements, the prisoners would rise up and take control of the island. Prisoners occasionally gave the guards trouble; any that did would be thrown into the dungeon and fed bread and water until he became calm again.[34]

Three days later, in a letter dated June 15th, Lt. Colonel Hoffman wrote to Secretary of War Edwin Stanton that he had just been at Fort Delaware and said that it had room for 2,000 prisoners. There were 600 there at the time, half of that number being prepared to be released on parole. He thought it was suitable for holding prisoners of war and recommended that barracks should be built to hold 3,000 more. He also thought that the island could possibly hold more prisoners. Colonel Hoffman also stated that he thought that the number of soldiers at the fort needed to be increased, so he suggested that the four companies already there be brought up to strength and a fifth company be added to successfully guard the prisoners. He also asked that Captain Gibson be given a promotion to either major or lieutenant-colonel to match the breadth of duties he was expected to perform as commander of Fort Delaware.[35]

Captain Gibson not only had to worry about the prisoners and what to do with them, but he also had to protect himself from a personal attack. On June 23, 1862, a group of men wrote a letter to President Lincoln claiming that Gibson was a Rebel sympathizer, that a great majority of the people at the fort were also sympathizers, and that anyone who was loyal to the government there was shunned. They also stated that at a recent election at Delaware City, all but one of the laborers from the fort voted for a Southern sympathizer. They then concluded their letter by demanding that Captain Gibson be removed from command and replaced with someone who was loyal to the federal government and would "encourage, instead of opposing the loyal Citizens of the state of Delaware."[36] The charges were investigated and found to be without merit.

On July 3, 1862, Captain Gibson wrote to Col. Hoffman concerning the clothing needs of the prisoners because he thought the matter was pressing. He requested "1,000 blouses (or any substitute), 500 blankets, 1,000 shirts, 500 shoes (pairs), 300 caps (or any substitute), 1,000 pants."[37] The problem did not end with the clothes. The conditions in which the prisoners lived were not ideal. The barracks for the prisoners were dirty, the food was bad, and the men held there were malnourished. They also had to deal with the twin problems of living in unhealthy conditions and suffering from contagious diseases.[38]

Col. Hoffman sent a circular around to all of the prison camps in the North four days later containing rules and regulations. Among the regulations were that the commander of the prison was responsible for the well-being of prisoners and guards alike and must send a written report to Col. Hoffman at the end of the month reporting on the status of the prisoners (deaths, escapes, etc.). A general fund to help prisoners was permitted to be created by the profits from selling any surplus food the prisoners had to the commissary, and the sutler was under the jurisdiction of the commanding officer who would make sure that he only sold quality items and at reasonable rates. Visitors would only be tolerated if they had business with the commanding officer and left as soon as their business was done. Prisoners who were seriously ill were the only ones allowed visits from family members. Prisoners were only allowed to write a one page letter on regular paper about personal matters or the letter would be destroyed. Finally, prisoners would only be paroled or released by either the order of the War Department or the commissioner general of prisoners.[39]

The concerns that there were not enough soldiers to guard the prisoners and that they might stage a jail break came to pass on July 15, 1862, when 19 Rebels escaped during the night. The suggestions made by Col. Hoffman after his visit had not been acted upon. Accusations and blame flew between the fort and the government flew between them fast and furious, especially after 200 more prisoners escaped the next evening. Additional troops and a steam guard boat were sent to the fort to help the less than 300 man force prevent any more escapes from the more than 3,000 prisoners held there. There was also another escape attempt on the 15th that was thwarted by the guards. Prisoners had a partially built raft hidden that was built from the wood being used to build a privy. Captain Gibson was also ordered to prevent civilians from landing on the island, except for those people who were working for the federal government, and to make sure that the civilians were not allowed to speak to the prisoners since the government was afraid that the prisoners could get outside help in escaping as those who broke out of prison on the 15th had.[40]

While some prisoners were escaping in one way, others were leaving by a more permanent means. There was a sickness going around in the camp that affected both guards and prisoners alike. One Union soldier wrote that he had a fever and although his skin had begun to peel off, he had not yet gone to the hospital and did not know when he would get there. He also said that there was "nothing to do but bury the rebels, we bury one every day and sometimes three and four."[41]

In the last week of July 1862, there was a great deal of activity in Washington concerning Fort Delaware. Lorenzo Thomas, who had been recently appointed agent for the North for the exchange of prisoners, was trying to arrange for transportation to carry the 3,000 prisoners of war held at the fort to Aiken's, on the James River, to be exchanged. Three steamers were located for the job and sent to Fort Delaware.

The *Atlantic, Merrimac,* and the *Coatzacoalcos* were each capable of carrying and cooking for 1,000 men. General Thomas went to the fort to personally accompany the prisoners to the exchange point. The government provided the transports, but Captain Gibson was ordered to provide guards for the prisoners since there were no available soldiers to do the job. Major General John Dix felt that Gibson could provide three companies to guard the prisoners on the steamboats because he was getting rid of his prisoners and could spare the men.[42]

Captain Gibson was transferred to Washington in late July and replaced by Major Henry S. Burton.[43] It was about at this time that the exchange cartel began to really affect the prison population. In early August 1862, Major Burton was ordered by Lorenzo Thomas, the Adjutant-General in Washington, to give the "oath of allegiance to the prisoners left behind for that purpose; discharge them and send list of them here. Send the French privateersmen under a proper escort, with any other prisoners of war well enough, to Fort Monroe to report to General Dix."[44] Approximately 3,000 prisoners were exchanged and 3,000 Union soldiers who had been held prisoner were brought back to the fort in exchange.[45] On September 17, a steamer landed with over 600 paroled soldiers who had been held at Richmond, Va. They were sent to Fort Delaware by Assistant Adjutant-General E. D. Townsend to stay there until their paroles came through. Ironically, they were housed in the barracks that recently paroled Rebel soldiers had stayed in.[46] More prisoners arrived on September 18th, 19th, and 21st,[47] but on September 24, 1862, Major Burton was ordered by General Thomas, by way of the Secretary of War, Edwin M. Stanton, to "send all the prisoners of war from rebel army to Fort Monroe to be exchanged. Put them on parole first. Release on taking oath of allegiance those who wish."[48] By October 29th, there were about 100 deserters at the fort and they ran away every chance they had. There were also, as one Union soldier put it, "no rebels here at all any more and we don't expect any."[49]

The soldier's prediction was far from accurate, because within a year, Fort Delaware was filled to capacity with prisoners and this was due to the breakdown of the exchange cartel and the suspension of the writ of habeas corpus.

Exchanges and the Writ of Habeas Corpus

On April 27, 1861, Lincoln ordered Lt. Gen. Winfield Scott to release the following statement:

> You are engaged in repressing an insurrection against the laws of the United States. If at any point on or in the vicinity of the military line which is now used between the city of Philadelphia via Perryville, Annapolis City and Annapolis Junction you find resistance which renders it necessary to suspend the writ of habeas corpus for the public safety, you personally or through the officer in command at the point where resistance occurs are authorized to suspend that writ.[1]

A writ of habeas corpus orders the authorities to bring a prisoner before a court or judge. Habeas corpus means "you should have the body." It is an important part of the Constitution that protects the citizens of the United States from arbitrary imprisonment.[2] The idea of the suspension was to allow army officers to arrest and hold without trial anyone suspected of being a traitor if it was assumed that the courts and civil authorities were being sympathetic to treason. The suspension was enacted only two days after Federal troops entered Washington, D.C. The timing of this action was important. In the early days of the war, Lincoln was afraid that the capital would be cut off from the rest of the Union. If Washington was cut off, then any type of action would be considered pointless. The concern Lincoln had about this situation had merit because the capital of the North shared a border with a Confederate state, Virginia, and with Maryland, which had a strong pro-Southern faction. This left Lincoln in a weakened situation and unable to act in a decisive manner. When the troops finally arrived at the capital, Washington was no longer isolated and those fears had dissipated. Once he felt that he was on solid ground again, Lincoln was free to use his power to try and shore up the Union.[3]

Not everyone went along with the idea of the suspension. Chief Justice Roger B. Taney declared on May 26, 1861, that the military arrest of John Merryman in Maryland was illegal and Lincoln had no right to suspend the writ of habeas corpus. He then issued a writ on Merryman. The President, in turn, felt that he had the power to do so in cases of rebellion or invasion in the interest of public safety. Lincoln expanded the range of the suspension on July 2, 1861, to go along or near the military line between New York City and Washington, D.C. On October 14, 1861, he expanded its influence to stretch from Bangor, Me., to Washington if it was necessary to stop any suspected subversion.[4]

Secretary of State Seward was in charge of internal security at the outbreak of the war and was responsible for the political arrests that the suspension created in 1861. The responsibility for internal security was then given to Edwin Stanton when he became Secretary of War in January 1862. Before he was placed in charge, Stanton asked Lincoln's permission to release all but the most dangerous prisoners if they would promise not to help the enemy and not to sue the country for false imprisonment. The President agreed to his request and Stanton became quite popular for a time because of these actions, but it changed quickly when the arrests began again, especially in 1862 and 1863. The majority of those arrested as a result of the suspension were released within a matter of days or weeks. The suspension had allowed a great deal of latitude in dealing with the rebellion. Unfortunately, this kind of sweeping power led to abuses of it and some of the victims of these abuses ended up at Fort Delaware.[5]

Civil power had been suspended in Maryland and martial law established. In the fall of 1861, military squads went to Queen Anne and Talbot counties to arrest people for "disloyalty" if they did not vote for the Union candidate.[6] The Maryland armory at Easton was sacked on a Sunday by a company of Union soldiers, who carried off public and private property. Provost marshals were appointed and anyone who spoke out against the federal government was arrested.

The situation became so bad that a grand jury, presided over by the Hon. Richard B. Carmichael, judge of the Circuit Court, indicted the worst offenders for their misuse of authority and ordered them arrested in May 1862. They were not arrested immediately because they were out of town. On May 25, they returned to Easton with the help of the clerk of the court, Samuel T. Hopkins, and they brought with them J. K. McPhail of Baltimore, a hatmaker who had been appointed as a marshal. Their orders were to arrest Judge Carmichael.

On the 28th of May, McPhail and some policemen entered the judge's courtroom. The courthouse was mostly empty because of the ringing of the hotel dinner bell, but it was in session. McPhail and his men tried to arrest Carmichael while he sat on the bench, listening to a case. The judge demanded to see their papers and they, in turn, drew their pistols. They rushed the bench, beat the Judge with their weapons and dragged him from the courtroom. Isaac C. Powell, Esq., who was acting as a counsel that day, was arrested along with two others, while the other people in the courtroom were driven away with the threat of pistols. The four men received no trial and were thrown into prison.[7] General Lorenzo Thomas ordered Powell and William Nabb on September 27 to be sent from Fort Lafayette to Fort Delaware,[8] where they arrived on October 1, 1862. Judge Carmichael had arrived there a few days earlier, after spending six weeks at Fort McHenry and two months at Fort Lafayette.

Judge Carmichael sent President Lincoln a copy of what he had stated at the grand jury and informed him of the circumstances of his arrest. The President stated to Senator James A. Pierce of Maryland that he thought that Carmichael and the three men arrested with him should be set free, but that Secretary of War Stanton objected.[9] The objection became obvious when on October 29th, Major Burton received orders from Secretary Stanton that the order to release the judge be cancelled.[10]

While they were at Fort Delaware, the two men observed that Major Henry Burton, the commander of the fort, "deported himself toward the prisoners as an officer and a gentleman; and never descended from his position, in either capacity, to an act of meanness or oppression." He put the four men on parole and allowed them to roam freely on the grounds of the fort. He also allowed them to keep anything sent by friends that would make them more comfortable.

On December 4, 1862, Judge Carmichael was released from prison. He was never read the charges that were brought against him during the entire six months that he spent in Union prisons. Isaac Powell was released four days later by Col. Perkins, the new commander of the fort, when Stanton sent a letter to Perkins stating, "You will immediately release I.C.W. Powell, a prisoner, who is said to have been arrested at the same time as Judge Carmichael, and who is said to be now at Fort Delaware."[11]

The Hon. Madison Y. Johnson lived in Galena, Illinois, and practiced law there. He was also a personal friend of President Lincoln, having been a member of the Whig party with the future president. Mr. Johnson was a believer in striving for a peaceful solution to the conflict between the North and South. When the war broke out, he was still an advocate of peace. A mass meeting was held in Springfield, Ill., during the war and Mr. Johnson was the author of a peace resolution which was passed at the time. It said:

> Resolved, That the further offensive prosecution of the war tends to subvert the Constitution and Government, and entail upon the nation all the disastrous consequences of misrule and anarchy. That we are in favor of peace upon the basis of a restored Union; and for the accomplishment of which, we propose a National Convention to settle upon terms of peace, which shall have in view the restoration of the Union as it was, and the securing by constitutional amendments such rights to the States and the people thereof as honor and justice demand.

Apparently someone in the federal government took a dim view of Mr. Johnson's opinions because on August 28, 1862, while working as a defense council on a murder case, he was arrested while court was in session by a U.S. marshal on the order of Secretary of War Stanton. There was no warrant or charges brought up against him. After being sent to four different prisons, he was finally sent to Fort Delaware. Mr. Johnson's friends worked hard to either have him freed or to be put on trial. The Governor of Illinois tried to have him returned to Illinois for trial, but the request was refused. The reasoning was, since he was not charged with a crime, there was no case to try. If there was no case to try, then there was no reason to send Johnson back to Illinois. His friends refused to allow this setback to stop them and continued to fight for him. They were so persistent in their efforts to free him that Lincoln said to Mr. Hunkins, one of Johnson's friends, that "Mr. Johnson has given us more trouble than all the political prisoners." Their hard work paid off when Johnson was freed after staying at Fort Delaware for four months.[12]

Warren J. Reed was a schoolteacher and a justice of the peace for Murderkill Hundred, Kent County, Delaware. He was active in politics and an outspoken supporter of state's rights and free speech. In September 1862, two soldiers came to arrest Reed while he was teaching school. They showed him their weapons, told him that he was their prisoner, and ordered him to immediately shut down the school. He was not allowed to return to his home to pick up money or extra clothes, even though his home was only a mile away. Instead, he was put into a carriage and quickly taken to Felton Station on the Delaware Railroad. He was then transported to a hotel and left in a room with a guard. Reed was then placed on the Wilmington train when it arrived. One of the arresting soldiers sat beside him and the other one, with a companion, sat behind him. On arrival in Wilmington at 9:00 P.M., he was escorted by a squad of soldiers to a room on the 4th floor with some of the soldiers standing guard outside his room.

After breakfast, Reed was brought before Col. A.H. Grimshaw, the commander of a Delaware regiment. The prisoner demanded to know what the charges were against him. The colonel, in a voice barely above a whisper, said something like it was all right. Reed was then ordered to stand against a wall while information such as his height, weight, color of eyes, place of residence was being obtained. Then he heard someone outside cry out "All ready?" The answer was yes and Reed, with two other prisoners, was escorted outside, and taken away. The three prisoners had no idea where they were going until they arrived at Delaware City at around 2:00 P.M.

After eating at the hotel there, a small boat was hired to take the prisoners across the channel to Fort Delaware. The boatmen hired to take the men to the prison at first refused to go because the wind was blowing hard and the water was so rough that they thought that it was too dangerous to attempt the trip. The officer in charge insisted and Reed, with three to four others, was put on the boat and taken to the fort safely by dark. On arrival, they were immediately taken to the headquarters of Major Henry Burton, the commandant. He was not there at the time, but another officer had the prisoners taken to a room on the second floor, which was about forty feet by twenty feet in size. Exhausted by their journey, the prisoners immediately lay down on the floor and went to sleep. Reed used a piece of a broken box as a pillow and fell asleep with no blanket.

The next morning, Reed awoke at daybreak and looked around the room he had been placed in. He saw three rows of sleeping prisoners, stretched lengthwise on the floor, each covered with a blanket. There was no fire in the room to keep the men warm. All of the 25-30 men in the room were political prisoners. None of them had had a trial or been charged with a crime.

After a month, Reed was released thanks to friends writing to Secretary Stanton for his freedom. Stanton issued the release order, but George P. Fisher, a Delaware representative, with three other men, wrote letters to Major Burton asking him, on their responsibility, to keep Reed until they could get the release order overturned. Their reasoning was that there was going to be an election in the near future and they considered it vital that Reed stay at Fort Delaware because his release would be disastrous in their eyes. Burton ignored the letters and released Reed. The major may have ignored the letters, but the letter writers did not ignore him. By the following Monday, Burton was removed from his position and not given another command for fifteen months.[13]

Edward S. Sharpe was a doctor from Salem, N.J., who was on a steamboat traveling to Philadelphia in late 1862 when he made remarks complaining about President Lincoln's war policies. Three Army officers overheard him and immediately arrested Dr. Sharpe. They then commanded the captain of the boat to change direction and take them to Fort Delaware. The boat landed on Pea Patch Island and Dr. Sharpe was taken to the prison. Once word of Dr. Sharpe's arrest had gotten out, a group of prominent citizens from New Jersey went to the officers in charge of the fort to plead for Dr. Sharpe's release due to his background and the high standing he held in the community. He was released after being held three weeks.[14] His roommates in prison were Isaac Powell and Madison Johnson.[15]

The Rev. Isaac Handy was a Presbyterian minister from Virginia who, with his family, was visiting his father-in-law in Delaware on an unconditional legal pass in June 1863. He was ordered to report to Fort Delaware on June 21, 1863, to answer charges of being a chaplain in the Confederate Army and making disparaging remarks about the American flag. When he arrived at the fort, General Schoepf, the commandant, asked him if he ever made the remarks he was accused of and Handy did not deny that he said what he was accused of saying. With that, he was escorted to his new room, which was his home for the next fifteen months.

He was assigned to quarters on the second floor opposite the office of the commandant. After several prisoners invited him to room with them, he decided to go to No. 6 with a man named Shreve from Loudon County, Virginia. There were seven rooms in the section, and each opened up into one of two passages. William Bright of Wilmington, a member of the Methodist Church, was in No. 1. Dr. Handy suggested that Bright try to make arrangements for some sort of daily worship or a regular prayer meeting. Just before bedtime on his first night of captivity, Dr. Handy spoke to Mr. Bright again, who informed the reverend that a number of people wanted to have an evening service. Handy went to No. 7, the largest of the rooms, to discover 25 to 30 men assembled there. He read the 37th Psalm and everyone sang

The Rev. Isaac Handy, a political prisoner who used his fifteen months in prison to comfort and convert his fellow prisoners.

the hymn "When I can read my title clear." They then got down on their knees and gave thanks. After the service, Dr. Handy wrapped himself in a blanket and went to sleep on a board bed to end his first day in prison.

The next morning, he washed with brownish, filthy water, which was all he could get. He shared No. 6 with six other men: Captains Sol. R. Jackson and H.A. Ball, and Messrs. T. Jeff Shreve, John A. Atwood, James S. Pleasants, and Harrison Tibbets. The room was 12 by 18 feet with an alcove and a grated window. The window opened to the southwest and directly faced Delaware City. At the other end was a large opening, creating a draught directly through the building. On each side of the room were tiers of bunks. He could not see Delaware City because of a cluster of willow trees surrounding an ice-house, which was on an embankment near the fort. Looking down from his window, the new prisoner could see other prisoners doing various jobs such as carrying boards, rolling barrels of flour, and pushing wheelbarrows. The prisoners got two meals a day, three if they worked. The Union army recruited soldiers from the prisoners and 100 men became Yankee soldiers during the time the Rev. Handy was held at the fort.

The prayer meeting held that night had even more prisoners than that of the previous evening. The 94th Psalm was read and they sang "A Charge to keep I have."[16] Seeing the increased attendance in the worship service, the Rev. Handy realized that his calling while at Fort Delaware was to minister to the prisoners and keep them from straying from the straight and narrow while far away from home and family. He then threw himself into this work, in spite of his frail health, creating a religious library in his room and founding the Confederate States Christian Association for the Relief of Prisoners. This organization was created to help in the physical, spiritual, moral, and intellectual needs of the prisoners. He led many prisoners into the Christian faith with his daily prayer meetings. There were those prisoners who were put off by his long, gray hair, but by the time he was released in October 1864, he had gained the respect of everyone he came into contact with due to his deep faith, good works, and strong support of the Confederacy.[17]

The provost marshall, Col. Edwin Wilmer, was concerned with keeping the peace, as well as disloyalty and secessionist activities. There were 52 people arrested between June 8, 1863, and January 1, 1864. Most of them were released after they took the oath. A few of them were sent to Fort Delaware. An Irishman in Smyrna, Del., was sent to Fort Delaware for stating that "his heart beat for the C.S.A. and he wished all the men that went down to fight for the U.S.A. would be killed and thrown into ditches." Another man from Smyrna was arrested for saying, "I wish all the Union men were in hell. While old Abe is in office, we are sure to go to Hell." A dentist from Smyrna was sent to Fort Delaware for bragging that he had personally sent 25 recruits to the Confederacy, drinking to the health of Jeff Davis, and saying that the Union was a "damned despotism."[18]

Colonel Waring of Maryland was arrested and court-marshaled on three charges, even though he was a private citizen. He was accused of having Confederate mail in his house, of harboring Rebels, and being a spy. Reverdy Johnson was his defense council, but he was found guilty and sentenced to be imprisoned at Fort Delaware until the end of the war. His daughter, Mrs. Elizabeth Waring Duckett, went to Washington to talk to President Lincoln to ask his permission to visit him in prison. Lincoln gave her a card to give to Secretary Stanton so she could see him about the possibility of visiting her father. As soon as she was ushered into Stanton's office, he tore up the card and threw it on the floor. He refused to allow her to go to Fort Delaware and she left the office in a frustrated and angry state. She eventually learned that she could not get permission to go to the fort, but she found out how to get there anyway. She got a pass to leave Baltimore and took a canal boat to Pea Patch Island at night. On the boat, she met some recaptured prisoners who told her that General Schoepf had given her father the parole of the island and that the only way she could get to the prison was on a milk-boat which left for the island at five A.M. She took the boat, but the guards would not allow her to land. The colonel heard about her arrival and went to General Schoepf to ask permission for her to visit. Schoepf agreed to the request and allowed her to stay for two days.

She then returned in the fall of 1863, bringing her daughter with her. They stayed at a lodging house on the island outside the fort and her father was allowed to visit her there. During the visit, Mrs. Duckett's daughter took off on her own to explore the island. She wandered into the smallpox hospital set up on the island, unaware of what the yellow flag meant that waved above it. Fortunately, one of the Confederate surgeons found her and brought her back to her mother before she became ill.

In early 1864, Archbishop Hughes of New York wrote to Lincoln asking for Colonel Waring's release. Lincoln also received a petition from the Court of Appeals and another from important citizens of Maryland asking for the colonel's freedom. All of this finally convinced the President to sign the order releasing Colonel Waring.[19]

The other major reason for the increase in the number of prisoners being held by both sides was the breakdown of the exchange cartel in 1863. The exchange cartel had its problems right from the beginning. Exchanges worked if the number of prisoners being exchanged was limited, as it was during the first part of the war. However, as the war progressed and the number of prisoners increased, it became harder to keep track of how many prisoners needed to be exchanged, who was on parole, and how to make sure that both sides were playing by the rules. It was a time when men were expected to live by a code of honor, but it did not mean that there were not abuses of the system. One problem that occurred was that some soldiers would use the exchange system to take a break from soldiering. There were many cases of Union soldiers deliberately taking their time walking away after a battle so that they could be captured and held by Confederate forces until exchanged or paroled. Some even skipped being captured altogether and just forged a paper declaring that they were on parole and went home. The federal government, in the fall of 1862, decided to use this situation to its advantage and ordered that when the paroled soldiers were sent North to await their exchange, they would be sent to Minnesota to quell an Indian uprising. The soldiers, believing that going to fight Indians was a violation of their parole, refused to go on the grounds that they were being forced to break their word by engaging in military activities before their exchanges went into effect. The South also got wind of this situation and deliberately worded their paroles to prevent Union soldiers from fighting Indians. They hoped that Union troops would have to be pulled away from fighting the Confederacy to handle the situation. As it turned out, the uprising was put down before any paroled soldiers could be sent to Minnesota.[20]

The idea of returning prisoners to their respective sides ground to a halt in 1863 with the advent of two situations. First, the Confederate Congress in May of that year authorized their armies to either enslave or execute captured African-American soldiers and their officers. This kind of blackmail had worked before for the South. It also threatened to hold Union officers hostage. Such threats, along with strong public opinion in the North for a formal exchange system, had finally convinced President Lincoln to create the exchange cartel in the first place. However, this time, the strategy did not work. The Federal War Department suspended the cartel so that Rebel prisoners could be held as hostages against threats like these.

The second situation was the abuse of the parole system. When the decision to halt the cartel, combined with the big battles that took place in the second part of 1863, made the prison population swell to enormous proportions, large scale paroles took place to alleviate the problem. However, the way the South handled the paroles sealed the fate of the entire system. General Grant had discovered that some of the soldiers he captured at Chattanooga in November 1863 had been part of the 30,000 Rebel soldiers he had paroled when he captured Vicksburg and the 7000 Rebels that General Nathaniel Banks had paroled at Port Hudson four months before. The South declared that most of these soldiers had been exchanged and thereby were allowed to return to combat. They claimed that there had been difficulties in the paperwork, which is why the North did not know that the exchanges had been completed.[21] Whether or not the explanation was the truth was not important. What was important was that Grant had had enough of exchanges. It was then that he recommended that the exchange cartel be disbanded. In a letter to General Benjamin Butler on April 17, 1864, Grant explained his position on exchanges and paroles.

> 1st.: Touching the validity of the paroles of the prisoners captured at Vicksburg and Port Hudson.
> 2nd.: The status of colored prisoners.
> As to the first: No Arrangement for the exchange of prisoners will be acceded to that does not fully recognize the validity of these paroles, and provide for the release to us, of a sufficient number of prisoners now held by the Confederate Authorities to cancel any balance that may be in our favor by virtue of these paroles. Until there is released to us an equal number of officers and men as were captured and paroled at Vicksburg and Port Hudson, not another Confederate prisoner of war will be paroled or exchanged.
> As to the second. No distinction whatever will be made in the exchange between white and colored prisoners; the only question being, were they, at the time of their capture, in the military service of the United States. If they were, the same terms as to treatment while prisoners and conditions of release and exchange must be exacted and had, in the case of colored soldiers as in the case of white soldiers.
> Non-acquiescence by the Confederate Authorities in both or either of these propositions, will be regarded as a refusal on their part to agree to the further exchange of prisoners, and will be so treated by us.[22]

Grant also let his feelings about prisoners of war be known to Secretary of State William Seward. On August 19, 1864, he wrote to Seward stating:" We ought not to make a single exchange nor release a prisoner on any pretext whatever until the war closes. We have got to fight until the Military power of the South is exhausted and if we release or exchange prisoners captured it simply becomes a War of extermination."[23]

Extermination was not what Grant wanted, but living on "the Devil's Half-acre" at Pea Patch Island did not improve the life expectancy of anyone held there.

The Growth of the Prison Population

The winter of 1862 was slow for the men stationed at Fort Delaware because most of the prisoners had been exchanged or paroled. On November 29th, Major Burton was replaced by Lt. Col. Delevan D. Perkins. Lt. Col. Perkins had previously been the chief of staff for Gen. Nathaniel P. Banks.[1] Perkins, like his predecessor, was always polite to the prisoners under his charge. He began a habit of visiting the Confederate officers on a daily basis with his clerk, James N. Gemmil. The officers were held inside the fort during this time period. Perkins and Gemmil were always respectful of the needs of the prisoners and did their best to see that their stay was as pleasant as possible. Other Union officers also visited them and most of them were also kind and considerate to those held there.[2]

It may have been a slow time for the men stationed at Fort Delaware, but it was not without its problems. There was a controversy on December 16th among the men of Battery G of the Pittsburgh Heavy Artillery stationed on the island. A shipment of clothing came in that day which was for light artillery. The uniforms had small tight jackets and the men did not like them. They also did not like them for a more important reason than the way they looked. They felt that accepting the uniforms meant that they would then be considered light artillery and not heavy artillery. Soldiers in heavy artillery stayed at fortifications while those in light artillery were used on the battlefield. That was not what the majority of the Pittsburgh battery wanted. They swore that they would rather be arrested than become light artillery. However, their officers wanted the change because their pay would increase from $15 a month to $20. It turned out that the situation was

28

a moot point because Battery G was stationed at Fort Delaware until the end of the war.[3]

In January 1863, Fort Delaware earned an international reputation. On January 27, the Secretary of State, William H. Seward, wrote to Secretary of War Edwin Stanton concerning an unofficial contact he had received from the British consul in Philadelphia. The official had gone to Fort Delaware to visit two of his countrymen who were held there as deserters. The consul informed Seward of the conditions they were held in. Seward told Stanton that "The granite walls of the dungeons are represented to be wet with moisture, the stone floor damp and cold, the air impure and deathly, no bed or couches to lie upon and offensive vermin crawling in every direction. It is also represented that the prisoners are allowed no water with which to wash themselves or change of clothes and are on every side surrounded by filth and vermin." Seward thought the consul had exaggerated the conditions, but he still wanted to let Stanton know what was reported.[4]

Secretary Stanton wrote back to Seward the next day informing him that "orders have been issued for a immediate and through inspection into the conditions of the prisoners confined at Fort Delaware." He then wrote to Maj. Gen. R. C. Schenck, commanding at Baltimore, on the same day to order him to send "a competent officer" to inspect the prisoner quarters and make a full report and send it to the Department of War.[5] The British seamen were released soon after Stanton received the letter.[6]

The month of February saw several problems with desertions. On February 10th, a sentry at the number 4 guard post took Major Burton's barge and deserted with 10 members of the 157th Pennsylvania Volunteers. The provost marshal went with a group of men to find them, but they only found the barge. Two days later, nine more men from the 157th Pennsylvania deserted and eight prisoners escaped the same evening.[7]

As spring came, so came an increase in activity on the island. On March 28, 1863, Col. William Hoffman, commissary-general of prisoners, wrote to Lt. Col. Ludlow, the commissioner for exchange of prisoners, from Washington to inform him that Rebel officers from Washington, Fort McHenry, and Fort Delaware were ordered to Fort Monroe and all Rebel officers at the western prison camps would be sent to Fort Delaware. Lt. Col. Perkins was informed of this movement of prisoners three days later when Col. Hoffman warned him that 800-1000 prisoners would be arriving at his prison camp in a week to ten days.

The next day, Perkins received another letter from Hoffman stating that he would be receiving orders from the headquarters of the Middle Department instructing him to turn over all the Rebel officer prisoners to Ludlow to be exchanged. However, Perkins was ordered to "not include with them Capt. R.W. Baylor who is charged with serious crimes, nor any other officer who may be held on any other charge than that of being in the rebel army."[8] Captain Robert Baylor had been captured December 1862 and placed under arrest for the murder of a man under a flag of truce. He stayed at Fort Delaware until May 22, 1863, when he was sent to Harper's Ferry to be court-martialed. He was convicted and sentenced to death, but the death sentence was set aside by Secretary Stanton. He was exchanged in 1864.[9]

On the same day, Col. Hoffman ordered Capt. E.L. Webber, the commander of Camp Chase Prison in Columbus, Ohio, to send all Rebel officers to Fort Delaware. The order also applied to "the sick and wounded who are able to travel, but those who are too unwell to be moved will remain at Camp Chase till further orders."[10] Special Orders #115 was sent from W.P. Anderson, the assistant adjunctant general from the Department of the Ohio in Cincinnati, Ohio, by the order of Major General Burnside, confirming this move. It stated: "III. All rebel officers held as prisoners of war in this department will at once be sent under proper guard to Fort Delaware. A list of all prisoners so transferred will be forwarded to Colonel Hoffman, Third Infantry, commissary-general of prisoners, Washington, D.C.. The Quartermaster's Department will provide the necessary transportation." While the prisoners were being taken to the prison, the officers were on their parole. They were "not permitted to have communication with any person by the way nor to make purchases of any kind except something to eat."[11] The first group of 31 Rebel officers and 12 non-commissioned officers arrived on April 8th and the rest arrived five days later.[12]

With the war going into its second year, people in Washington were wondering how many men could be contained on the island. M. E. Meigs, quartermaster-general in Washington, D.C., sent a letter to Secretary of War Stanton on April 2, 1863, concerning his opinion about the availability of the fort to hold more prisoners. He made inquiries and found "that the total area of the island is 178 acres, of which there are 6¾ covered by the fort. The inhabitable part of the island exclusive of the fort is about 45 acres. There are barracks for 5000 persons already erected inside of the fort. On the upper end of the island it is estimated there is room to build barracks for about 10,000 more or to encamp 6,000."[13]

Lt. Col. Perkins was replaced as commander on April 2nd, 1863, by Col. Robert G. Buchanan of the 7th U.S. Infantry.[14] Col. Buchanan's greatest claim to fame up to that point was that in 1854, he forced Ulysses S. Grant to resign from the army due to an incident in California in which Grant was too drunk to perform his duties.[15] Buchanan had barely settled into his duties when Col. Hoffman advanced the idea of increasing the number of barracks for prisoners at the fort. Hoffman informed Secretary Stanton that he thought that Fort Delaware should be prepared to receive 10,000 prisoners. In the letter, Hoffman stated that he thought "that we may never have occasion to prepare for so many, but the chances are in favor of our having quite that number to take care of occasionally though it may be only for a short time, and it will probably be the best economy and certainly the most convenient course to be prepared permanently for any number that may be thrown in our hands at any one time."[16]

April 11, 1863, was a day that saw a great deal of activity directed toward Fort Delaware. Secretary Stanton agreed with the idea of expanding the facilities for holding prisoners. He directed Col. George H. Crosman, the assistant quartermaster-general stationed in Philadelphia, to have additional barracks for 5000 prisoners built on Pea Patch Island immediately. Col. Hoffman also mentioned the barracks to Stanton the same day, saying that he felt that changes should be made in the design of the barracks. It was:

> proposed to substitute shingles for felt roofing, probably to secure more durability and better security against leakage, but principally with a view to collect in wooden tanks all the rainwater that falls on them. Large quantities of water will be required for the prisoners if the barracks are ever fully occupied, and the Quartermaster-General is considering the propriety of employing a steam water-boat which perhaps will be considered as obviating the necessity of change in the roofing.[17]

Col. Hoffman also ordered Lt. Col. Martin Burke, the commanding officer of Fort Hamilton in New York Harbor, on the 11th to send prisoners of war from Fort Lafayette to Fort Delaware under the authority of the Navy Department for exchange. The Quartermaster's Department was to get transportation for the prisoners and General Brown, the commander of New York Harbor, was required to send a suitable guard. To avoid a large guard, the parole of the prisoners would be binding until they were exchanged. He also wrote to Lt. Col. Ludlow on the same day telling him that there were about 80 rebel officers being held at Fort Delaware and that 450 more prisoners were being sent there from Camp Chase, Ohio, in a day or two.[18]

The prisoners did arrive on the 12th, complaining of the treatment they had received as they were leaving their previous camp. Brig. Gen. T. J. Churchill of the Confederate Army sent a letter of protest the next morning to Col. Hoffman concerning what happened there. As Churchill and the other prisoners were leaving, their clothes were taken from them. Churchill had his luggage emptied, his overcoat, gloves, sash, combs, brushes, and spurs taken from him. The 300 to 400 other officers all had the same complaint, with some of them even having the shirts ripped from their backs. Their money held by the commandant was not returned to them upon leaving, making it impossible for them to buy replacement clothing. Col. Buchanan verified this by also sending a letter with Churchill's complaint stating that he had to issue 422 blankets to the prisoners and that he needed 30 more to take care of the others coming from Camp Chase since he had run out of blankets.[19]

Four days later, Hoffman answered Churchill and Buchanan about the incident. He said that this kind of conduct was not authorized and was in violation of General Orders #100, which governed the treatment of prisoners. However, he then used the rest of the letter to complain about the treatment the Union prisoners of war received at the hands of the Confederacy. He said that since Federal soldiers were treated the same way that Churchill and the others were treated, that nullified their complaints. He also stated that Rebel prisoners of war were always given clothes and blankets, their sick and wounded were always properly cared for, and in conclusion, he hoped that

> the humane example which has been set by the Government of the United States in its care for the welfare of prisoners of war may be followed by the Government

at Richmond, a course which cannot fail to greatly mitigate the hardships [that] must unavoidably be experienced by all who are so unfortunate as to be captured. Very respectfully, your obedient servant, W. Hoffman, Colonel, Third Infantry, Commissary-General of Prisoners.[20]

Lt. Col. Buchanan only stayed as commander at Fort Delaware for a few weeks and was replaced by Brig. Gen. Albin F. Schoepf. General Schoepf was born in Podgorze, Poland, in 1822.[21] He served with Kossuth during the revolts in Hungary in 1848. He was also a graduate of the Military Academy of Vienna. When Hungary attempted to gain its independence, Captain Schoepf resigned his commission and followed Generals Gorgei and Bem, who followed Kossuth. When the side that Schoepf fought for lost, he and Bem went to Turkey, where he became a bimbashi (major) and served as an artillery instructor.[22] He emigrated to the United States in 1851 and worked as a porter at a hotel in Washington D.C. While there, he became friends with Joseph Holt, the patent commissioner, who gave him a job as a draftsman at the patent office. When James Buchanan became President in 1857, he made Holt the Secretary of War. Holt, in turn, transferred Schoepf to the War Department.[23] At the beginning of the war, Schoepf was made a brigadier general because of the recommendation of the then general in chief Winfield Scott due to his previous background.[24] He commanded the Wildcat Brigade in Kentucky and Tennessee in the early part of the war, but resigned after being wounded. He rejoined the army in 1863 and was appointed commander of Fort Delaware in April of the same year and served in that capacity until January 1866.[25]

No sooner had Gen. Schoepf arrived at Fort Delaware than he received a letter from Col. Hoffman giving him instructions on the running of the prison and a glimpse into the future. He first discussed with Schoepf the plans for construction that were first mentioned while his predecessor was stationed there. Then he informed Schoepf that from that point on, Fort Delaware would become a major staging area for prisoners and that the rules and regulations that pertained to a prison needed to be strictly enforced for that reason.[26]

The need to build housing for the anticipated expansion of the prison population was a topic that continued to be explored. On April 15 and 16, 1863, Col. Hoffman went to Fort Delaware for an inspection of the barracks. He agreed with Col. Buchanan that the barracks erected the year before were not good enough for

Gen. Albin F. Schoepf, commander of Fort Delaware from 1863 to 1866.

holding prisoners. He believed that he did not have to make a decision about them quickly because they were not needed at that point.[27] He went back to Washington and on April 25, wrote to Col. Crosman about the project. In the letter, he stated that it had been decided that wooden tanks would be used to collect rainwater from the roofs of the prisoners' barracks. He also said that water would be carried over from the mainland to help with the expected increase of prisoners. In addition, he laid out the changes in the barracks that he wanted. He said that the barracks already in place had their floor on the ground. The floor was always very damp, which made them uncomfortable and unhealthy. Col. Hoffman felt that the buildings were tall enough so that the floor could be raised fifteen to eighteen inches off of the ground and there would still be enough space from the floor to the eaves to allow three tiers of bunks, which would be about nine feet in height. It was also his experience that ventilation by an opening in the roof through its whole length just below the ridge would not be practical because in stormy weather, rain and snow would blow in, making the barracks wet and uncomfortable. He preferred to have square ventilators placed fifteen or twenty feet apart set into the comb of the roof with shutters on the four sides, which he felt would be more effective.[28]

On May 15, 1863, Col. Hoffman wrote to Lt. Col. Ludlow to inform him that he could hold 2,000 paroled prisoners in Washington and 5,000 at Annapolis. Any extra had to be sent to Fort Delaware. He also stated that there were 1,100 prisoners at Fort Delaware and they would be sent to Ludlow whenever he requested them.[29] The prisoners held at Fort Delaware were sent away to City Point for exchange on May 21 to the great joy of guards and prisoners alike.[30]

Even though Col. Hoffman had warned Gen. Schoepf that Fort Delaware would become a major staging area for prisoners, he still was not sure if they would be staying for any length of time. Joseph R. Smith, the acting Surgeon General, asked Col. Hoffman on June 7, 1863, about how many prisoners he was planning to keep at Fort Delaware and how long they would be staying there so that he could calculate what kind of hospital arrangements he would have to make on the island. Hoffman replied the next day that barracks for 8,000 to 10,000 prisoners were being erected there and a hospital corresponding in size would be built. He was not sure if that large a number of prisoners would ever be collected there, and how long they remained would depend on circumstances which could not be foreseen. He felt if provisions were made for the usual proportion of sick in 5,000 men for forty-five days, Smith would have enough time to obtain any additional supplies that would be required.[31]

As fast as prisoners were removed from the fort, more came in. On June 9, 1863, Col. Hoffman ordered Gen. Schoepf to send all of the enlisted men he received from the west to City Point along with duplicate parole rolls signed and a roll for Hoffman's office. The rolls were to be made out by regiments and companies.[32] On the same day, the fort received 1,994 prisoners from Vicksburg. They were dirty, tired, and saying that they were willing to take the Oath of Allegiance. The next day, Schoepf wrote back to Hoffman to let him know how many prisoners he had and told him that he had plenty of room for 4,000 more prisoners.[33]

PRISON BARRACKS
1864

POW barracks.

Perhaps Schoepf spoke a little too hastily because by June 15, he had written to Brig. Gen. William A. Hammond, the Surgeon General, stating that he had 4,000 prisoners and needed one or two more surgeons stationed at the fort. He said that there were too many sick people for two acting assistant surgeons to handle.[34] The influx of prisoners continued when over 710 prisoners came in on the 14th and 1,500 more the next day. Many of them were sick and 3 had died.[35] Within the month, Schoepf had written to Major Gen. Robert C. Schenck, who had visited the fort in June, telling him that he had 9,040 prisoners and could not take any more.[36]

Apparently, the large number of prisoners being held at the fort made more than just Gen. Schoepf nervous. During the month of June, there were several rumors of plots to take over the garrison. On the 17th, three Confederate officers who were under parole and given the run of the island went to a Union officer and turned in their paroles. They told him that they had no further need of them. Immediately, it was assumed that the prisoners were planning to take over the island. Gen. Schoepf had the three men placed under close confinement. The guards were very excited about the stories being passed around and were prepared to thwart any such plot, which did not come about. On the 28th, a dispatch boat from Philadelphia arrived in the evening. Those on board told the garrison that the Rebels who lived in Delaware were planning to give the prisoners weapons and free them. This rumor fueled a great deal of activity. The guards were increased to 100 men and two gunboats waited on the Delaware River for the first sign of trouble. Only a few troops were allowed outside the walls of the fort. Troops paraded inside the walls and the cannons were loaded. The gunboats fired off a few shots and stirred up the island's population. The Union soldiers made a great show of their might to discourage any takeover plot. Whether or not the plot was real, no uprising occurred.

Other Rebels were busy at this time, but not with a plot to take over the island. Some of the prisoners were taking the Oath of Allegiance and joining the Union army. Those who joined were placed in the 1st Delaware Heavy Artillery at the fort. The 1st Delaware was under the command of Capt. Ahl, who also served as Gen. Schoepf's assistant adjunctant general. Sergeant Abraham G. Wolf was made a lieutenant in this battery and was in charge of the prisoners There were four prisoners who enlisted in the army on the 23rd and more during the next few days.[37]

General Hammond received another letter several weeks after Col. Hoffman contacted him expressing some concerns about the conditions on the island. Reverdy Johnson wrote a letter from Baltimore dated July 4, 1863, complaining about the conditions that had developed at the prison. In it, he said:

> A friend writes me that the crowded state of the prisoners at Fort Delaware and the brackishness of the drinking water is proving very fatal to the occupants. He says they are dying at the rate of from ten to fifteen a day. Can this be so? I advise you of it that if you find it true you may direct the means of arresting it. If suffered it will be a libel on our good name. I do not know if the matter falls within your province, but if not, I am sure you will let those who should attend to it know what is said. Let me hear from you as soon as you can conveniently.[38]

Water was definitely a problem at the prison as Mr. Johnson stated in his letter. In the original setup of Fort Delaware, water was supplied by rainwater coming off the roof. It ran from the roof through a filtering system made up of 6 inches of sand, 2 feet of earth, 9 inches of gravel, and several layers of bricks. This was a sufficient supply of water when the fort was occupied by just soldiers. However, when the prisoners began arriving, a different arrangement had to be created. When the prisoners barracks were built, rainwater was also collected from the roofs to augment the water supply. This proved to not be enough water to care for the needs of the prisoners, so on July 11th, a steam water boat was ordered to Fort Delaware. The boat was assigned to go to the Brandywine River and bring water back to the fort. Unfortunately, the water from the Brandywine was not filtered, and it left a sandy sediment several inches thick in the cisterns. This made the water bad for drinking, creating diarrhea and much sickness among the prisoners.[39]

One of the reasons that the prison was so crowded was that Maj. Gen. Schenck ordered Gen. Schoepf not to send prisoners to City Point as he was going to do originally. Schenck defended his decision by stating that he was told that the prisoners would be used in the defense of Richmond upon their release. Not only were the prisoners not sent to City Point, but 1,100 more prisoners were sent to the island from Baltimore three days later on the 8th.[40]

The change of plans concerning the transfer of prisoners to City Point was not the only reason for the continued growth of the prison population in the first week of July. The island was charged with excitement over the reports coming in from Pennsylvania about the great battle raging there. It was the main topic of conversation at the fort.[41] It was also the focus of those living in the area. When Lee's army came through the North in June 1863, the citizens of Delaware panicked. The 5th and 6th Delaware Regiments were called out to watch the rail lines of the Philadel-

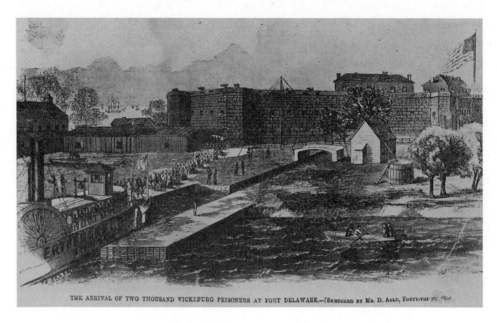

THE ARRIVAL OF TWO THOUSAND VICKSBURG PRISONERS AT FORT DELAWARE.—[SKETCHED BY MR. D. AULD, FORTY-THIRD

2,000 prisoners arriving from Vicksburg.

phia, Wilmington, and Baltimore Railroad and help guard the prisoners at Fort Delaware. There was an emergency meeting of the citizens of Wilmington on June 29 to plan for the defense of the city. On June 30, the mayor of Wilmington asked all men to volunteer for some sort of military service.

The Fourth of July was a quiet one in Wilmington because of the threat of invasion. The services at City Hall, which included the reading of the Declaration of Independence, was sparsely attended. Later in the day, word began to filter in that Lee had been defeated. The mood at the fort and the surrounding area changed. Happy people crowded the streets of Wilmington.[42] The troops at the fort celebrated with a 35 heavy gun salute and fireworks. There were also 1,900 prisoners transferred out that day. Their presence was not missed because two days later, prisoners from the battle of Gettysburg and the siege of Vicksburg, which ended on the 4th, began arriving. The first wave brought in 1,200 Rebels and 2,800 more the next day. In addition to the prisoners who came from Baltimore, 1,000 came on the 10th, 1,000 more on the 11th, 260 on the 13th, and 700 more Confederate prisoners on the 14th. With this many men coming into the prison in such a short period of time, there were bound to be some problems.[43]

During this time, in which there was a tremendous number of prisoners coming onto the island, the issue of the barracks came up again in an unexpected way. Gen. Schoepf contacted Gen. Meigs on the 7th to report on the new barracks. He said that they were "built strictly according to contract" and the workmanship and materials used were acceptable. However, due to the "spongy nature of the soil and the rains combined," the foundation props began to sink as soon as he put prisoners into them. Some sunk nearly a foot, which weakened the building. Schoepf knew he was to receive 8,000 more prisoners in the near future and he was afraid if he put them in the barracks, the building might tip over and many prisoners would be killed. He was also concerned that the hospital which was to be built would suffer the same fate. He requested that Col. Crosman be ordered to send an architect to Fort Delaware to correct these problems, which he was ordered to do four days later.[44]

The overcrowded conditions at Fort Delaware caused the Confederate government to look into what was going on there. In a letter to Confederate Secretary of War James A. Seddon, dated July 30th, Confederate Surgeon General S.P. Moore complained about the conditions at the prison. A former prisoner had told Moore about the situation and had convinced him that the increase in deaths at the island was caused by a combination of overcrowding, unhealthy food, and bad water. He asked Secretary Seddon to contact the Federal authorities to see if they could do something to improve the situation. A copy of this letter was also sent to Brig. Gen. S.A. Meredith, the Union agent of exchange, by his Confederate counterpart, Robert Ould, with a cover letter which ended by asking: "Can nothing be done to stop the fearful mortality at Fort Delaware? Is it intended to fill our land with mourning by such means of subjugation?"[45]

The situation was looked into and on August 19, 1863, Gen. Schoepf wrote to Col. Hoffman and reported on this issue. Schoepf thought that the prisoners were as healthy as they would be at any other place. The death rate was lower than that of a regular city of 10,000 people, which was the number of prisoners Fort Delaware held at that time. He also felt that the months of July and August were especially hard on those men who were already worn out physically, such as the prisoners received from Vicksburg after its surrender on July 4, 1863. The water was collected from Brandywine Creek, which Schoepf stated was known for its pure water, by a steam pump and placed into tanks near the barracks. It was used for cooking and drinking by Union soldiers and prisoners. He also said that the food for the prisoners was the same as that given to the guards. The prisoners got fresh meat four times a week and fresh vegetables were given out when they could be brought in.

The general also sent a letter to Hoffman from the Rebel surgeons dated the same day stating that they looked at the death lists of the fort from July 1, 1863, to August 19, 1863. During that time period, 180 prisoners had died, which averaged out to 4 a day. They thought that the rate was small, considering that there were 10,000 prisoners there at that time. The surgeons thought that Schoepf was doing his best to keep the prisoners healthy. The sick were being treated as well as possible, new hospitals were being built to hold more prisoners, and the prisoners were not being forced to drink water from the ditches on Fort Delaware as was earlier reported. The water boat that came twice a day brought enough water for everyone, plus they also had the rain water that collected from the roofs for the prisoners' use. The barracks were also kept as clean as possible under the circumstances. This report was written and signed by R.R. Goode, surgeon and medical director, E. Holt Jones, medical inspector, Thomas W. Foster, surgeon, and W.W. Cleves, surgeon.[46]

At the same time this report was sent to Washington, another one also arrived.

Col. Hoffman had ordered Surgeon Charles H. Crane to inspect the Rebel hospitals at Davids Island, N.Y., Chester, Pa., Fort Delaware, Gettysburg, Pa., and the West Hospital in Baltimore, Md., to see how healthy they were and to find out "how far the regulations for the government of officers in charge of prisoners of war are carried out." Once that was discovered, Crane was suppose to then write a report to Hoffman.[47] In the meantime, Medical-Inspector Lieutenant Colonel Cuyler sent a report about Fort Delaware to Medical Inspector-General Joseph K. Barnes. This report told of "numerous cases of low form of disease" which was blamed partially on "the crowded conditions of the prison." Barnes sent the report to Brig. Gen. W.A. Hammond; in it a number of suggestions were made on how to improve the prison. He felt that the recommendations could be completed with a small amount of money from the prisoners. The suggestions to improve the sanitary conditions were as follows:

> Improving ventilation by making openings flush with the floor of barracks at intervals of fifteen feet; additional windows at ends of buildings; reducing the number of bunks by removing one tier; constructing wooden troughs in or near the buildings for washing faces and hands; urinals at convenient distances, with movable soil tubs or latrines, for use of sick in quarters at night, the distance to the sinks being considerable; ditches and drains to be kept free, and the interior of barracks whitewashed at least every six weeks. The prisoners have no bedding, and so little clothing that it is almost impossible to enforce cleanliness of person.[48]

Fort Delaware was rapidly becoming a bad place to be thanks to overcrowding, the breakdown of the exchange system, and the suspension of the writ of habeas corpus. It was not a calculated effort on anyone's part to torment the prisoners on Pea Patch Island. However, due to the breakdown of a system that was ill prepared to handle the influx of prisoners into camps that were not created to hold the large numbers of captured soldiers generated by the war, many prisoners suffered. It was that way in prison camps on both sides of the Mason-Dixon Line, but that was cold comfort to the men who lived on the Devil's Half Acre.

⚔ 5 ⚜

Life on the
Devil's Half Acre

Fort Delaware was shaped like a granite pentagon. It had 100 guns mounted on three tiers of casements that guarded both channels of the Delaware River, which was about one mile wide. A moat surrounded the fort, which was filled with water. The whole island could have been flooded with four or five feet of water by opening the flood gates. The fort itself sat on the southeast corner of the island. When the federal government decided to build the fort, a levee was built to surround the island and close out the tides. This made the island livable. However, the soil was so black, loamy, and porous that one prisoner feared walking too hard on it in case that the ground opened up like quicksand. That quip was not much of an exaggeration. The fort was situated on ten acres of reclaimed swamp and five feet below water level. The river would sometimes seep through the levee and into the ground so that on rainy days, the island would become a sea of mud. The ditches, or "canals," connecting in all directions to the moat, would, at low tide, have just enough water in them to float the trash and waste from thousands of men out into the Delaware River. This made Fort Delaware a breeding ground for cholera. There were also no trees or shrubs for shade. In the summer, the heat would make the ground crack and the surface of the stream would sizzle. There was nothing during the winter to protect them from the winds that came off the river and ripped through the clothes of guards and prisoners alike. The noise of the winds would also mix with the sounds of icebergs crashing in the river during February and March which made it sound like the storms would sweep the fort into the waters.[1]

Prisoners were held in large pens under the guns of the fort. These were formed by creating an enclosure shaped like a parallelogram with one long line of one-story pine barracks which ran along the northeast and half of the south side of the fort. The other half of the south side was taken up by the cookhouse. The west side had a high fence that had a parapet manned by three guards.[2] This enclosure, or court-yard, was divided into two separate yards by two lines of high plank fences. These fences had a parapet running along the top so that guards could walk on it to keep watch over the prisoners. The fences were ten feet apart to keep the officers, who were held in the smaller pen closer to the fort, and enlisted men, who were in the larger and more crowded pen, separated. There were also gates placed in the fences that opened into the two pens.

The row of barracks was situated under one roof but separated into rooms called divisions. These rooms were numbered 1 to 40. The barracks were made up of long planks standing on end in line that ran around three sides of a square. The floors were "rough as a stable," the roof leaked, the weather boarding was so open that a man could put his hand between most of the planks, and snow drifts collected on the beds at night in the winter.[3] Each division had a lamp burning dimly all night long and to touch it would mean that prisoner's death. Lights out, except for the lamp, was at 8:00 P.M. and there was no talking allowed after that time. This rule was not always strictly enforced by the guard who patrolled behind the divisions.[4]

Each division was twenty feet long by ten feet wide and held 100 men. Inside the division was a center aisle, which was five feet wide. The aisle contained a table and a stove in the middle.[5] The stove had enough coal to keep it red hot and in the winter, the prisoners were packed in like sardines around it. The other men walked the floor and waited their turn. When a man would get warm, someone behind him would ask, "Captain, give me your place when you are warm." This request was made of everyone.[6] The prisoners were not allowed any bedding and only one blanket. Everything else was taken away. They would lie on one half of the blanket and cover themselves with the other half. The rest of the space was taken up with three tiers of shelves. The first tier was four feet off of the ground and the other two tiers were four feet apart up to the roof. Each shelf on the tier was six feet wide. At night, 50 men on each north and south wall slept on the shelves, side by side, heads against the wall, and their feet toward the center. The men could only get up to the upper tiers by climbing up the support beams, which were only long pieces of scantling going from floor to ceiling. Cross-pieces were fastened to these supports to form a ladder, but they were soon worn out because of their continuous use. The larger pris-oners had to be careful on these flimsy ladders in case they broke, which would send them ten to fifteen feet to the floor, the table, or onto the stove in the aisle.

Even if a prisoner did not come crashing down onto someone or something, there were still other problems with climbing up and down on ladders made of thin pieces of wood. The occupants of the lower tiers had their blankets, clothes, faces, and food sprayed with mud, trash, vermin, and anything else that was attached to the boots of the person going up and down the ladder. Also, if a man spilled water, coffee, or ink on the upper tier, which was called "upstairs," that meant that grav-

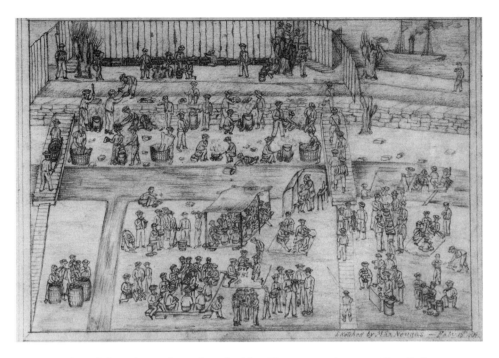

Drawing of the prisoners' pen done by Max Neugas, a prisoner at Fort Delaware.

ity would help them share it with their bunkmates below. This type of closeness to that many people was a problem when someone was sick. One prisoner remembered lying for a week directly under a man who had smallpox and later helping to lift him down after he died. The men on the lower tier did not have to deal with some of the rain leaks or breathe air so bad that it would make a man feel like his lungs had frozen up inside of him as the "high livers" did. On the other hand, the "floor men" were the most uncomfortable. They dealt with the dripping from higher men and breathing in the dampness from the wet ground under the open, badly constructed floor.[7] These conditions made the barracks much less healthy to live in than inside the fort. Diarrhea, sore-throats and bad food happened more often in the wooden barracks than within the walls of the fort.[8]

All valuables were taken from the prisoners upon arrival at the fort. If a prisoner wanted to have anything of value, he needed to hide it. Capt. Henry C. Dickinson hid his money and valuables in the grass as he stood on the lawns outside of the hospitals waiting to be searched, counted, and called for the rolls.[9] Once all of this was done, the gates of the pen were opened and the guards told the new prisoners to "hunt holes to sleep in." As soon as they entered, someone would spot them and call out "Fresh Fish! Fresh Fish!" At that point, any prisoner already being held in the pen would rush from their bunks to see them and ask them for the latest news from the outside world. Each old prisoner would grab a new man and overwhelm him with questions about anything. Any topic was fair game, such as the military, politics, and questions that could be considered civil and uncivil of a total stranger.

One new prisoner remembered ending up at Division 34, which was positioned directly over one of the ditches that crisscrossed the yard. These dirty ditches were used for washing. The floor of the barracks was rough and uneven like a pile of rails and the floorboards were so far apart that a person could have dropped a marble through the cracks into the water below.

The barracks all had one door and two windows, which opened out to the pen. There were narrow plank walks which ran around the square in front of the doors. On the northeast corner of the pen was the main gate. There was a small box near the entrance which was for the prisoners to deposit their letters for mailing.[10] The prisoners received mail regularly. Letters sent to a prisoner could not be more than one page in length. Each division assigned one man to be their postmaster. Every evening, when a signal was given, the postmasters went to the hole in the wall on the west side to collect the incoming mail. If any letters had money in them, the envelope was delivered to the addressee and the money was exchanged for checks that could only be given to the sutler. If a check was sent, even if it was marked as good by a bank, it was held and sutler checks were given to the prisoner minus a ten per cent fee for collection. The Union officials wanted to limit the amount of real money prisoners had so that they would be unable to bribe a guard.[11]

There was also an opening nearby called the "Surgeon's window." It was here that the doctor would come once a day or once every three or four days to check on the prisoners. The line was so long that the patients would have to wait for hours in

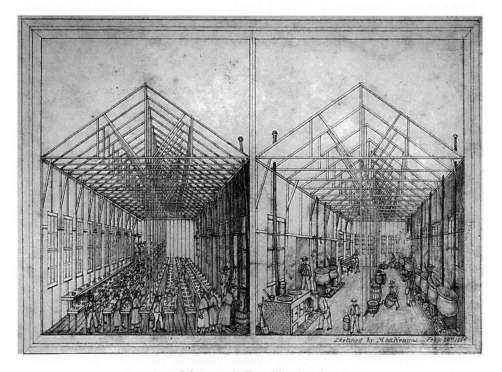

Drawing of the mess hall and kitchen by Neugas.

the weather to see the doctor. The doctor would then prescribe bread pills, magnesia, quinine, or a white powder that the prisoners believed to be sifted flour, to cure the patients.

The plank walkways in front of the barracks led to the dining room. It was a room in the western corner of the square where there were ten long tables, two feet wide, made up of rough planks. At 8:30 A.M. and 2:00 P.M., the prisoners would hear a shout and the various divisions would line up in twos behind their chiefs of division and march down the plank walkways to the dining room, which was also known as the cook house.[12] One prisoner described this walk through the "Devil's Half Acre" to the dining room: "during the cold and pitiless blasts of winter as they swept over the bay and chilled our feeble frames; during the scorching summer and autumn months, when no protection was allowed us from the burning sun, and the pestilence-laden, damp, dark, deathly winds."[13] Once there, a guard "boss" would stand in the doorway and send half of the prisoners to the left of the tables and the other half to the right. The food was already placed on the tables 18 inches apart. There was no place to sit, so the men had to line themselves up properly so that everyone had a portion in front of him. This type of jockeying for position meant that it took a great deal of time before everyone was inside. Some prisoners did not stay to eat, but preferred to take the food back to their barracks. There were several reasons for this. First, they would have to leave the dining room if they wanted to sit down while they ate. Second, if they stayed, they would have to eat quickly in fear of someone else grabbing their share. Another reason was that some prisoners liked to not eat all of their meal at once so that they could save it for later to have a third meal.[14] If they did not do that and they did not have money to buy food from the sutler or have food sent to them from someone from the outside, a prisoner's third meal of the day was, in the words of Major J. Ogden Murray, "wind."[15]

The meals the prisoners protected so carefully were a 3 inch long, 1 inch thick piece of cornbread, yellow in color, a small piece of bacon or beef, and "a cup of decoction of logwood and beans called coffee" for breakfast.[16] Dinner offered a little bit more. It contained the bread again and two to three ounces of "loud-smelling pickled beef—'red horse' as it was called—and a tin cup of miserable stuff, called soup, so mean that I could not swallow it".[17] The meat was fat and had the potential of being good, but it was killed the day before and brought in about 9:00 A.M. It was covered with green flies and usually so bad that it could not be eaten.[18] The cooks claimed that the soup they served was rice soup, but the prisoners had their doubts. In the opinion of the men who ate it, the soup was made up of rotten water, rice hulls, dozens of half inch long white worms in every cupful, grit, hair, with an occasional grain of corn or piece of rice. The cup was normally half full, or half empty depending on the attitude of the prisoner. There were times when bean soup would replace the rice soup, but the quality and quantity were the same. The running gag of the prisoners was that "the soup was too weak to drown the rice worms and pea bugs, which, however, came to their death by starvation."[19]

Pea bugs were not the only ones who had fears about starving to death on Fort

Delaware. The dairy rations were so small that some prisoners actually felt tired from walking around the prison grounds. Captain Thomas Pinckney wrote that when he took his daily walk around the grounds, he "would time myself to note the rate of my waning strength, the burden of my thoughts being, 'At this rate how long can I hold out?' and 'How near must the end be?'"[20]

There was a sutler on the island who sold food and other items the prisoners could use to survive, such as coffee pots, pans, and wood. If a prisoner had enough money, he could buy goods from the sutler and have enough to eat. There was even an ice cream saloon attached to the sutler's shop at one time until he was ordered to shut it down. The sutler was from New England and only sold such items that he could get top dollar for, since he had no competition. He had several assistants working for him and they were generally considered by the prisoners as little more than vultures.[21] In October 1864, the sutler claimed that it was against orders from Washington to run his shop in the prison and he had to use bribes to stay in business. Therefore, he had to pass on the extra cost of bribes to his customers, which is why his prices were so high. He charged $.60 for a pound of butter, $4.00 a bushel for Irish potatoes, $2.50 a gallon for molasses, $2.25 a pound for tea, and $1.25 a plug for tobacco, to name the prices for just some of his items.

There was another way that the soldiers supplemented their supply of food. Pea Patch Island had a thriving population of rats. They were not the average house rat, but a larger version of water rat. Some sections of the grounds were riddled with rat holes. The men would wait quietly near a breathing hole with clubs in their hands. When one of the unsuspecting rats would appear, it would be attacked for the chance of having a dinner made up of "fresh meat and rat soup." This dietary supplement was easy to obtain, with at least one or more rats usually caught at the same time.

Officers were not above enjoying this type of meal. When served either deviled or stewed, rat was said to look like squirrel meat. The flesh was white and when several were served on a plate with a great deal of dressing, it looked rather appetizing. When a fellow soldier objected to one rat fancier to the eating of rats, the culinary adventurer replied: "Why, you eat wagon loads of hogs, and everybody knows a rat is cleaner than a hog. Rats are just as dainty as squirrels or chickens. Try a piece?"[22]

Some Rebel officers caused hard feelings with their fellow prisoners because of their ability to get outside help. These fortunate prisoners were able to obtain either food from the outside or the money to buy food from the sutlers on the island. Instead of sharing their extra food, some officers would keep it until it spoiled and then throw it into the ditch. Two to five men would band together in a mess and share what they had with each other and hire someone to cook the food and make the coffee in exchange for sharing their rations with them. Eating all that they received was one thing; it was considered quite another thing to feast and be wasteful while their fellow prisoners were hunting rats or rooting through the garbage looking for their leftovers. This feeling of resentment also applied to receiving clothing. Once again, the lucky ones were able to get a regular supply of clothing and keep two or more suits of clothes for themselves without trying to share some of what they did not need with those who were constantly patching the same set of clothes.[23]

Water was a big problem for the prisoners of Fort Delaware. The demand for water was barely filled during the rainy season, but the supply in the summer and fall was not enough for the prisoners. At first, the water supply came from the rain water flowing from the roofs and collected in two wooden tanks. The purity of the water was questionable. When there were steady rains, the supply was relatively clean. However, when there was no rain for a few weeks, the water would become stagnant and putrid. When the lids of the barrels were opened, the thirsty prisoner would be treated to the sight of a swarming mass of wiggletails and white worms in his drinking water. There was no way to strain the water or purify it. Another problem was that the lower the amount of water in the tanks, the more they stank. The whole situation caused one prisoner to sum it all up by saying, "It isn't natural to take one's fresh meat and water so closely mixed."[24]

Another problem with the water situation was the position of the fort in the first place. The surface of the island was little better than mud. It was porous and damp when it rained and hard as a rock when there were long stretches of dry weather. When there are thousands of prisoners placed on an island which is several feet below sea level, flat as a board, with no shade, in the summer the prisoners will bake like a plate full of cookies. Therefore, despite the smell and taste of the water, and the number of bugs in it, when there was none left in the tanks, everyone wanted that water. Especially in July and August, the heat could be so intense that there were days where "men by hundreds are seen sweltering on their backs, fairly gasping for breath, like fish dying on a sand beach." Outside water was brought in from the nearby Brandywine River on a water boat to try to relieve the situation. However, the boat did not go far enough upriver to get fresh water and the result was that the water shipped in was not much better that the water from the Delaware that came up through the ditches.[25]

When the prisoners' barracks were first created, man-made channels were built using the fact that at high tide, the island was five feet below sea level. The river was held back by dykes that surrounded the island. Two ditches four feet wide and two feet deep were built on the western side of the island and stretched from the moat to the other canal. It went under the officers' barracks and through the privates' pen with flood gates on either end. The gate in the outer canal was opened once a day when high tide occurred until the water from the bay filled the channel. The water would gradually fill up the smaller ditches, which would wash away all of the waste since all trash was thrown into them. This water was never clean, but this was what the prisoners used for bathing, washing their clothes, pans, dishes, and, when the water supply ran out, drinking. From dawn to close to noon every day, each side of the ditch was filled with thousands of men in various states of undress, splashing themselves with water covered with green "frog foam" in an effort to get clean. The purity was not helped by not only the waste being dumped into the water, but also by the constant dipping of thousands of buckets and pans into the ditches.[26] The water was so bad that even a slight wound washed in it would become inflamed and mortified. Amputation and/or death followed.[27]

The issue of the cleanliness of the fort continued from another angle. Robert Ould, agent of exchange, C.S.A., wrote to Brig. Gen. Meredith, agent of exchange, U.S.A., about it also on August 28. In his contact with Meredith, Ould sent a statement from an unnamed writer concerning the treatment of Rebel prisoners. Ould asked for a proper report to be made about it and if the statement about the fort was false, then Ould said that the Confederate government would deal with the writer themselves.[28]

On September 1, 1863, Hoffman sent a copy of the report to Gen. Schoepf. He told Schoepf to do with the report what he saw fit. Hoffman thought it would not cost much to fix things and suggested that the prison fund could pay for the repairs. He did not think it was a good idea to get rid of the one tier of bunks because they might need them for more prisoners. If the prison became too crowded, the excess could be sent to Point Lookout, Md. At that time, he also offered to transfer 1,000 or 1,500 prisoners on Schoepf's recommendation.[29]

On September 11, Col. Hoffman received the report from Crane. He had arrived at Fort Delaware on September 3, 1863, and gave the report of his inspection on the overall condition of the fort. Crane stated that there were 8,000 prisoners there and:

> they have been much crowded together, sick and well, in the same barracks, which it has been impossible to keep clean. The opening of a new hospital at this post which contains 600 beds will improve the condition of affairs very much, and the separation of the sick will improve their sanitary condition immensely. The patients were being moved the day I was there very much to their relief. Greater facilities for cooking are needed, and rigid policing in the neighborhood of the kitchens, mess-rooms, and throughout the barracks cannot be too strictly enforced. General Schoepf informs me that he was able to procure everything that was needed and wanted for nothing. He appears to be very zealous and attentive in the discharge of his duties and gives all his time to a personal supervision of the wants of those under his charge and labors to improve their condition. I do not consider Fort Delaware a desirable location, in a sanitary point of view, for a large depot of prisoners. The ground is wet and marshy and the locality favorable for the development of malarious diseases. There have been many deaths at this place from typhoid fever, the result of their being crowded together in large numbers in a confined space.[30]

Complaints about the treatment of the prisoners were passed on to Gen. Schoepf by Col. Hoffman. Schoepf defended himself to Hoffman on Sept. 15, 1863, by telling him that he was following the orders that Hoffman had given him. The orders were concerned with the visiting of prisoners and the type of clothing that the prisoners were allowed to receive. He wrote out the orders as Special Orders No. 165 to inform those on the island of the regulations. Schoepf also had the orders printed in the Philadelphia and Baltimore papers because many people from the two towns were constantly sending the prisoners large amounts of clothing that could be made into uniforms which would help in any escape attempt.[31]

The prisoners did receive a large amount of clothing, food, and other items from family and friends to make their stay in the prison more comfortable. The boxes containing these things were shipped by express and handed out to the prisoners twice a week. Every box was always opened in full view of the prisoners and examined carefully. The guards searched the cans of fruit and bottles for whiskey. Any clothing sent was searched for money, contraband letters, or anything else that would be considered illegal for prisoners to have in their possession. If there was an abundance of a certain item of clothing sent to a specific prisoner, it was immediately confiscated. The same was true of any type of high quality clothing or hat. When clothing was given to a prisoner, he was immediately expected to take off his old clothes and put on the new. The guards were not completely successful in this endeavor because many prisoners would put on their new clothes and hide their old ones. All very old clothes were kept and passed along from friend to friend just in case the guards did manage to take the clothes away.[32]

The ever expanding prison population on Pea Patch Island raised questions not only of where the prisoners would be placed, but also what was to be done about supplies for them. In September 1863, Captain G. S. Clark, the commissary of subsistence of volunteers at the fort, expressed his opinion to General Schoepf on what was needed on the island to care for everyone. He felt that there was a shortage of storehouses for goods, especially if the fort was to hold a large number of prisoners during the winter. The situation was made more pressing because the Delaware River had been known to freeze over in the winter, which would shut them off from the mainland for two months. He wanted to have supplies for 12,000 men. He thought it was necessary to have storehouses capable of holding 7,000 barrels to supply the needs of everyone on the island.[33]

A few days later, Col. Hoffman contacted Gen. Schoepf about this problem. He told Schoepf that he should be prepared to hold a full complement of prisoners during the winter and that he agreed that a sufficient number of storehouses needed to be built. However, he believed that it was an exaggeration that the fort could be cut off from the rest of the world for two months in the winter. He authorized the use of the prison fund to pay for the construction of a storehouse, as well as the supplies that would be held in them, stoves for the prisoners' quarters and warmer clothes for them.[34]

There were still complaints within the federal government about the fitness of Fort Delaware to hold prisoners of war. In early October 1863, Assistant Surgeon H.R. Silliman wrote to Surgeon J. Simpson, the medical director of the Middle Department from Baltimore, sending the list of the number of dead prisoners of war from the month of September. He felt that the number was terrible and proof that it was an unfit place to keep large numbers of prisoners. The acting medical director, George Suckley, passed this letter on to Col. Hoffman with his own note stating that he wanted Hoffman to notice that out of the 7,000 prisoners not sick or wounded when they were sent to Fort Delaware, 300 had died in the previous month. Suckley also thought that the fort was not a healthy place for prisoners and that common decency dictated that a better place be found for a prison camp.[35]

The question of cleanliness at Fort Delaware continued with the outbreak of smallpox in the prison. Smallpox, one of the eruptive fevers, was the third highest cause of death among Confederate soldiers held in the North. The others were measles, scarlet fever, and erysipelas, which killed Major Sanders in 1858. Vaccinations were understood and accepted on principle. However, the vaccines were unreliable because they were made from shed scabs. This caused problems in the creation of a vaccine because the scabs were sometimes too old to be of use, since they had lost their charge of virus. There was also the chance that the scabs were contaminated, which occurred often. This caused infections and large, ugly ulcers on the area in which the vaccinations were given. However, the vaccinations did help and it was better to have an ulcer than smallpox.

One of the reasons that smallpox was so prevalent was that many of the farm boys who went off to fight in the Civil War had never been exposed to the disease as children or had vaccinations to fight it, as opposed to men who grew up in the larger cities and were exposed early to viruses. Someone who never had the disease or was never vaccinated was a breeding ground for microbial growth. In the field, an entire regiment or brigade could be attacked by the smallpox disease rendering thousands of men useless with fevers or chills. In the confines of a prison, the results were devastating.[36]

On October 26, 1863, Brig. Gen. Gilman Marston from Point Lookout, Md., told Col. Hoffman that every group of prisoners he received from Fort Delaware had cases of smallpox. There were 26 in the last group of men that arrived. He did not want any more prisoners from there because their arrival frightened his troops and the civilian workers. Hoffman passed this information on to the Surgeon General's office and the next day, he received a reply saying that no more prisoners were to be transferred from Fort Delaware until the disease was beaten. The Surgeon General's office had not received any word from Fort Delaware mentioning an outbreak of the disease. It was decided that if it became prevalent on Pea Patch Island, the prisoners who were sick would be separated and isolated as much as possible.[37]

On the 28th, Hoffman wrote to Schoepf telling him about the statements made by Gen. Marston. Hoffman wanted to know if smallpox was prevalent at the fort and how many cases of the disease were there. Schoepf answered Hoffman's questions the next day by saying that there were 130 cases of smallpox at Fort Delaware, but most of them were mild. He also stated that the number of smallpox cases was decreasing and the disease was entirely among the prisoners. The prisoners who were suffering from the disease were being kept in a contagious hospital made just for such cases. Schoepf closed by saying that he was told by Dr. H. R. Silliman, his post surgeon, that the first case of smallpox came from the prison at Camp Chase, Ohio.[38]

The general also wrote to Hoffman on November 7 and gave him a more detailed report on the smallpox situation. Schoepf told him that when he assumed command of Fort Delaware, there were 14 cases of smallpox and the disease had been there more or less ever since. Dr. Silliman was working on getting rid of the disease altogether. The general believed that it was a combination of smallpox with other diseases that caused the deaths. He was also happy that the number of deaths was decreasing. Deaths were on the average of 2½ a day. Preventative measures were taken to slow down the outbreak of the disease. The barracks were cleaned and whitewashed. Chloride of lime and Ridgewood disinfecting powder were sprinkled through the barracks to kill the disease. In addition, the prisoners were turned out once a day and kept out and moving for several hours. Smallpox vaccine and the instruments to administer it were given to the Confederate surgeons, who were sent into the barracks to give the prisoners the medicine. Every man not vaccinated in the preceding twelve months was given one. Finally, every man who arrived at the fort and who entered the hospital was required to receive a vaccination.[39]

Col. Hoffman's concern about the smallpox situation compelled him to send Surgeon A.M. Clark to visit Fort Delaware on November 12, 1863. He was ordered to inspect the hospital and the general sanitary conditions of the prisoners in the barracks. Hoffman wanted to know how bad the smallpox outbreak was and what was being done to fight it. Clark was ordered to report his findings to Hoffman in person with a written report.[40] Clark arrived at the fort, which at that time carried a complement of 800 guards to watch the 2,846 enlisted men, 33 commissioned officers, and the 52 civilians being held there as prisoners. His report stated that he felt that the prison was well run, with the exceptions of poor drainage and the lack of things for the prisoners to do to occupy themselves. He also felt that improvements on the ventilation in the barracks was necessary, as well as a better system for the prisoners to wash their clothes.

Surgeon Clark addressed the situation concerning the smallpox outbreak. He stated that he thought that the "smallpox hospital is overcrowded at present, but this will soon be obviated, for the disease is rapidly on the decrease." Clark also thought that the "smallpox hospital is located too near the general hospital, nearly adjoining it, but this the limits of the island render necessary. Additional materials for vaccination should be obtained and every man on reaching the island vaccinated. This is the only sure means of eventually eradicating the disease." He ended his report with this assessment:

> I have to report that in my opinion this post is an utterly unfit location for a prison, much more for a hospital. Lying so low, its level being some six feet below high tide, it is impossible to properly drain it or to prevent its surface being constantly marshy and wet. The island is traversed by ditches connecting with the main ditch encircling the island, and with the moat around the fort, and intended to be constantly full of water, changing with the tide. The moat is in process of repair, and during this the water is partially shut off, rendering the ditches partially dry. From the stagnant mud and partially stagnant water a constant, and in some cases a most offensive effluvia is constantly given off, rendering the atmosphere in a high degree unhealthy. Some of these ditches run directly underneath the barracks. The influence of such an atmosphere on a large number of men congregated together, and whose vital powers are depressed, as those of prisoners naturally are, cannot but be injurious.
>
> I would respectfully suggest that at this as at other posts where prisoners are confined some system of labor be devised, light it may be, but still sufficient to

occupy their minds and bodies, and thus obviate the depressing influence which confinement and want of occupation necessarily exercise. I am convinced that if this were done the general condition of the prisoners would be much improved and the numbers on the sick list rapidly diminished.

In many of the prisons which I have visited I have heard the men begging for work as a means of passing away time, and at Camp Douglas, where many of the prisoners were employed on the sewer and in erecting the new fence around the camp, these were by far the most cheerful and presented the best appearance. At every post I think that by some judiciously devised plan sufficient work could be found for all the prisoners to answer this purpose, if enforced by the commanding officer. At present I am convinced that idleness and ennui are more pregnant sources of disease than any other to be found in our various prisons.[41]

Idle hands may be the devil's tools, and on the Devil's Half Acre, those particular tools were sadly numerous among the many whose very lives depended on being busy.

6

Hope and Survival on the Devil's Half Acre

To be placed in a prison camp hundreds of miles from home and loved ones can easily sap a man's strength, both physically and emotionally. It is hard to keep one's spirits up when he eats food that is inadequate at best and lives in a building that might have a ditch flowing underneath it to go along with the mud and water that sometimes covers the floor. However, many of the men who entered Fort Delaware as prisoners did survive the experience, some better than others, however. The survival techniques of these men were as varied as the prisoners themselves. What they seemed to have in common was a willingness to make the best of a bad situation and reasonably good health when they arrived. Being healthy on their arrival gave prisoners the strength to deal with sickness and a lack of healthy food. At the same time, it was equally important to be able to stay busy doing something so that the mind and body stayed active.

Surgeon Clark reported that the prisoners at Camp Douglas and other prisons were begging for work to pass the time. The prisoners at Fort Delaware also wanted something to do to pass the time. Some prisoners worked at various jobs around the island, such as picking up boards and working on improvements in the fort. If they did this, they earned an extra ration a day, which was a strong motivator.[1] One of the projects that they worked on was the building of an Episcopal Church on the island. The cornerstone was laid on September 12, 1863, and the structure was completely built by prison labor.[2] The laborers were mostly made up of a group of condemned criminals who were on the island doing hard time for crimes ranging from desertion to murder. They were forced to transport heavy loads of stone or wood to be used to

51

repair buildings or the dykes. However, there were also political prisoners among this group. Captain William H. Gordon from West Virginia, charged with recruiting for the Confederate Army behind Union lines, and Mr. E.J. Debett were stripped of their clothes, given used Federal Army uniforms, and thrown in with the chain gang to help with the construction. Lt. Randolph Shotwell watched from a nearby window as Capt. Gordon went by. Gordon was paired with a convict and pulling a heavy cart with 50 other men. A Union guard, with a stick in his hand and sitting on a pile of concrete blocks, watched the laborers. He kept up a constant stream of abuse at the prisoners, saying "Pull, d — n you, pull! What the h — l you hanging back for?"[3] The prisoners worked for a long time hauling lumber for a half-mile to build the church and a hospital for the prisoners. They were promised that they would be paid for their labor, but they never received any money.[4] Not only that, but once the framed Gothic chapel was built and consecrated by Bishop Alfred Lee of the Diocese of Delaware, no prisoner was permitted to worship there.[5]

There were other types of work going on that were not created by the federal authorities. Many prisoners found ways of keeping busy that fit in with their particular skills. Some men applied themselves as barbers or shoe cobblers for their fellow inmates. The tools they had were not always perfect and they depended on the wealthier prisoners for payment. The form of payment could either be money, scraps of food, or a sutler's check.[6] There was one barber in particular, Captain Meadows, who had an excellent place for men's care. It was covered with blankets for protection from the elements, equipped with sharp razors and scissors, and offered a shampoo as well. This, combined with his reputation as a skillful barber, made going to Capt. Meadows a rare luxury.

Others set themselves up as washermen and ironers. There were many such men in the prison. They worked the hardest and received the least amount of money. They did their best to clean clothes from the water in the ditches, usually working within ten feet of the sinks. This type of work environment was particularly rough for these men. The smell from this area due to the sinks was terrible.[7] This was the same water in which prisoners washed themselves and that cooks used to make coffee and soup. Because of all the various ways the ditch water was used, its surface became a mixture of soapsuds and green foam.[8]

There were also men who sold things such as ice cream,[9] lemonade, beer, and cakes. The beer sellers would set their stands up at cool spots in the pen and sell lemon or ginger cakes to go along with the beer. They would buy one half bushel of corn for a dollar and one gallon of molasses for a dollar and a half to make thirty-two gallons. Some ginger and water were thrown in, the mix was allowed to ferment, and it was then sold for five cents a pint.[10] It was "villainous at best, but extra-villainous when heated to a luke warm temperature by hours under a vertical sun." This drink would not win any awards, but because of the lack of good drinking water and the fear of contracting scurvy due to the steady diet of dry crackers and salt meat, there was a craving for acid drinks and the "small beer" fit the bill. Some prisoners even sold their clothes to get the money to buy it.[11] On October 13 and 14, 1863, H. Wright and J. Boyd were arrested for buying prisoners' old clothes soon after they had received a shipment of new from Weir S. Mitchell, a doctor who had recently inspected the fort and had sent the clothes to help out the more unfortunate prisoners.[12]

Other prisoners worked as craftsmen. These men made rings, pins, buttons, chains, charms, and puzzles out of any piece of bone, horn, brass tack, tin, wire, or copper they could find.[13] Gutta-percha was another material that was put to good use. Gutta-percha was first discovered as a by-product of the rubber making process. It was a light and imperishable material used to make jewelry in the early Victorian era, which covered the years 1837–1860.[14] Buttons made out of gutta-percha were used at the fort for material to make items such as rings, watch seals, and chains. They were boiled to bring out the shape. The common tools for this type of work were a regular knife, files, a small hammer, awls made out of needles, sandpaper, and a piece of leather greased and rubbed in the shell dust found on the island or on an emery board.[15] These elaborate and beautiful pieces, along with miniature machines, toys, violins, banjos, and wall ornaments, were sold to the richer prisoners or to the guards. The guards would buy large quantities of these goods and sell them to the Yankee visitors who came to the island.[16] In particular, fans made out of white pine and trimmed with silk of different colors were in great demand with Northern ladies. Some of these fans sold for $2.50 each.[17] The "Confederate Jewelry" was sometimes sent to the women who sent the craftsmen food, money, clothes, or who just kept their spirits up by writing to them. Most of those women were from Maryland, which had a very strong pro-Southern faction. The jewelry was also sent to the makers' wives and sweethearts.[18] The Union soldiers would also ask the prisoners to make specific pieces so they could send them as presents to their friends and loved ones. Lieut. Sidney Wailes of the Purnell Legion, for example, had a ring and a "small curiosity in the shape of a fan made out of solid wood" for a lady and tried to get a Masonic ring made for her father, but the prisoner who was going to make it was transferred to another prison before he had a chance to make it.[19]

One such artificer was Capt. James N. Bosang of the 4th Virginia Infantry. Capt. Bosang got his start when a new prisoner asked him to make rings out of gutta-percha buttons. Bosang agreed to make a ring with a heart set in it with one button and he wanted another button as payment. He had no idea how to do it, but he wanted that button. He then went to Capt. Bob Stuart, a maker of rings, and borrowed a knife and a file. He made the ring using a piece of oyster shell for the heart set. His client was happy with the finished product and paid him the extra button. Bosang then made another ring with the other button and sold it for $.75 to Capt. W.F. Nicholson. Feeling very good about actually having money, he went to the sutler and bought a file for $.25, 5 buttons for $.25, tobacco for $.10, meal for $.10, and kept the other 5 cents. Using this side business, he was able to regularly purchase a little extra to eat.

Four to six weeks later, two new prisoners arrived with shoemaker's tools. Bosang saw that they knew very little about using their tools, so he went to them and proposed a business deal. They would provide the materials and he would do the work, with the three of them sharing the profits equally. Their clients would be the wealthier prisoners, who could afford to pay for their services. This provided the opportunity for Bosang and his fellow craftsmen to have a better life at Fort

A violin made by a prisoner at Fort Delaware. Now in Fort Delaware Society Library.

Delaware. Bosang started footing boots, which was putting new feet to old legs, for $15.00 a pair, split three ways. He did a pair a day and had more work than he could do. He started to live well, had a bunk-mate do his cooking, and ate when he had nothing to do.

The good times ended when Bosang caught pneumonia due to working too far away from the fire. It came quickly and he was sent to the hospital, where he was delirious for some time. Finally, he woke up hungry and the nurse brought him half a soft boiled egg and a small piece of toast. He offered the nurse $.50 if he brought him something for dinner. He promised he would and brought Bosang back two thick slices of fat pork and a pint cup of greasy soup. The nurse was a Rebel prisoner who had taken the Oath of Allegiance to the Union. Such prisoners were called galvanized Yankees. Bosang paid the nurse to continue smuggling food to him. He ended up spending most of his money doing this. When he finally got better and was released from the hospital, he found out that his shoe making partners had been sent away and had taken their tools with them. Bosang then went back into the gutta-percha jewelry business.[20]

Another prisoner who used his hands to good advantage was John Boone. He arrived at Fort Delaware in March 1864. Boone carved rings, breastpins, military insignias, and other things to pass the time and to make money. He made these things for guards and prisoners alike with a pen knife, a file, and a turning lathe that he made himself. Boone once said: "I can make about $.40 a day when I get the work to do." He used this money to buy things that he needed, such as food. He said: "We have access to sutlers from whom we can get most anything we want if we have the money.... I have found out since I have been in prison what it is to be without money.... The sutler has commenced selling melons and peaches, but I would rather not see them as I have no money."[21]

Money was the great equalizer at Fort Delaware. Prisoners who had money had a much better experience during their confinement than those who did not. Men with financial resources at their disposal did not have to worry about what kind of food was being offered by the Yankees. They could buy extra food from the sutlers and even hire someone to prepare their meals. This lead to another way prisoners were able to survive in prison. Some men were hired by other prisoners to be their cooks. A group of prisoners who had money would pool their resources and hire someone to prepare their food and in return, the cook would receive free food. This was a custom that was carried over from before they were captured. During the Civil War, there was no such thing as a mess hall and the men in the field had to do their own cooking. Many times, men were designated as cooks for their companies. This kind of job made life for the cooks more bearable because they were allowed to share in the bounty they prepared for others.[22]

Having someone on the outside was another way that prisoners were able to deal with the rigors of prison life. Anyone who had a friend or family member living in the North was able to ask for the things he needed and have them sent to him. When Confederate Gen. Jeff Thompson first came to Fort Delaware, he started writing to friends in Philadelphia, New York, Baltimore, and Boston to procure clothes and other items to make his stay more comfortable. He also received many presents from the ladies of New Castle and Delaware City, as well as many useful things from friends and relatives. He not only made sure that he and his mess were well taken care of in the comfort department, he also made sure that he received enough items to help other prisoners in need as well. Gen. Thompson had a conversation with one of the chaplains of the post a few days after his arrival. The Episcopal minister informed him that some ladies from New York wanted to know if they could send Thompson anything that would increase his comfort. He said the only thing that he needed was a pillow, which was sent to him the next day. He sent back a thank you poem about the pillow and soon everyone in his entire mess had pillows.[23]

Thompson's mess included Major-General Franklin Gardner, Brig.-Gen. James J. Archer, who was wounded and captured at Gettysburg, and officers from Brig.-Gen. John H. Morgan's command, such as his brothers Colonel Richard C. and Captain Charlton H. Morgan, his brother-in-law Basil Duke, and Colonel J.B. McCreary, a future governor of Kentucky and U.S. senator. The comfort these prisoners lived in while at Fort Delaware was proof that any prisoner who had enough money could live quite well while held there. The conditions they lived in were in stark contrast to the way many of the prisoners existed. Lieut. McHenry Howard, who stayed in their mess for a period of time, mentioned in his recollections about how the members of the mess lived. They took their meals in a lower room of the fort and they were prepared by an enlisted Union prisoner. Howard remembered how surprised he was when he first went to their table. They had real coffee, condensed milk, and had ice cream for dessert. The water they drank did have what Howard called "wiggle waggles" in it, but they were considered harmless and were killed by a mixture of whiskey or brandy. The alcohol was bought from the sutler. It was incredible to Howard that they were allowed to keep a bottle on a shelf in their room to be used anytime they felt "disposed."[24]

One person in particular that was on the outside helping the prisoners was Margaret Anna Parker Knobeloch. Mrs. Knobeloch contacted Secretary Stanton in 1862 to ask his permission to provide aid to Rebel prisoners being held near her home in Philadelphia. The money for this aid would come from Rebels living in Europe. Her husband, John Knobeloch, went home to Germany to avoid being drafted into the Union army and would be able to make the necessary contacts there in Europe. Surprisingly, considering his reputation as someone who had no sympathy for Confederates or their cause, Stanton granted Mrs. Knobeloch's request. She then spent the rest of the war helping Rebel prisoners in hospitals and Fort Delaware.[25]

The prisoners also passed the time by continuing their education. A prisoner could study the law, medicine, or theology, which was taught by the Rev. Handy.[26] Lectures were given on many different types of subjects. There was one British sea captain who was able to draw large crowds to his lectures on his travels to the Orient and Europe.[27] Foreign languages were also taught. Studying another language was not just a way to pass the time of day. Some prisoners were looking ahead to the time after the defeat of the Confederacy when they might have to live in exile. Acquiring a working knowledge of a foreign language like German, would be an important skill for them to master.[28] Officers from Louisiana taught French and Capt. Henderson of that state taught Latin and Greek to a class of twelve.[29]

There were very few things that the guards and prisoners had in common, but one of them was that they both used reading as a way to fight boredom. The prisoners were not allowed to have any books that dealt with military strategy, military history, or geography.[30] However, books on religious topics and novels were permitted. A box of books was sent by a Mrs. A.W. Emley of Philadelphia, Pa., that arrived on June 20, 1864; it contained one hundred and two hymn books and sixty Bibles. Several prisoners broke the box apart and used it to make a set of book shelves. This package was the basis of a prison library set up by the Rev. Handy for the use of the prisoners. Handy frowned on the habit of prisoners' reading novels as a way to pass the time, but it did not stop them from enjoying them.[31] One of the books that the prisoners read was *Les Miserables* by Victor Hugo, or as it was also called, "Lee's Miserables."[32]

Having a person on the outside sending in supplies was great for those who had that, but the best kind of outside help was the kind that got a prisoner released. President Lincoln was contacted many times to free someone from Fort Delaware. On August 29, 1863, Lincoln asked Secretary Stanton to free "Robert Howard and Junius B. Alexander, now prisoners of war at Fort Delaware. They are both privates, and the latter only eighteen years of age as represented to me. They wish to take the oath, give bond, and be discharged."[33] He also wrote to Stanton on December 23, 1863, concerning James C. Gates. He had been captured at Gettysburg, and Lincoln told Stanton to "Let James C. Gates, a prisoner of War at Fort Delaware, take the oath of allegiance and be discharged."

Mr. Lincoln also stepped in when it came to other types of prisoners. Pvt. John Connor of the 1st D.C. Infantry was being held at Fort Delaware for desertion. Lincoln ordered Connor to return to his regiment and informed him that when he served his term, made up lost time, or was otherwise discharged, he would be pardoned.[34] Lincoln was also made aware of the story of five Quakers held at the fort. Thomas Hinshaw, his brother Jacob, and Nathan and Cyrus Barker were forced to travel with the 52nd North Carolina Regiment in spite of their pacifist beliefs. They ended up as part of the Rebel force that advanced on Gettysburg. The men became separated from the Confederates after the battle and went to find fellow Quakers. Even though the North and South were at war, the Quakers were not so split. The Pennsylvania Quakers took in their Southern brothers and cared for them. This did not last long because word spread throughout the area that the Quakers were hiding "four rebel soldiers." On July 10, the Federal cavalry came and took the men to Fort Delaware. Five days later, they arrived at the fort and were greeted by William B. Hockett, another Quaker being held there. Fortunately for the five men, nearby Quakers heard about their capture and immediately started working toward their release. Thomas Evans, Samuel Hilles, and James B. Graves traveled to Washington to see the President and Secretary Stanton to ask for their release. Lincoln granted their release because he held the Quakers in high regard and at one time said that "Any man who is a Quaker is not to be considered as a prisoner of war." Stanton sent a telegram to General Schoepf ordering their release. They were brought before the general and asked to sign the Oaths of Allegiance before they could leave. Being Quakers, they could not take an oath. Schoepf then changed the wording of the oath so that it became an affirmation of allegiance. The five men then felt free to sign the documents and were released.[35]

There were some men held on the island who were not as industrious or did not have the emotional strength to deal with life in prison. These unfortunate men, who had no one on the outside to help them, were known as walkers. They would wander around the yard all day without stopping. Some of them would walk around with their heads down and their arms behind them, looking as if they were lost in thought. Other walkers would walk in pairs and never stop talking. Some would walk around puffing and blowing, slapping their hands together, and saying: "Taking exercise." It might be easy to assume that these men were lazy or emotionally weak. That may have been the case, but then again, maybe not. It is possible that at least some of them were affected by a constant exposure to brackish drinking water, which left many of the prisoners weak and disoriented. Whatever the reason for their actions, they were the prisoners who suffered the most.

Everyone who stayed busy did not necessarily have a job. Games were a big part of occupying time on the island. While some prisoners were wandering around the yard all day, others were spending the same amount of time playing games. Chess, whist, draughts, backgammon, and dominoes were very popular. Throughout the barracks, from one division to another, could be heard the sounds of men saying "Your move! Shake the dice! Jump your man! Checkmate!" Games of chess were sometimes played between divisions and there were messengers who ran between them delivering the moves. These games could go on for days.[36] Several of the men were first-class players and one in particular, Lieut. Fry, was very impressive. His first six moves were basic ones, then he would study the board, plan his attack, and he very rarely checked his opponent until he was ready to mate. His moves did not seem to be formidable at first, but their true purpose was only seen when it was too late.[37]

Whist, one of the more popular games played in prison, was a card game played with four people. There were two teams of two people who played against each other. The partners sat across from one another and the four players were named for the four points on the compass, with north and south together against east and west.[38] The champion whist player was Lieut. C.R. Darricott of Richmond, Va. He played his trumps strong, led from an ace, and tried to make his tricks at the end of the game.

Other games were also played, such as old sledge, base, knucks,[39] and, if the weather was good, marbles. Care-worn soldiers could be seen outside playing the game and fighting over the marbles like children.[40] When the weather was very hot, Lieut. Wolfe, the adjutant-general of the fort, would amuse a crowd of prisoners by hooking up a hose and watering down the housetops and the yard, which soaked all those playing there.[41]

Leading a soldier's life is a good way for a man to risk not only his physical well-being, but his spiritual as well. There are a lot of bad habits a man can get into when he is far from home. One of the most prevalent bad habits in the Civil War was gambling. There was so much gambling going on in the Confederate armies that General Robert E. Lee released an order in November 1862 in which he declared that he was shocked to discover how widespread it was. To understand why gambling was so out of favor by polite society in the South, it must be remembered that the South was a very evangelical and pious society. They took the Bible very seriously and its interpretation was literal. Anyone who broke any of the Ten Commandments was considered a sinner. The more religious members of the Rebel armies were appalled at the amount of gambling going on around them.[42] Card-playing, or "throwing the paper,"[43] was the most common form of gambling. A deck of cards, some of which had pictures of President Jefferson Davis and high-ranking Confederate generals on them, was a popular item in camp. As the war went on, it was harder to get a fresh pack of cards. Soldiers would get them from prisoners or dead soldiers on the field.[44]

Gambling may not have been the most positive way to keep busy, but many men gained some measure of relief from the boredom and suffering of their everyday existence with its presence.[45] Faro, keno, poker, vingt et un (blackjack), euchre, seven-up, casino, and reno were the games of choice. The betting was normally low. The average bet was five cents and a bet of twenty-five cents was considered "a fearful risk." Fortunately, there were very few arguments between gamblers.[46] The gaming tables were numerous and always busy. Capt. Coffee from Mississippi was the most popular of the faro dealers. He always had impeccable manners and attracted the biggest crowds. Before his capture, he only gambled for fun and not for profit. At

Fort Delaware, rumor had it that his first victim was a Yankee guard. At Capt. Coffee's table, Rebel or Federal money was accepted. No one really knew how much money he had, but once, when barracks and prisoners were being searched for contraband, he hid a gold watch, one hundred and eleven dollars in gold, and several hundred dollars in notes in the grass. One of the guards saw where he had hidden it and took it.

The men really involved in gambling would sometimes write to someone on the outside to beg for money, or they would send for clothing and, when it arrived, sell it to raise the money to play again. The most popular game on the island was keno. Some Rebel officers revolved their entire lives around it. The dealer was paid one dollar for calling out the numbers. The players would take a large card with twenty-four figures in six rows running from one to sixty. Some players were not happy with one card, so they would have two. When all of the players were ready, the dealer put the figures in a bag. He would shake up the bag, pull them out one at a time, and call them out to the waiting players. Each man would look at his card and, if he had the figure, put a button or copper piece on it. The person who got one row of six first would yell out "keno," and win the money. The dealers had their own way of calling out the numbers. Any number under 13 was called "figure" something—"figure 1, 7, 8, 12," and so on—any multiple of 10 was announced by saying "flat," such as "40 flat," but the rest of the numbers were just said normally.[47]

Many times, the sounds of gambling mixed with the sounds of prayer. The gambling tables and the prayer meetings were so close together that when the dealer shouted out: "Make your bets, gentlemen!" the religious speaker would counter with, "Avoid the paths of sin!" with a side reference to the "gay gambolier." There were no hard feelings on either side and sometimes, when a dealer was broke, he would go to one of the many prayer meetings in the fort until he was able to "borrow a stake."[48] Gambling was so popular that the Rev. Handy remembered falling asleep in his bunk one night with a card table at his feet and the table was surrounded by players.[49]

One time where the spiritual life collided with the gambling life is mentioned in the "Reminiscences of Gen. Basil W. Duke, C.S.A." The general, of Gen. John Morgan's command, wrote of a prisoner who, within a month of his capture, proved to be an unequaled card player. He then decided to convert his barracks into a gaming saloon. There were twelve tables set up for keno and faro. He appointed one of his roommates to each table and he was the general manager. The room was packed with gamblers from reveille to taps and all branches of the military had a great deal of representation.

This captain had a strong sense of propriety as he did a love of gambling. He worked hard so that no one would be offended by the actions of anyone in his saloon. He had been brought up in a strictly religious household and he never allowed gambling in his quarters before noon on Sundays. He used to clean up the area and arrange it so that worship services could be held there. A man of the cloth was always invited to hold services there and he assisted with the services as much as possible.

One day, the captain learned that two ministers had been brought in with a new group of prisoners. He immediately went to pay his respects and invited them to come to his barracks the next Sunday and conduct worship services. He also told them that there would be an enthusiastic group waiting for them. The two accepted the invitation, but they made a mistake concerning the time of their arrival. They showed up in the afternoon instead of the morning. They did find an enthusiastic group, but the enthusiasm they displayed was for matters less than spiritual. The captain had been called away and left a lieutenant in charge of the room. The lieutenant, not knowing who they were, immediately approached the clergymen and invited them to make themselves at home and "take a hand." The stunned ministers explained that they had been invited by the captain to come and assist in the services taking place in the barracks. Hearing this, the still unsuspecting lieutenant thought that they had been hired by the captain to be dealers. Therefore, he told them in a friendly manner: "Oh, very well, thar's a faro and a keno table both idle; take charge of them." That was the straw that broke the back of the clergymen's patience. Not only did they finally realize what was going on around them, but they also felt that they had been insulted. When the captain found out what had happened, he was furious at the lieutenant and confronted him.

> "'You blamed wedge-headed ape with a hunk of mouldy limberger cheese where your brains ought to be, couldn't you see that those gentlemen were preachers?'"
> "'No I couldn't,' answered the lieutenant, "you didn't tell me anything about them, and I thought from their looks that they belonged to the profesh.'"[50]

Of the many ways prisoners had of coping with captivity and keeping their spirits up, religion was one of the strongest. Because Fort Delaware held political prisoners as well as captured soldiers, the prison had its share of ministers who had been arrested for their pro-South opinions. The Rev. Handy was depressed when he first was placed on the island. That attitude changed when he was approached by several prisoners who wanted to have some sort of religious direction. He soon felt that his imprisonment was a blessing in disguise. Handy felt that it was his duty to try to give the prisoners the ability to worship, even in prison, and to try to convert as many as possible to the Lord. He started out with his first prayer meeting being attended by twenty-five to thirty prisoners.[51] He was warned more than once by other prisoners that because he was making himself known by his works, it was possible that he might be at risk of lengthening his incarceration. The thought of this did not deter Handy from his mission and he continued until the day of his release.[52]

Not only was the Rev. Handy approached by prisoners needing religious instruction, but also by the guards. On September 29, 1863, he was asked by a private in Capt. Ahl's command to preach to the Union officer's men that night. He was willing to go, but he remembered before he left that he had a pass that only permitted him to be out until eight o'clock at night. He did not want to disappoint the soldiers, but he thought it would be best to ask Gen. Schoepf's permission.[53]

There were religious services held every Sunday. They would either be held in a barracks or in the open air, weather permitting. There were several ministers in the prison who held services for their fellow prisoners, such as Capts. A.M. Samford and Thomas W. Harris from the Methodist Church. The Rev. Handy was also busy holding a divinity class, as well as a Bible class and a daily prayer meeting at noon. The prayer meeting was held in the yard. Handy, who was not a large man, had to use a box, a stool, or a tub as his pulpit. The prisoners in attendance would sit in circles around him. There would also be groups of prisoners who would stand or sit nearby so as to listen while not participating. Less than twenty feet away were rows of gambling tables with a large crowd surrounding them. Some of the tables would stop during the services, but others would not. Past these two groups would march the walkers. Above all of this would watch the sentries on the parapets, taking it all in.

The prayer meeting would start out with a hymn. The men would sing in their hoarse, untrained voices and would make up for their lack of singing talents with their enthusiasm and conviction. After the hymn would be prayers and comments from the minister or his assistants. Interest in these meetings grew as time went on and at one point, nearly one fourth of the prisoners were involved in some form of worship.[54]

One of the largest services that the Rev. Handy ever held in Fort Delaware was on June 26, 1864. On that morning, every available inch of his division was filled with listeners for his sermon on "The nature, and importance of a public confession of Christ." The usual Bible study class was suspended for the day because of the communion and baptism service that was planned for that afternoon. Handy wanted to hold the services outside to accommodate the large number of people he was expecting. In the afternoon, just before the service was to begin, the wind began to blow and it started to rain. The weather improved and the service was set up. Benches were put in place for those who wanted to kneel in prayer. Most of the congregation sat on the ground and eight prisoners were baptized. These men had tried for some time to convince Handy to baptize them. He had originally refused to do it because he wanted to keep his services non-denominational. However, he finally agreed to their request. The eight men were happy with the service and Handy felt that it was a great day for men of different beliefs to get together and worship the Lord without interference from the Union soldiers.[55]

Unfortunately, there were times when the religious services would be interrupted. Occasionally, the prison sergeant would hurry into the pen just at the time the Rev. Handy would be holding services. He would start screaming at the prisoners: "Get out! Get out! Fall into line! Roll Call!" This would break up the services just as they were getting started. Handy did send a note to General Schoepf to complain about the intrusion, but nothing was ever done to stop the sergeant.[56]

The pen, or the Devil's Half Acre, was not only home to the gamblers, ministers, and the walkers, but also to those men, such as the craftsmen, who set up shop to offer their services. Boards from boxes sent to the prisoners were joined together as uprights and the blankets that they used on their bunks at night were stretched out to screen the proprietor and client from the burning sun.[57] This arrangement was not done in a haphazard way. The barracks were arranged neatly into streets. One street might have men setting up a large box to show off the food they were selling. On top of the box would be rations of bread and meat. One of the rations would go for ten cents or so many chews of tobacco. Another place would have bread, molasses, and red hot coffee. A sop of molasses and a cup of coffee would go for five cents. Sometimes during the course of the day, hundreds of men would handle the same piece of bread on display until it became black.[58]

News from the outside world was hard to get. The prisoners rarely saw a newspaper. The only paper they were allowed to read was the *Philadelphia Enquirer*. It was brought in by a sergeant and sold to the prisoners. However, the *Enquirer* was not sold every day. When there was news of a Rebel defeat, it was allowed to be sold. When there was news of Southern successes, no one was allowed to read the paper. That bit of censorship could be gotten around with a well-placed bribe to a sentinel.[59] Restrictions on letters coming into the prison were was also carefully adhered to. If a letter was sent to a prisoner that had the smallest amount of information about the outside world, unless it was about family matters, the prisoner would never receive it.[60]

The prisoners enjoyed any distraction from their captivity. One of the ways they passed the time was with athletic contests. Sports were very popular in the U.S. during this time period, with boxing being one of the most popular before the beginning of the Civil War.[61] In one case at Fort Delaware, the men had a boxing match for fun. A prisoner borrowed a pair of gloves from another prisoner and challenged a man named Pearson to a match. Both prisoners claimed to have some knowledge of how to box and since they were about the same size, they decided to fight. Pearson came across as a man who knew how to box and soon subdued his opponent. A man named Welsh, who was also called "Reddy," stepped forward and challenged Pearson. Welsh was soon dispatched by Pearson. The next man who wanted to fight Pearson was a Capt. Long. The champion agreed and soon the two men went at it. Long, who was much smaller than his opponent, was able to beat Pearson by the tactic of sticking his head into Pearson's stomach and punching him in the face, eyes, and nose. The boxers ended up with sore noses and headaches, and were short of breath.[62]

It might be wondered why the commandant of the fort would allow so many different activities to go on in the prison. Gen. Schoepf had a simple reason for permitting the religious services, gambling, etc. to go on. He felt that if the prisoners were busy doing these activities, they were too busy to plan an escape.[63] That might have worked with some of the prisoners, but it certainly was not a foolproof solution to the problem. The outside world was tantalizingly close to the prisoners. The island was less than a mile away from the mainland and it was well known that if a prisoner could safely get to either the Delaware or New Jersey side, he had a good chance of making his escape. These two states both had a system in place that could get Rebel prisoners back to the South.[64] Having that kind of knowledge gave some prisoners hope that if they could get off of the island, they could go home.

Captain Stanislaus Mlotkowski was a Union officer who never failed to treat the Confederates with respect, shaking the hands of the Rebel officers, and telling them that a prisoner had the right and duty to try to escape, unless he was on parole.[65] Many of the prisoners at the fort agreed with that attitude and did their best to escape. One of the favorite tricks used by an escaping prisoner was finding a canteen or other type of container to use as a floatation device to help them swim the Delaware River to freedom. The prisoners would seal the container with a cork, wax, or even a bullet begged from a guard and melted down. Some sort of life preserver was necessary to swim the Delaware. There was a counter current in the river that made swimming difficult. Sharks in the water also added to the danger of escape. They were attracted to the sinks and the other debris that came from the island.

Captain Henry C. Dickerson examined the sinks on his first night at Fort Delaware and noted that a hole could be cut through them and a man could escape in this manner. Apparently, some of his fellow prisoners agreed with him because seventeen of them made their escape through the sinks that night. When the guards found the hole, they had it reinforced with wooden bars so that no one else could escape through it. A few days later, the wooden bars were cut through and three officers escaped. One of them drowned, but nothing else was heard of from the other two. Large sills were then placed in the opening to stop the escapes. A platform was also built behind the sinks with a sentry on watch, and another guard manned a large railroad reflector that lit up the surrounding area.

These precautions did not prevent the prisoners from trying to escape. The knack to escaping from the sinks was that a prisoner had to wait for the tide to be up at the same time it was dark in the early evening. A month after the guards fixed the hole, six prisoners nearly cut through when the guards discovered them and fired a shot. This raised such an alarm that it was impossible to make an escape effort.[66]

The toilet situation was a substantial problem for the prison system for several reasons. Both Union and Rebel prisoner of war camps built their "sinks," the official name for toilets, over the nearest body of running water. This was a concept first used in Roman times because running water carried away impurities. This idea was not very successful when large groups of men stayed in one place permanently. The dangers of the antiquated system became apparent to the engineers and surgeons on both sides, but not before lives were lost because of the buildup of germs in the area of confinement.

This situation was made worse because of the lack of chamber pots or commodes. Prisons did not have enough cups, plates, pots, pans, or buckets for eating, let alone receptacles for use as toilets. Only hospitals had commodes. Everyone else had to use the sinks. The ones at Fort Delaware were frameworks, some open and some like rows of outhouses. These sinks were built away from the center of camp for obvious reasons. However, their placement also gave prisoners a means of escape. Prisoners were known to slip into the water and be off. To stop this, they were not allowed to use the sinks after dark without the permission of a guard. When escapes were plentiful, guards had to escort prisoners to and from the toilets. There could be as many as 200 prisoners to a guard. An outbreak of diarrhea would run everyone ragged.[67]

Some prisoners used other less smelly means to try to escape. At one time, many of the Union officers liked to walk through the prisoners' barracks out of curiosity. On one Fourth of July, one of Morgan's men decided to take advantage of this habit. He dressed up like a Federal officer and walked past the guard, who had thought that he had entered by another way. Once he was out of sight of the guard, the prisoner decided to reconnoiter the island in an attempt to find a way to the mainland. He found a steamboat that had brought a large group of people over to the island from Philadelphia for a picnic. It was scheduled to leave that evening. He then went back to his barracks, dressed up two of his friends like himself, had Captain Morgan forge papers with Gen. Schoepf's name on it to go to the boat, and the three of them marched out. By the time they had arrived to where the boat was moored, it had already left. Two of the men decided to hide in a woodpile, while the third escapee went to the hotel on the island that was used by people visiting their loved ones in prison. The two men in the woodpile were soon found out. Their partner was discovered when he was invited to go to a wine supper, but refused. This had made him look suspicious and soon the third escapee was returned to his barracks.

The next day, the man who had first walked out was taken to Gen. Schoepf's office. The prisoner was asked where he had received the pass he had on him when he had been captured. He refused to answer, so Schoepf threatened to hang him up by his thumbs unless he told the general exactly where he got the pass from. The man refused to tell where he got the pass from. A guard began to hang him by his thumbs, but the general changed his mind and put him into the dungeon instead. The next day, he was brought back to the general and asked again who had helped them. When the man again refused to answer, Schoepf let him go and said to him: "Sir, I honor you for your fidelity to your friends." After this incident, the number of Yankee visits to the barracks dropped dramatically.

Another incident where someone used quick, bold action to try for their freedom happened one night when Dickinson was returning from the sinks. He saw two officers walking near the privates' sutler shop. When the search beam passed them, one officer grabbed the other's foot and boosted him into the "whitewashed" camp. This was where the galvanized Yankees lived who were Confederate soldiers who had taken the Oath of Allegiance and had joined the Union army. They were under far fewer restrictions than the prisoners and it was assumed that the officer had made good his escape.

There were ditches which ran under some of the divisions. They were considered by the prisoners to be a health hazard. However, the guards could also have considered the ditches a problem since they also provided the prisoners with a way out. In particular, there was a ditch which ran under Division 30 within a few inches of the floor. The prisoners examined it and figured out that it was possible for a man to work his way through the ditch. He could then go under where the guards walked their beat and make his way to the main ditch. Once at the main ditch, he could get to the bay near the fort on the New Jersey side and freedom. Canteens were prepared and four men, Captains Parkins and Patton and two others, went through the ditch at night. They headed toward the fort, but there were too many guards between them and the fort. Therefore, they crawled out of the ditch and hid under the baker's shop, which was near Division 31, all day. Meanwhile, the other prisoners thought that the four men had made their escape since no one had heard anything about them. This led five other men to try to escape the same way. As the second man was under the guard's beat, he made a noise that the guard heard. He then called his corporal over and said: "There's either a 'Reb' or a damned big rat under there." The guards made a search and found one man by poking him with a stick. He was ordered to come out and a second prisoner was soon found. The two prisoners who were still under Division 30 got back up before anything happened to them. The first prisoner who had already passed the guard kept going. One guard threatened to kill the two men he captured and had raised his weapon as if he was going to shoot, but another guard came over and talked him out of it.

While this was going on, the men who were waiting under the baker's shop had finally arrived at the east end of the fort. Some of them had gotten into the water and were waiting for the rest of the escaped prisoners. One prisoner stumbled in the water and a guard heard him. The guard then shouted out: "Corporal of the guard, double quick." Hearing that, the ones in the water figured it was time to leave and successfully escaped. One of the three men who escaped went to New York and the other two went South. The three of them also sent letters from their new homes to Fort Delaware to let their former cellmates know that they had made it to safety.[68]

Charles Rivenbark, of the 1st North Carolina Regiment, tells the story of the time he was selected to cut through a wall. He used a jeweler's saw to cut through the 4 to 6 boards that made up the wall, which was within 22 feet of a sentry's post. One hundred and thirty prisoners had flotation devices out of two canteens each sealed shut with cork and wax. All of the prisoners escaped except for one man, who drowned, and Rivenbark. He was the last man to leave and when he was ready to go, he found that somebody had stolen his life preserver. He had to go back to his bunk before he was found out. As he lay there, he heard shouts and later found out that a group of officers from another part of the prison had done the exact same thing as Rivenbark's group on the same night. Rivenbark was later in on a scheme to build a boat to use for an escape. The prisoners used knife-saws and screws to build it. Just as they had finished the eight-man boat, two guards came into the barracks, tore up the floorboards, found the boat, and then destroyed it.[69]

Despite the best efforts of the guards, prisoners continued to attempt to escape. On the night of August 12, 1863, A.L. Brooks, C.J. Fuller, and J.D. Marian of the 9th Georgia, William E. Glassy of the 18th Mississippi, John Dorsey from Stuart's Horse Artillery, and another man from Philadelphia all broke out of the prison. It was a very dark night and the men were able to leave the camp and slip into the water unseen. They all had well-corked homemade life preservers made out of four can-teens each. The Philadelphia man did not make it because he could not swim, even though he had eight canteens strapped to him. The other five men landed safely. Three of them came to shore near Delaware City. Those men hid in a cornfield all night, and the next evening, they headed south. Before they went on their way, they introduced themselves to a farmer, who helped them by giving them a good supper. They continued south, going into Kent County. The people there gave them money and new clothes. The pattern of citizens helping them continued until they reached the Confederate lines. Once in Richmond, they proceeded to express their gratitude toward the generous people of Maryland and Delaware who went out of their way to help them.[70]

Three days later, the guards were severely rebuked by Gen. Schoepf for this escape and others that had occurred around this time. Four Rebels were captured on the 13th by Capt. Thoroughgood of the schooner W.H. Sherman, and two more Rebel lieutenants escaped from the hospital on the 14th. There were orders given to shoot any guard caught sitting down while on duty. This was not a popular order and one guard was "fully determined not to stand for four hours and to shoot first if any shooting was done."

On September 4, two members of Battery G, Pittsburgh Heavy Artillery and one from Battery A were arrested, put in the guard house, and sentenced to digging graves for one month after three prisoners had escaped on their watch.[71] Burials originally were done on the far side of the island in two plots.[72] There were head boards and fences at the cemetery. The graves there were shallow ones, due to the makeup of the island, and were covered with layers of quick lime and earth four feet thick.[73] However, as the prison population grew, so did the number of burials, which was too much for the island cemetery to handle. An eighty-six acre farm across the river in New Jersey at Finn's Point was chosen to take care of the situation.[74] Finn's Point had been bought by the federal government in 1837 and from it the Finn's Point Battery for the defense of Philadelphia had been created. Part of this land was set aside to bury the prisoners who died on Pea Patch Island.[75] The dead were brought over to the mainland by the "coffin detail."[76] People who lived in the area at the time long remembered the sight of the bodies being put into open trenches and having dirt thrown over them after a brief ceremony.[77] The cemetery on the island was still used in the winter when it was difficult to get across the river. One hundred and forty-two men were buried there[78] and later taken to Finn's Point at the end of the war. Altogether, 2,436 Confederate prisoners of war and 135 Union soldiers[79] who died on the island were taken across the river to, in the words of Sgt. Charles W. Rivenbark, "the burial ground, and there, in the rude holes we dug for them, reposes the body of many a gallant Southern man, whose noble heart once throbbed only for truth and honor and liberty and love and home; whose unrecorded greatness and valor will only be known at the great final day when the graves shall give up their dead and justice at last be meted out to all."[80]

In the month of November 1863, there were two incidents involving prisoners trying to use boats to escape. On November 14, five prisoners tried to escape using a boat. Three of them were drowned and the other two were picked up by the Northern soldiers. The other incident in November was on the 25th. One man tried to escape using a sloop, but he was discovered and arrested.[81]

Trying to swim across the river was a tempting thought. However, it was easier said than done. Only an expert swimmer could chance the swim to the mainland if he had on a life preserver and had the help of the tides. Otherwise, a prisoner would be swept out to sea and drowned.[82] Capt. Dickinson also tried to get a boat to use to escape, since he was not a strong swimmer. He had bribed, or as Dickinson put it, "bought up," one guard and the man was trying to get a boat for him. Unfortunately for Dickinson, the Yankee soldiers who guarded the boats were one hundred day men and could not be bought.

When prisoners tried to escape, the ones still at the fort tried to help them by giving the Union soldiers misinformation. The guards had a roll call every day. The prisoners would try to convince the guards that an escaped prisoner was still on the island.[83] It was not as difficult as might be imagined, since incorrect roles of incoming prisoners was a longstanding problem at Fort Delaware. There would be names of prisoners who never arrived or who had been paroled on the same list as Rebels still on the island. Therefore, it was easy for the guards to be confused about the identity of prisoners.[84]

People have always been able to endure the harshest of conditions if they managed to keep their sense of humor. The life of a prisoner was not an easy one, but that still did not stop some prisoners from having some fun while they were there. Once, when Col. Perkins was the commandant of the fort, Capt. Robert Baylor of the Baylor Light Horse, decided to play a prank on two men, Mr. Jackson and Mr. Solomon of Philadelphia. The two men had just been arrested and thrown into the prison on charges of being contrabandists. Capt. Baylor posed as Col. Perkins, Capt. John Murray as his adjutant and six or seven of their companions pretended to be his escort. They approached the two men in their rooms within the fort's walls and demanded to know everything about their blockade business or else they would be killed. The disguised prisoners then insisted that they take the Oath of Allegiance. Solomon agreed immediately to take the oath, but Jackson refused. Solomon was then taken out of the room, marched down the hallway, and placed in a five foot square closet. Murray then said in an authoritarian voice, after the closet door was closed: "Sentinel, if he moves in there, shoot him." The pranksters then went back to their own rooms, leaving Solomon in the closet all night. Jackson, because he had resisted taking the oath, was treated well. The next morning, the men told Col. Perkins' clerk, Gemmil, what had happened. Gemmil then went to release Solomon from his closet prison.

Another time, there was a prisoner named Lieut. Tormey from the 1st Maryland. He was very full of himself and liked to brag about the many lady friends he had in Baltimore. There was one that he talked about so much that Capt. Murray and Capt. George Baylor of the Baylor Light Horse soon got to know her about as well as Tormey himself. They then decided to play a practical joke on him. They enlisted the help of Gemmil, who readily agreed, and then wrote a passionate letter in the style of his sweetheart. They then had Gemmil copy it, stamp it, and deliver it to Tormey. When he received it, Tormey's spirits rose considerably. He was so pleased with the letter that he could no longer keep it to himself. He then went to Baylor and Murray to tell them of the letter. Tormey spent the next couple of days trying to write the perfect response to the object of his affections. He then gave the letter to Gemmil to be mailed. Gemmil made a copy, which he gave to his coconspirators, and mailed the original. No one knew if she ever received it or sent a letter back. However, Murray and Baylor did send a letter back and kept up a regular correspondence going with Tormey for weeks. The regular letters from his "sweetheart" kept Tormey in high spirits and they thought that the letters did him as much good as real letters from home. Tormey eventually found out about the prank a few days before the jokers left the island, but he took it well. The same could not be said about Lieut. Purvis, who, when he found out that the same trick was being played on him by the two men, refused to speak to Capt. Murray or the two Baylors until the day of their departure. He then forgave them.[85]

Playing jokes on each other in a prison might not seem to be the thing to do, but it helped to pass the time and made life just a little easier to deal with. One trick was to put pieces of wood or coal between the sheets or under the pillow of a fellow prisoner. Two prisoners were caught in a "sell" when they ran all the way to the kitchen after they heard someone call that it was dinnertime, only to find out that they were a half hour early.

April Fool's Day was a big day for the prisoners. Newspapers were left hanging from coattails, signs were attached to backs, false calls were made, and many a mysterious vessel appeared in the river. The Rev. Handy had a trick played on him when there was a box delivered to his quarters. He was in the middle of a conversation when the box arrived. He was expecting two boxes, but this was not the size of either that he was expecting. He was still thinking about his conversation and:

> the restrained smiles of the several visitors entirely escaped my notice. Beginning, at length, to open the box, I took from it, first, a second-hand gray shirt: and proceeding downwards, the character of the articles grew more and more mysterious. I was just exclaiming "what in the world —," as I put my hand upon a large bundle of old rags, and it was not until this moment, that I saw I was "sold." Nelson being the first to shout, I instantly suspected him of being the father of the joke. The whole company was now in ecstasy. The laugh became uproarious. I had immediately pounced upon Nelson, and enjoying the fun, myself, chased him around the room, at the toe of my boot — anon shaking him lustily. Everybody screamed, clapped, and I verily believe, cried with delight. It was a scene for a Hogarth. Every man who witnessed it will remember it for years to come. It turned out, after all, that Nelson had nothing to do with the matter. The whole thing had been concocted by Tibbetts, who knew that I was anxiously expecting a couple of boxes. Both he, and his convict accomplice, performed their parts well — for nobody would have dreamed, from their straight countenances, that they had the slightest idea of mischief. A Latin poet has written Dulce et decorum

est desipere in loco; and a wiser and better than he has said, "There is a time to laugh."[86]

The island was not completely separated from the rest of the world. There would be many times that the island and its prisoners would get visitors. The Quaker ladies of Salem, N.J., along with other church groups, made up gifts for the prisoners as well as for local boys who were fighting the Rebels. They sent to the island "stockings, mittens, pillows, long johns winter underwear, envelopes of cornstarch and farina, crackers" to help prisoners in need.[87] The Masons would come over once a week to hold meetings of instruction to its members who were prisoners.[88] They were a powerful organization during the war and its members were on both sides of the conflict. Their wide-ranging membership was helpful to more than one prisoner, which once again proved that it was beneficial for a prisoner to have a friend on the outside. When Capt. Bosang was first captured on May 18, 1864, before he arrived at Fort Delaware, a Union colonel noticed that he was a Mason by the ring he wore on his finger. The colonel, as well as a lieutenant colonel and a major who held Bosang captive, were also Masons and treated him with great kindness. Before he was transferred to Fredericksburg, they asked him if he had any money. Bosang said that he did not, so they asked him as a fellow Mason to accept $5.00, which he did. When he arrived at Belle Plain, a guard wanted to take his money when he was searched. He told the guard how he got the money and a nearby lieutenant, who was also a Mason, overheard the conversation and told the guard to give back the money and leave him alone. He invited Bosang into his tent for a drink of whiskey, but he refused because he did not drink. He did ask if he could take some back for his fellow prisoners. The lieutenant gave him a pint cup to take back with him, which was enjoyed by all.[89]

There was a ban on any visitors unless they were on government business or visiting a prisoner.[90] However, that rule was ignored many times in many different ways. Once, Lieut. McHenry Howard, who was being held within the fort at the time, was in a room when suddenly a gray-haired old man and a group of schoolgirls walked in and calmly looked him and his fellow prisoners over. They then left as quietly as they came. After they went on to the next room, Lieut. Howard started complaining about the intrusion. Capt. Ahl overheard him and appeared at the door. Howard then said: "Captain Ahl, we are glad at any time to give any Northern people information about friends in the South or any other proper information, but we protest against being exhibited like wild animals." Apparently, Capt. Ahl did not appreciate being lectured by a prisoner, because a short time later, Lieut. Howard found himself out of the relative comfort of the fort and thrown into the officers' barracks.[91]

The Rev. Handy recalled a time when the prisoners were excited by a group of visitors who came to the island. The visitors, most of whom were female, had relatives and friends among the soldiers stationed at the fort. The women seemed to have a good time walking along the ramparts, going through the barracks, and looking at the prisoners as they walked toward the water cisterns to fill up their canteens.

On more than one occasion, guest speakers would come to the fort to talk with the prisoners. The Rev. Dr. George Junkin came in June 1864 to preach as a part of the Christian Commission. He had moved from his home in Lexington, Ky., at the beginning of the war so as to not be disloyal to the Union. That action made many of the prisoners unwilling to listen to anything he had to say. A council of prisoners was held upon his arrival to discuss the situation. It was agreed that they would listen to the Rev. Junkin out of respect because he was the father of the first Mrs. Stonewall Jackson.[92] On the 11th, he spoke to the prisoners and handed out tracts for them to read. There was always a shortage of reading material and they made a rush for the reverend when he passed them out. It was so bad that Dr. Junkin had to beat them back with a cane.[93]

The U.S. Christian Commission did not have a good reputation among the prisoners. They felt that its main concern was not to save souls, but to convince Confederate soldiers to return to the Union. Some of the prisoners did not like some of the tracts handed out by the commission. The ones that they objected to were more political than religious. However, this did not stop some prisoners from rejecting all of the tracts whether or not they contained what might be considered offensive material. Once, after receiving a tract called "The Blood of Jesus," one young Rebel ripped it up and made "a vile use of the paper." The young man was rebuked into blushing when another prisoner named Capt. Gordon asked him: "Would you refuse to receive a valuable medicine from the hands of the Yankees, if dying with disease?"

Later in June, the Rev. Dr. Breckinridge came to the pen with Gen. Schoepf and some other Union officers. He went to Division 27, where the majority of the prisoners were from Kentucky, like the Rev. Breckinridge. Gen. Schoepf introduced the reverend and said that he would be glad to see the officers of his state and talk with them. The few who came forward did so more for curiosity than for a religious conversation. While he was talking to the prisoners, he remarked about their good appearance and made the suggestion that the prisoners must be "well treated and well fed." A prisoner quickly replied that: "We can assure you, it is not the result of Fort Delaware rations." To back up that statement, Capt. William J. Mitchell immediately held up the bread and meat which was his portion of his previous meal. The general and the reverend were surprised by the small portion and Schoepf told Mitchell to get it weighed at the sutler's shop. He then promised that he would do something about the situation.[94]

Nothing was done about the rations. However, the perception of Dr. Breckinridge brought up an interesting point. Men like the reverend would see the prisoners and say that they must be doing well, while others would see the prisoners as being in abject misery. This difference of opinion became more pronounced as the war went on and conditions at Fort Delaware declined.

❧ 7 ❧

Difference of Opinion — The Other Side of the Dead Line

The difference of opinion about Fort Delaware among even the Federal authorities was shown several weeks after Surgeon Clark reported his findings about the prison. Lieut. Col. William Irvine of the 10th New York Cavalry had been ordered by Maj. Gen. E.A. Hitchcock, the commissioner for the exchange of prisoners, to inspect Fort Delaware concerning the treatment of Rebel prisoners held there. On December 5, 1863, he sent his report to Washington. Irvine interviewed the Confederate surgeons, the enlisted men in groups, with one-on-one interviews, their non-commissioned officers, and prisoners in the hospital. His findings were that the Rebels held at the prison were as well treated as any Union soldier in the field or in a hospital. The barracks were:

> well constructed, well-lighted, and well ventilated, the floors sufficiently high between joints for two tiers of bunks on either side of a middle passageway seven feet wide. In the passageway at suitable intervals were put up four large coal stoves in each one of the barracks. The tiers of bunks are also four and a half feet between joints, six and a half feet deep, and inclining slightly toward the passageway. The ventilation is through the roof. A sufficient number of ventilators constructed in the ordinary manner are common to all the buildings constituting the men's quarters, mess-rooms, kitchens, bakery, and hospital wards. Visiting next the kitchens, I found them exceedingly neat and well-ordered, ample in size, and furnished with kettles set in arches, and cooking ranges with all necessary furnishings and utensils. The bake-house I found to be a model one in all respects, as

well constructed and convenient as any post bakery I have ever seen outside of Washington and ample in its accommodations. I examined the bread, which I found to be of excellent quality, made of two parts wheat and one of corn meal. The mess rooms are constructed like the sleeping barracks, somewhat wider, with tiers of stationary tables with sufficient intervals between them.

These buildings have all been constructed on the same general plan, including also the hospital ward, of the same material, and are as good in all respects as are provided for our soldiers at recruiting depots and camps of instruction. The grounds are well ditched, and plank and brick walks have been constructed to and from every point necessary to be visited. I saw the men at their dinner and noticed their fare; everything served to them was as good and abundant as the rations supplied to our soldiers, including onions, potatoes, and cabbage once a day habitually. ...Finding the well men without cause of complaint, I next visited the prison hospital. Each of the hospital barracks constituted a ward, with a mess-room at the head for convalescents and a surgeon's office across a hall opposite. I found them clean, comfortable, and well ordered in all respects, with ample room and accommodations for the sick. They are arranged with one tier of single beds on either side of a sufficiently wide passageway, and are heated with coal stoves; the walls were whitewashed, the bedding clean, the attendants tidy in appearance, and everything indicated that the sick were as comfortable as possible. I talked to the sick, with the convalescent, and with the attendants, and to all inquiries received the same general replies, that they were well cared for and as comfortable as they could be made. The sick are allowed to have the attendance of their own surgeons if they so desire, and I found in the different wards rebel surgeons attending some of their sick.

Lieut. Col. Irvine went on to discuss the water situation. He mentioned that the:

water, which is supplied from Brandywine Creek every day or once in two days, is kept in large iron tanks convenient to and sufficient for all the uses of the post, the garrison included. These tanks are of the capacity of sixty barrels or more, and are tapped with faucets at the base all around the tanks, as near together as practicable, so that a dozen or more persons can draw water at the same time. They are coated with a white paint and in warm weather keep the water cool as any hydrant water. I tasted the water and found it as sweet as Potomac Creek or James River water.[1]

There was definitely a difference of opinion concerning the purity of the water the prisoners had at their disposal. It could have been due to when and where Lieut. Col. Irvine tasted the water. If he tasted water from inside the fort, where the general officers and political prisoners were kept, the water was "conducted through a cistern on top of the building. The fixtures are now complete; and we can obtain clear, and good tasted water, by turning a cock at the head of the stairway. The arrangement for washing is, also, pretty snug for a prison, and the luxury of a bath gives us a fair start for the day."[2] However, if he tried water from the prison barracks, that might have been a different story. As one prisoner wrote:

The supply of drinking water, was rarely equal to the demand even in the rainy season, but in the summer and fall it was totally inadequate to the barest needs for thirst and cooking; while the quality was at times nearly nauseating. At first the total supply was contained in two wooden tanks, situated in the corners of the barracks, and filled by rain water from the roofs.

When the rains were frequent the tanks were kept tolerably pure; but when several weeks elapsed without showers, they became putrid, as any barrel of rain-water will, and on opening the top of either, the contents would appear to be fairly swarming with wiggletails and white worms. There was no strainer, nor had we any means of filtering it, nor purification.

When the contents of the tanks grew low even the smell of the water was sickening, to say nothing of the knowledge that one was emptying into his stomach a positively rotten fluid alive with animalculae [*sic*].[3]

The Federal inspector may have been pleased with the prison, but that opinion was not shared by everyone. Dr. Haynie, one of Gen. Morgan's surgeons, wrote a song that described his feelings about the conditions that went against what Lieut.-Col. Clark had to say about Fort Delaware. It was called "The Wailings at Fort Delaware." Part of the song went as follows:

> Oh, here we are confined, at Fort Delaware,
> With nothing to drink but a little lager beer;
> Infested by vermin, as much as we can bear —
> Oh, Jeff; can't you help us get away from here?
>
> Spoiled beef and bad soup is our daily fare
> And to complain is more than any dare;
> They will buck us and gag us and case us in a cell,
> There to bear the anguish and torments of hell.
>
> The room for eating is anything but clean,
> The filth upon the benches is plainly to be seen;
> The smell of putrefaction rises on the air,
> To fill out and refill our bill of fare.
>
> The sick are well treated, as Southern surgeons say;
> And the losses by death are scarcely four per day —
> It's diarrhea mixture for scurvy and smallpox,
> And every other disease of Pandora's box.
>
> Oh, look at the graveyard on the Jersey shore
> At the hundreds who ne'er will return more.
> Oh, could they come back again to testify
> Against the lying devils who lived to see them die!
>
> Our kindness to prisoners you can't deny;
> It's no Dutch falsehood, nor a Yankee trick —
> We have the proof on hand, on which you may rely,
> From Southern surgeons who daily see the sick.
>
> Oh, speak out, young soldiers, and let your country hear
> All about your treatment at Fort Delaware —
> How they work you in the wagons, when weary and sad,
> With only half rations, when plenty they had.[4]

Despite the better opinions about the conditions at Fort Delaware, Col. Hoffman was still concerned about them. Three hundred men had died at the fort during the month of September and 330 in October 1863. He again asked Schoepf about the situation in December, to which he replied that the cases of smallpox were decreasing and the disease was changing its form. He said that the death rate was very low. In January 1864, the cases dropped from 178 to 84, of which 60 would be discharged by the next Saturday. By March 1 of that year, Gen. Schoepf said that the smallpox situation was over and the barracks were repaired, renovated, and ready to accept 4,000 more prisoners on top of what he already had.[5]

General Schoepf had a rather confusing reputation at Fort Delaware. Both the guards and the prisoners were divided on how they felt about him. He was very supportive of the Purnell Legion when they were stationed at the fort—he made sure that their officers had large rooms and had large quarters built for the rest of the men. He also granted all leaves which were requested of him.[6] However, he was also a strict disciplinarian, which did not sit very well with some of the soldiers under his command. The soldiers who did not like him were even talking about revolting and committing violence against Schoepf. Part of the group that was disgruntled about Schoepf had as their captain, Charles Chaille-Long. When he got wind of the plot against Schoepf, Long confronted his men. He gave the soldiers in question a tongue-lashing, telling them that he was ashamed of them, and threatened to quit the army immediately. He then ordered them to their quarters. Rebellious spirit broken, the men did as they were told and that was the end of the planned uprising. The next day, Long was ordered to Schoepf's office and was placed on his staff as the commissary of musters.[7] To ensure that the urge to rebel did not return, the 5th Delaware Regiment was sent to the fort to reinforce the garrison.[8] The 5th Delaware stayed until August 6, 1863. The next day, the 6th Delaware took their places and stayed until August 22, when they were replaced by the Purnell Legion.[9]

Even though Gen. Schoepf was supportive of the Purnell Legion as a whole, it did not mean that his relationship with every member was a positive one. There was a captain from the legion who had been in trouble in the past for attempting to attack a deaf and mute child, who was the daughter of a sergeant on the island. He had also been placed under arrest for insulting a lady. Gen. Schoepf had been the major witness against him in the insult incident. After his release, the captain had refused to acknowledge his superior officer, even when directly spoken to by Schoepf. On September 29, 1863, Gen. Schoepf happened to have the occasion to walk past the captain and he raised his hat in greeting. The captain refused to pay attention. Schoepf, angered by the insult, grabbed the other man's head, tore his hat off, and threw it to the ground. This enraged the captain and he returned the favor by grabbing Schoepf's hat and doing the same thing. Schoepf answered back by immediately placing him under arrest.[10]

The general was not the most popular man on the island. Some of the prisoners called him "General Terror"[11] or "a Hessian brute"[12] or said that he had no administrative abilities and that the "veriest simpleton in Dixie would have reduced the plan of governing the prison to more order and simplicity."[13] However, there were others who had dealings with him that considered him distant but honorable. One such person who might have thought of him in that way was Henry Hall Brogden. Mr. Brogden was a sergeant in the Signal Corps in Richmond, Va.,[14] who had been asked to go to New York City for the Confederate War Department. On May 3, 1863, on his way back, he was captured and sent to Fort McHenry for the crime of crossing Union lines without permission. He was sent to Fort Delaware for a few days in July 1863 when Lee was on the move. He met Gen. Schoepf then and felt that he was treated well by him at the time.

Brogden was returned to Fort Delaware in December 1863. Gen. Schoepf insisted on giving him the run of the island, due to his bad health, from reveille to retreat without parole. In March 1864, he wrote to a friend, with Schoepf's permission, to arrange for an exchange.[15] On April 30, 1864, his aunt sent him a note stating that President Lincoln had ordered Brogden to be sent to City Point for exchange with someone of the same rank.[16] However, the exchange paper was not in the envelope with the note. He requested and received an interview with Gen. Schoepf to ask about the letter. The general said that he had read the letter as per his duty, but there was no letter of exchange enclosed. Brogden went back to his room to look for the exchange paper, but could not find it. He went back to the commandant and asked if he had a waste basket or was one emptied recently. Schoepf said that it was recently emptied and rang for his orderly. The orderly came and said that he had not emptied the basket yet because the moat was empty and he was waiting for the tide to come in. The basket was brought back, the general kicked it over, and told Brogden to look for it himself.

A few minutes later, he found the paper in the waste basket. Brogden felt as though he was going to faint and Schoepf looked even worse. Schoepf apologized deeply for his carelessness and asked when he could be ready to leave. Brogden said immediately, but the general said that he could not send him until the next morning, he would be in time to catch the evening boat from Baltimore to Fortress Monroe, where he would be exchanged. Capt. Ahl sent for him later and told him that he would be leaving on the 7:00 A.M. boat to catch the Baltimore train at Wilmington. Ahl asked him to wear civilian dress while traveling, but the only decent thing he had was his uniform, so that is what he wore.[17]

Gen. Schoepf also liked to visit the officers' barracks. Every few days, he would visit the generals held at the fort. He would always knock before entering their quarters and talk with them in an informal and friendly manner. The war was freely talked about and one time, when the Rebel officers had said that the South could never be beaten, Schoepf replied after listening politely: "Gentlemen, I think you are mistaken and underrate the determination and resources of the North."[18]

On another occasion, Gen. Schoepf got together with the officers who had the parole of the island. He sat with them for at least an hour in the sutler's private room. It was a pleasant visit and eventually, the conversation turned toward the treatment of the prisoners. Schoepf told them that it was always important to him to treat the prisoners with kindness and with the consideration due them. He also said that if he were ever taken prisoner, he would hope to fall into the hands of Gen. Morgan and his officers. He thought that he would receive the very best treatment from them, just as he had given them while they stayed at Fort Delaware. Everyone in the room enjoyed the meeting and it ended with a friendly glass between them.[19]

Even though Gen. Schoepf would visit the Rebel generals on a regular basis, there were many complaints from the other prisoners that he was a hard man to get to. They believed that he was a good man and willing to grant favors.[20] The proof of that was when the wife of Capt. Gibbon, Gen. Morgan's adjutant general, received a permit to visit her husband. They were entertained for three days at Schoepf's home on the island and shown every kindness and courtesy.[21] However, they also believed that he allowed Capt. Ahl to run the day-to-day operation of the fort.[22] Capt. George W. Ahl, the adjutant general of the fort, was unanimously considered by the prisoners to be the worst of the guards. Ahl came from Allegheny County, Pa.,[23] and was promoted to captain in July 1863 to command an independent artillery company made up of former Rebel prisoners who had taken the Oath of Allegiance. He was accused of being "a cold-blooded, heartless, cruel, and cowardly South-hater." He treated all of the prisoners with contempt and it was thought by the prisoners that any mistreatment they suffered at Fort Delaware was either directly from him or with his permission. It was thought that he held Gen. Schoepf back from treating the prisoners better and that there were complaints going to Washington about "too lenient treatment of rebels" by Schoepf and Ahl agreed with the complaints.[24] Ahl made sure that all communications between the prisoners and Gen. Schoepf was severely restricted. Only those messages that Ahl wanted to go to Schoepf got to the general's desk. He was so hated by the prisoners that they used to say that all in Ahl, he was "Ahl-fired mean."[25]

Capt. Ahl, or as he was also called, Ape Ahl,[26] was not alone in his actions towards the prisoners. Lieut. A.G. Wolf. who was from Philadelphia and arrived on the island in September 1862,[27] was the assistant provost marshal in charge of the officers' section. He was considered "a coarse, brutal creature, with all the mean, cowardly, and cruel instincts of the beast from which his name is taken; a fellow without culture, refinement, or gentility, who took much delight in insulting the Confederate officers that the misfortunes of war had made prisoners."[28] He tried to come across as a businesslike man, but it was believed that he had no head for business and was too fond of his whiskey. The lack of respect that the prisoners had for him did not mean that they treated him with disrespect. Many of the officers tried to stay on good terms with him, even to the point of acting subservient to him. Whenever he entered the pen, it was the signal for the prisoners to rush to him for favors and news from the outside world. He was the eyes and ears of the camp, since he read every incoming letter and forbade all the guards from talking to the prisoners, and any information from the prisoners to Gen. Schoepf went through him first. The sutler got along very well with Wolf and his men, allowing them to help themselves to cigars or anything else he kept in stock.[29] Wolf, his assistants, and the Rebel soldiers who took the Oath of Allegiance made life miserable for the prisoners. Major John Ogden Murray and his bunk-mates, Lieut. Bob Bowie and Capt. Tom Roche, would sneak into the enlisted men's camp after taps and listen to the stories of their abuse. The prisoners could not complain to the Union authorities about their treatment because the complaints never got any farther than Capt. Ahl.[30]

One example of this was the case of Capt. Henry Dickinson. The captain was a prisoner and had learned that his brother was a prisoner in the enlisted men's barracks. He was refused permission to see him by Capt. Ahl and Lieut. Wolf. Dickinson did keep in touch with his brother by writing to him through the mail. Dickinson tried to explain that his brother was sick and that he only wanted to see him for a few minutes, but he was turned down. Altogether, he asked the Union authorities to let him see his brother nine times. It was two days before Dickinson was supposed to leave the fort that he received permission to see his brother. He had gone to see Gen. Schoepf and told him that he had "repeatedly asked for an interview with my brother in the privates' prison. I expect as you know to leave in a short time, and may get home before he does. Shall I then say we stayed within a few feet of each other all summer, but I never saw him?" Gen. Schoepf turned to his orderly and ordered him to tell Lieut. Wolf to let him see his brother. Dickinson was able to visit with him for an hour in private.[31]

Major Murray and his friends were not the only ones sneaking around the prisoners' quarters. Occasionally, Lieut. Wolf would dress in a Rebel uniform and walk among the prisoners, going from division to division listening for any information he could pick up. His attempts to gather information did not go undetected. One of the officers in Division 30 spotted him one evening. He did not let on to the others that Wolf was among them, but, instead, proceeded to give everyone his opinion of sneak thieves. He also said that he did not like "such fellows as the Wolf, who tries to play Fox, but isn't half as smart as the damned Dutchman." Upon hearing this, Wolf looked around anxiously for a few moments and then got out as quickly and as quietly as he could.[32]

One guard that stood out above the others was a Vermont Yankee by the name of Adam or Adams. He was also mentioned in one diary by the name of Fox and was called the "damned Dutchman." He was also called "Old Hike." Whatever his name was, the prisoners remembered him well. Sgt. Charles W. Rivenbark from North Carolina, who was captured at Gettysburg and spent two years at Fort Delaware, wrote many years later about him. "Hike" had first been sent to Fort Delaware as a prisoner. He had been charged with being the first man to get back to Washington after the First Battle of Bull Run. He was convicted and sentenced to imprisonment at the fort. Somehow, he managed to get promoted and was a type of supervisor and considered a "devil's agent in general."[33] Captain Dickinson agreed with this negative statement by saying that Fox "was utterly repulsive to humanity," and no one in the pen spoke to him willingly.[34] His command to the prisoners for every occasion was: "Hike out! hike out! you d — — d rebel sons of — — — -!" Once a week he would "hike out" the prisoners to search them, their bunks, and clothes for any contraband material. Any sick prisoners not able to move quickly would be hit by the heavy stick he carried with him.

Soaps, knives, forks, bottles, an extra piece of wood or coal was "hiked." "Old Hike" seized any opportunity to do swindles, cheats, and tricks on the prisoners. He took any Yankee jacket or pants, no matter how the prisoner managed to get them, and promised to exchange them for Confederate clothing. The promises were never kept. One time, he had 500 prisoners strip and told them that they were getting new clothes. As soon as they stripped down to their shirts, he ordered them to go "right face, forward, double-quick, march! and back through the cold mud and water to our own cheerless barracks." They then had to scrounge around for more clothes in a barracks with one stove and one barrow-load of coal that had to last for a day.

One day, "Hike" came to the prisoners when the tide was very high and the wind and waves were rough and raised an alarm that the levee was falling apart. "Hike out! hike out, you d——d rebel sons of b——-s, or you will all be drowned. Run, run!" When the prisoners came out in the ice, snow, and mud, many shoeless and nearly naked, they found out that the only danger was that a pile of wood and some of the sutler's goods were going to get wet. They were forced to work for several hours, cold and hungry, to move the items to safety.

"Hike" got along very well with another guard named Campbell, who was from Mississippi. He had been taken prisoner and sent to Fort Delaware, but he took the oath and became a Yankee lieutenant. The prisoners assumed that the two of them got along because they both liked to torment the Rebels. Campbell liked to tell them that various Confederate officials and generals had been killed, captured, or deserted. He also liked to say that Southern women and children were starving or were only kept from this by selling themselves to Yankees and southern "loyalists." On another occasion, two prisoners, one from Maryland and the other from Tennessee, bribed Campbell with a gold watch and $100 to allow them to escape. They were smuggled aboard a steamer, but Campbell then hunted them down and brought them back in handcuffs at gunpoint. He also kept the money and the watch.[35]

Occasionally, a prisoner needed to be punished and there were several means at the guards' disposal to do this. One form of punishment was called "marking time." The offending prisoner had to stand still until given permission to move, no matter how long. [36] Bucking and gagging was also a common form of punishment for prisoners. It consisted of tying a stick or bayonet in a man's mouth, tying his hands together, slipping them over his knees and running a stick through the space beneath the knees. A ball and chain was also used to keep prisoners in one place. Most of the balls weighed 12 pounds, but some of them were as heavy as 32 pounds. The chains that went with them were about 6 feet long, although they were some-times shorter.[37] Whatever the length and weight, they kept the prisoner from running away. They also made it obvious when the shackled prisoner moved around. The Rev. Handy complained that the rattling of the chains of the prisoners in the kitchens would keep him awake.

The guards carried out inspections of the barracks on an irregular basis. This was done to ensure that they did not have anything against regulations in their possession. If the barracks were acceptable, the guards would say "Post No.——, all vigilant."[38] They were expected to do this in turn when signaled from the guardhouse. This was done as a safety measure for the guards in case a prisoner attacked them while they were carrying out the inspections.

There was a time when the orders for the treatment of prisoners were not posted for anyone to see. For many prisoners, the first idea anyone had that they had broken a rule was when they had a rifle cocked at them. This led to many prisoners being confused about what was right and what was wrong. One time, around sunset after a hot day, a guard was heard to tell the prisoners: "Go to your quarters, you devils you." The next day, the prisoners were kept marching until it was pitch dark. The guards on the parapets would call down to the prisoners if they saw them with a knife that they liked. Another time, Capt. B. Lewis was reading a newspaper and mentioned that the Confederate army had won a battle. A guard heard this, presented bayonet and ordered him to mark time. Capt. Lewis refused and the guard threw his bayonet at him. Capt. Lewis caught it and the guard demanded again that he to mark time. It was at this point that Lieut. Wolf came up to the two men. Because he was a friend of Capt. Lewis, Wolf did not react as he would normally and took Lewis's side in the argument.[39]

Not every guard had problems with the prisoners. Stanislaus Mlotkowski was a young Polish artist who arrived at Fort Delaware on September 19, 1861, as a part of the 130 men of Independent Battery A who were assigned to the island as reinforcements. On March 1, 1862, he was promoted to captain and put in charge of Battery A. He regularly brought his company together on the parade grounds to practice and every Fourth of July was greeted with a 36 gun salute from them. However, because the focus of his company's efforts had by 1864 turned more towards guarding the prisoners in the wooden barracks, Capt. Mlotkowski came into greater contact with the prisoners than he had originally. Unlike Ahl and Wolf, he treated "the Rebels with kindness; cordially shakes hands with the Confederate officers, and admits that a Prisoner not only has a right to make his escape, if not on parole, but that his duty to his government requires him to do so, if possible. His fairness, his respect for the rights of others, and his determination to recognize the goodness of human beings were exemplary." For example, he once gave Captain Robert Baylor of the 12th Virginia Cavalry a silk tobacco purse made by his wife and tobacco as a present. He also sent five blankets to the Rebels and thought that some of the Rebels had "tam bad physiosiques."[40]

That kind of attitude made him very popular with the prisoners. He was never accused of any mistreatment of the prisoners and none of the men under his command were ever known to be abusive or hit prisoners over the head with their bayonets. He was considered to be a man of above average intelligence and never complained to his superior officers when his men were used as guards instead of what they were trained for.[41]

The difference in how the guards treated the prisoners came about from one important aspect of their character. Any guard that had been in a combat situation treated the Rebels with respect and courtesy. The ones who were abusive to the prisoners were men who had never been in a battle and who used their position to gain a certain measure of revenge on those that they thought were disloyal to the country and deserving of punishment.[42]

Whether or not the guards were abusive, the routine of prison life got to them as easily as it did to the Rebels. They had to find their own ways to stay busy and amuse themselves just like the prisoners when they were not on duty. Reading was a way to relieve the boredom. Unlike the prisoners, the men stationed at Fort Delaware were allowed to read military histories as well as the best sellers of the day. They also had a library that they could get books from. There were parties at Mrs. Patterson's hotel that the guards attended, and sometimes they got into fights there, especially during the holidays. Many of the guards celebrated the Christmas season by getting drunk during Christmas Eve. Several fights broke out and one man, John Toland, was badly beaten by six members of the 5th Maryland. The next night, there was a party at Mrs. Patterson's hotel on the island which lasted until dawn. New Year's Eve was celebrated in much the same way with the beer shop open for business, many of the guards drunk, and more fighting. New Year's Day 1864 was quiet. In the evening, there was another party at Mrs. Patterson's hotel. As one soldier wrote: "Some 7 or 8 Irish girls are there, a dozen boys and two fiddles, we conclude to be jolly, went to dancing, kept up till morning but had two quarrels and near bursting up." The wind was blowing hard, which made it a cold night. It became so cold the next day that the guards were relieved from their posts every two hours instead of every four.

Fortunately, the guards were able to occasionally leave the confines of the fort. Passes were granted and the soldiers would cross over to the New Jersey side and visit Salem, N.J., and sometimes spend the night at the Nelson House. They would also visit the Delaware side of the river and go to Delaware City or the nearby towns of New Castle and Wilmington. They were also able to visit Philadelphia. They would go to see the sights, since many of them had never been away from home before. They might come back a little worse for wear due to drinking or fights.

Drinking was a problem among the guards. Being stationed on a reclaimed swamp far from the action with time on one's hands and away from home for the first time did not make for a good combination. There were many drunken fights between guards. Sometimes the fights were little more than grabbing each other's clothes. Other times, they became worse. A man named Helmsley was killed because of a drunken brawl. For some of the guards, getting drunk meant staying drunk for several days. The holidays, like Christmas, New Year's, etc., were prime days for drunken guards. During one fight at the beer shop, the provost marshal was knocked down. Two of the men involved were arrested and placed on the chain gang. Another fight ended up with one man hit in the mouth with a bayonet, two placed in cells, and one more bucked and gagged.[43]

Alcohol was not hard to get for the prisoners and guards alike. Dr. Stone would visit the prisoners and prescribe alcohol to help them for illnesses such as a cough or a kidney problem. Even if some patients were not sick, a bottle of "spirits" would be required to restore the patient to full health. The ability to have alcohol was so abused that all prescriptions that entailed using alcohol had to be countersigned by Capt. Ahl. This precaution did not put a dent in the sutler's alcohol business and there was so much of the "ardent" circulating throughout the prison that both prisoners and guards alike were able to get drunk occasionally. Gen. Schoepf received reports of some Rebel officers getting drunk and went to the Confederate officers' quarters to speak about this topic:

> There now, gentlemen! you see how it is — I am obliged to notice the matter. I know that a little of the "ardent" is necessary to keep body and soul together; and I have given the sutler orders to let you have it; but you must not get drunk. If anybody, however, does get too much, you must not let him walk about the "pen." I want you to take him to his bunk immediately: and you must keep him there until he gets sober.

Schoepf's response to the drinking situation earned him three cheers from the officers and made him, at least for one day, a popular man among the prisoners.

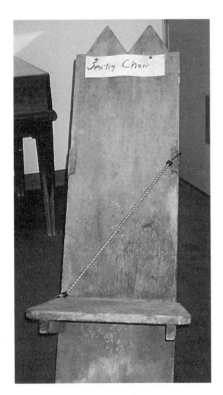

A chair used by sentries at Fort Delaware. Now in Fort Delaware Society Library.

Tolerating drunken officers seemed to be a trait that was a part of being in the army. Gen. Vance, who had been captured in January 1864, was a Christian and as such, found that one of the hardest things to deal with in the army was with the social pressure to drink. He felt that the idea of drinking in the army was so strong that an officer who resisted taking a drink was not only rare, but was considered somewhat odd and unnecessarily pious.[44]

On February 15, 1864, Gen. Schoepf was notified that Gen. M. Jeff Thompson was being sent to Fort Delaware from Point Lookout, Md., and he should be kept apart from the enlisted prisoners.[45] Gen. Thompson soon arrived at Delaware City escorted by Capt. William Patterson. To cross over to the island, Thompson and Patterson had to rent a yawl to navigate past the cakes of ice that filled the Delaware River. After he arrived, Gen. Thompson was concerned about the reputation of Gen. Schoepf because of what the Gettysburg prisoners had told him about their captor. He soon found out that his fears were groundless. Gen. Schoepf met with him soon after his arrival and informed him that his orders were to treat him with courtesy. Schoepf told Thompson that he could have his parole of the island if he gave his word not to try to escape. Thompson promised and the parole was granted. It was in place for several months until Col. Hoffman came for a visit and discovered that Thompson and his roommates had the run of the island. Hoffman had their paroles cancelled and the officers confined to their rooms. They were only able to come out to take some exercise by swimming in the Delaware River under the watchful eyes of the guards.[46] Thompson became very popular with the guards because he was a well spoken, witty man. They enjoyed trying to get as close as possible to him so that they could listen to his humorous stories and expressions.[47]

How Gen. Thompson and his mess lived while on the island helped to cause a difference of opinion on the conditions in which the prisoners lived while at the prison. Thirty years after the war ended, someone wrote a letter to the *Wilmington Morning News* refuting the reputation of Fort Delaware as a "notorious hole of horrors." The writer, who signed the letter "L.E.W.," stated that he saw no sign of horror in the prison. The higher-ranking officers who lived in the casement, like Basil Duke, lived very comfortably. L.E.W. did not see prisoners begging for work to give

Col. Basil Duke, a member of Gen. Morgan's staff, whose lifestyle as a prisoner was incorrectly considered by some visitors to be typical of all prisoners'.

them something to do and thought that they appeared to be healthy. He saw them at work, in the barracks, and at meals and they seemed to be fine. He also said that the hospital was clean and better than the army hospital in Wilmington.[48]

On March 3, 1864, Col. Hoffman sent a directive by the authority of Secretary Stanton to the commanders of the Northern prison camps. It contained a set of rules by which the sutlers could operate at the prisons and a list of articles that they could sell to the prisoners. Hoffman stated that a large sutler's store was not expected to be established at each prison:

> but merely a small room where supplies for a day or two may be kept on hand. None but the articles enumerated on the list can be sold, and every precaution must be taken to prevent abuse of the privilege, either by the person permitted to sell or the prisoners. No sale should be made before 8 o'clock in the morning or after half an hour before sunset. As prisoners are not permitted to have money in their possession, all sales should be made on orders of the commanding officer or

office in whose hands is deposited the money belonging to prisoners, and these orders should be paid as often as once a week, if practicable.

The enclosure that went out with Col. Hoffman's letter listed the items which were permitted by the Federal government to be sold at the sutler's shop in the Federal prisons. They were:

> Tobacco, cigars, pipes, snuff, steel pens, paper, envelopes, lead pencils, pen knives, postage stamps, buttons, tape, thread, sewing cotton, pins and needles, handkerchiefs, suspenders, socks, underclothes, caps, shoes, towels, looking glasses, brushes, combs, clothes brooms, pocket knives, scissors. Groceries: Crushed sugar, syrup, family soap, butter, lard, smoked beef, beef tongues, bologna sausage, corn meal, nutmegs, pepper, mustard, table salt, salt fish, crackers, cheese pickles, sauces, meats and fish in cans, vegetables, dried fruits, syrups, lemons, nuts, apples, matches, yeast powders. Table furniture: Crockery, glassware, tinware.[49]

Col. G.K. Johnson of the Medical Inspector's Office came to Fort Delaware on February 29, 1864, to inspect the hospital and the prison. The purpose of this visit was to discover what the conditions on Pea Patch Island were and to implement improvements if needed. The report that came from this inspection was sent to Col. Hoffman and a copy of it was sent to Gen. Schoepf on March 8. It first focused on the hospital, covering the period between November 1, 1863, to February 1, 1864. Of the 2,747 prisoners held during this time, 856 became ill each month. There was an average of 611 men sick daily with an average of 22.2 percent. The mortality rate was 311 prisoners in three months, bringing the monthly average to 103⅔. The diseases that killed these men were smallpox, which claimed 112 in three months; diarrhea, 60; pneumonia, 45; scurvy, 15; typhoid fever, 12; erysipelas, 11; dysentery, 10; and typho-malarial fever, 9.

Col. Johnson also did a survey on the health of the garrison stationed at the fort. At the time, there were 1,068 Union soldiers on duty on the island. During each of the three months included in this report, 163⅓ soldiers became ill for a daily average of 44, which came to 4.1 percent of the total garrison. There were 14 deaths in three months for a monthly average of 4⅔. These deaths were caused by much of the same diseases that took the lives of the prisoners. Smallpox claimed 8 men, with typhoid fever and diarrhea killing one soldier each. No causes were given for the other three deaths.

He went on to look at the prisoners' barracks. At the time of his visit, Col. Johnson noted that only one of the barracks was being used to house the prisoners. This was due to the smaller number of prisoners being held on the island. The decision was made to put the 1,505 remaining men in one barracks to save on fuel. However, doing this did not translate into comfort for the prisoners. The colonel found that the barracks were damp and not very warm. He also suspected that it was that way during the winter as well. He felt that the barracks and the privies were kept moderately clean. He noticed that some of the men:

perhaps a large majority, were comfortably clad. Some had a moderate and still others an insufficient supply of clothing. The garments of a few were ragged and filthy. Each man had one blanket, but I observed no other bedding nor straw. Nearly all of the men show a marked neglect of personal cleanliness. Some of them seem vigorous and well, many look only moderately well, while a considerable number have an unhealthy, a cachectic appearance.

The inspection also included the amount of food the prisoners received. The following items were given to the prisoners during the month of January. These figures were broken down to show that:

coffee was issued of 5 pounds 9⁹⁄₁₀ ounces daily for every 100 men, being 2 pounds 6⁶⁄₁₀ ounces less daily than the regular ration. Of bread (made of seven parts of flour and two of meal) 18 ounces were issued daily to each man. Sugar is issued at the rate of about 11 pounds daily for 100 men, being 4 pounds daily less than the full ration. Of fresh beef each man gets 18 pounds 5³⁄₁₀ ounces during thirty-one days, or 9½ ounces daily. Of salt meat, including pork, bacon, and salt beef, each man gets 9 pounds 3 ounces during thirty-one days, or 4⁷⁄₁₀ ounces daily. Potatoes— Of these each man gets 10 pounds 15⁵⁄₁₀ ounces per month, or 5⁵⁄₁₀ ounces daily. Onions— Of these a fraction more than 1 pound per month to each man was issued. Beans— Of these 1 pound 9 ounces were issued during thirty-one days to each man, or ²⁵⁄₄₁ of 1 ounce daily. It should be added that cucumber pickles were also issued and used by the men during the month, but to what extent I do not know.

Col. Johnson addressed the problem of the health of the prisoners and what could be done to correct the situation. He felt that the prisoners' health was already weakened by the hard service they had seen before their capture. He did not ignore the emotional state of the prisoners while in captivity. He said that being held prisoner brought about:

nostalgia, disappointment, anxiety, a listless, monotonous life, absence of discipline and of regular exercise and occupation, all of which are lowering and disease inviting influences. Looking for the more proximate causes we find, first that the island on which the men are quartered is low, damp, and to some extent miasmatic; second, that 1,505 men are congregated in one common barrack with insufficient space, thus engendering crowd with its evils; third, that the temperature of the quarters is too low. This cause, combined with humidity, particularly encourages scurvy and other cachectic troubles; fourth, the diet may, I suppose, be considered fair, both as to quantity and quality. Under favorable or ordinary circumstances it probably would not lead to scurvy, but in this case, considering the other distempering influences, the diet, I apprehend, has not been quite sufficient in quantity, nor composed quite largely enough of vegetables. These facts and views suggest at once the proper preventive and sanitary measures, and these, which I respectfully recommend, are as follows: First. That during the continuances of cold weather the quarters be kept comfortably warm; those men, few in number, who have insufficient clothing should be sought out and clad. Second. The congregation of so many men in one barrack should be avoided. The 1,505 men now thus together should be put into at least two barracks; there is no difficulty in doing this since there are several unoccupied buildings. They were thus concentrated in order to economize fuel, but this motive should not outweigh sanitary considerations. Third. Ventilation of quarters and policing of quarters and grounds should be carefully attended to. While there is at present no marked neglect of policing, yet too much care cannot be given to it. Fourth. The diet needs to be improved. The present issue of bread I regard as sufficient, but the coffee should be for the present, and until further health shall prevail, increased to the full ration, perhaps a small increase in the meat ration would be desirable; but the quality of vegetables especially should be increased particularly of good, sound potatoes and onions. The proper extent of this increase can only determined by careful observation on the spot, but I think the two articles last named should be at first increased 33 per cent. The mode of cooking and serving these vegetables also deserves attention. At present I believe they all are put into soup. If some of them were well cooked and eaten solid advantage would result.

The accumulated savings from the ration, amounting, I think on the 1st of February to $23,000, afford abundant means for the proposed increase.[50]

The difference of opinion between Col. Irvine and Col. Johnson consisted of Irvine seeing nothing wrong at the prison and Johnson seeing problems and creating solutions to them. These differences were not helped by those who stated their opinions as if they were fact. One example of opinion being substituted for fact was when Col. George W. McCook of the 157th Ohio National Guard went to a dinner party. While he was there, he informed the dinner guests that not only did the Confederate prisoners at Fort Delaware eat rats, but that they actually preferred them to regular food when there was an ample supply of rations being issued by the Union soldiers.[51] Anyone hearing a story like that would be hard pressed to work up any sympathy for the Southern captives. Those who based their opinions on their emotions and others who based their opinions on the facts would always have a difference of opinion on the state of the prisoners.

Whether or not everyone agreed on the conditions at fort Delaware, the prisoners still continued to try to escape. On March 10 and 13, Rebel prisoners made two separate attempts. There were 10 prisoners captured on the 10th while trying to escape and a plot was discovered on the 13th in which prisoners were going to attempt to capture a steamer and use it to escape. At the same time, the 5th Maryland arrived to begin their guard duties. Their commander, Col. William Schley, insisted on a dress parade when he arrived on the 16th, complete with inspection and battalion drills, even though it was a cold and wet day.[52]

To stop the escape attempts, a large Drummond light was placed on the west bank of the island. It was placed in front of the barracks and facing toward the Delaware shore. It was able to illuminate the water and the river bank for a distance of 100 yards. The hope was that the lamp would create enough light so that escaping prisoners would be easier to spot, and thus it would discourage the attempts.[53]

A directive sent out by Col. Hoffman by order of Secretary Stanton to all the prison camps on March 18, 1864, instructed the camp commanders how to deal with prisoners who disobeyed the rules. They were told that:

> hereafter, when a prisoner of war is shot by a sentinel for violating the regulations of the post, immediately order a board of officers to investigate all the cir-

cumstances of the case to show that the act was justifiable, a full report of which will be forwarded with your remarks. It is necessary that both the guards and the prisoners should be fully informed of the regulations or orders by which they are governed, and when a sentinel finds it necessary to fire upon a prisoner he must be able to show that he was governed strictly by the orders he received, and that the prisoner or prisoners willfully disregarded his cautions or orders. Rigid discipline must be preserved among the prisoners, but great care must be observed that no wanton excesses or cruelties are committed under the plea of enforcing orders. Should a prisoner be wounded by a sentinel he will immediately be taken to the hospital, where he must have proper attention from the surgeon in charge.

Someone else had a plan concerning the prisoners of Fort Delaware. On March 11, 1864, the commissioner for exchange, Maj. Gen. Benjamin Butler, had asked Col. Hoffman to send all the prisoners from Fort Delaware and elsewhere to Point Lookout, Md. Butler made this request just in case prisoner exchanges were resumed. He believed that they might happen soon and having all of the prisoners there would make the exchanges easier to accomplish. Ten days later, Gen. Butler received an answer from Secretary Stanton. The idea was rejected because Stanton thought that Fort Delaware was a safer place to hold prisoners than Point Lookout. In fact, three days earlier, Col. Hoffman ordered prisoners held in the Ohio penitentiary and Camp Chase to be transported to Fort Delaware.[54]

One of the men who came in from the Ohio penitentiary was Capt. Charlton Morgan, brother of Col. Dick Morgan, who was already being held at Fort Delaware. When he arrived, he told stories about the treatment the officers of Morgan's brigade received at the penitentiary. They were all stripped naked:

> and scrubbed by a negro man, who used a hard brush; and that the same water was used for twenty or thirty persons. When Gen. Morgan was scoured, the women of the establishment gathered about the windows and witnessed the whole operation, as he stood in the wash-tub. It was also common for females to come into the room, without the least reserve, when the men would be standing in their drawers, or lying, half-naked, in their beds. Merion, the Penitentiary turnkey, according to the Captain, is the son of convict parents, and prides himself on being an Atheist. Once, when a prisoner requested the use of a Bible, was peremptorily refused. The prisoners were not allowed public religious services, even on the Sabbath.

Public religious services were not banned at Fort Delaware. On the contrary, they were encouraged. On April 2, 1864, the Rev. Handy was summoned to Gen. Schoepf's office. He was then informed that he had his parole returned to him and that it would be in effect from reveille to sundown. They then discussed ways in which sermons could be preached in the barracks to the Confederate officers. The general also asked Handy not to encourage the prisoners to escape and to try to convert as many of them to the Union cause as possible. Handy had no intention of doing that, but he appreciated the ability to move around within the prison.

On the night of April 9, there was a terrible storm on the island.[55] It had rained heavily several days before,[56] but on this night, the water rose to the point that it came over the banks. At Post No. 12, the guard on duty there stood in water that was knee deep until he was relieved by another sentry. That guard was not as rigid in his duty as the man he replaced and found higher ground. Two prisoners from Tennessee were adjusting some boards on the walkway leading to the privies to cover some low spots when they were challenged by a guard. The men did not hear him and continued their work. The guard fired upon them; he wounded one of them badly, and the other man was killed.[57]

On April 26, 1864, Gen Schoepf sent a message to Col. Hoffman concerning the arrival of new prisoners. He mentioned that Col. Hoffman had asked him how many more men can the prison hold and his reply was 1,500 prisoners. Schoepf had thought that all of the prisoners from Johnson's Island would be sent to him and he had plans to place them in the unoccupied barracks he had on the island. Instead, only 335 men were sent. Gen. Schoepf was concerned that if the federal government wanted the Rebel officers held there to be separated from the enlisted men, there would not be enough room to continue that practice because of the new arrivals. He did not have enough room in the fort itself to hold the officers. He wanted to know if Col. Hoffman still wanted the prisoners separated; could he either send all of the officers away to another prison or should only officers be sent to the island from that point on? The barracks were able to hold about 1,000 enlisted men. Hoffman wrote Schoepf back two days later to inform him that Johnson's Island had as many officers as it could hold and it might be necessary to hold a thousand more in the weeks to come and he could not think of a better place to hold them than Fort Delaware. Hoffman told him to be prepared for them and if the island got crowded with enlisted men, Hoffman might transfer them to another prison.[58]

The island was not completely isolated from the rest of the world. Visitors would come to see their loved ones. In May 1864, the father of Lieut. McHenry Howard came to the fort to see if he could get a chance to see his son. Col. William Schley, the commander of the 5th Maryland Regiment, which was in charge of the island, happened to be in Gen. Schoepf's office at the time Howard's father asked permission to see him. Before Gen. Schoepf gave an answer, Col. Schley pulled the general aside and told him that the prisoner's father was "the most obnoxious man in the State of Maryland" and protested his ability to see his son. Schoepf went along with Schley and refused to allow the father to see the son unless he signed the Oath of Allegiance. The father turned around, left the fort, and picked up his waiting family without seeing his son. Two months later, Lieut. Howard had a problem with receiving the money that his father had sent him. His father wrote to Gen. Schoepf about the problem and the general sent for Howard. The two men talked and Schoepf told him that he regretted not letting his family come to visit. He told Howard that there were many spies around him and they sent negative reports about him to Washington, D.C., on a regular basis. Therefore, he felt that he had to play it safe and not grant permission for the visit. He also told Howard that in the future, if someone was going to send him money, he should have the envelope addressed to or through him and Howard could come and pick it up at any time. Schoepf then asked him if he wanted to leave the barracks he stayed at to come inside the fort. Howard said yes and soon he was back in the fort.[59]

Col. Schley made his presence known again in the same month. On May 30, the colonel got into a fight with Capt. Crissman, who was also of the 5th Maryland. The exchange became so heated that Schley pulled a pistol on Crissman. Fortunately for the captain, Schley decided not to use his gun.[60]

Three days before his visit, there were orders to clean and fix up the prison before Col. Hoffman's arrival. The prisoners were taken out of their barracks so that the buildings could be whitewashed. They stood out in the hot sun for hours while this was taking place. Later, they were led out to the river to take a bath. Guards lined the shoreline to make sure no one escaped.[61] Inspectors like this were not a rarity. The federal government sent health inspectors to Fort Delaware once a month. These were not surprise inspections and the prison was always cleaned before they arrived. Beans and meat were put into the soup served to the prisoners so that the fort would receive a good report.[62] It could be argued that Gen. Schoepf deliberately created an illusion for the inspectors that the conditions were not all that bad so that he would not get into trouble with his superiors. Then again, it is not unusual for anyone to spend time making things look better when they know that their supervisors are coming to check them out. Any way the situation could be looked at, regular inspections proved that the prison and its conditions were not being ignored by the Union.

Cleanliness was a topic that Gen. Schoepf felt strongly about. On June 1, 1864, Schoepf issued Special Order No. 157, which, in part, covered the problem of keeping the prison as clean and healthy as possible. The guards were ordered to stop any prisoner from "committing any 'Nuisance' in or about their barracks" as well as keeping them from escaping and being abusive to the guards. The consequences of that kind of behavior were very specific. The order stated that if the guard should "detect any prisoner in violating these instructions, he must order him three distinct times to halt! and if the prisoner obeys the order, the sentinel must call for the Corporal of the guard, and have the prisoner placed in arrest — but should the prisoner fail to halt, when so ordered, the sentinel must enforce his order by bayonet or ball." Gen. Schoepf did not want prisoners to make a "nuisance," or relieve themselves, in places other than the sinks because of the risks to public health and cleanliness. This order was not given or treated lightly. One prisoner was killed when he made a "nuisance" on the river bank and was ordered to stop. He called the guard "a Yankee son of a bitch," and continued what he was doing. The guard shot him and he later died from his wound.[63]

On June 2, 1864, Gen. Schoepf suggested to Col. Hoffman that he should be allowed to have the frame buildings inside the fort removed. They had caught fire once before and the general was concerned that they might catch fire again. His concern was also fueled by the fact that the buildings were very close to the magazines, making them a real danger to the fort. They were also home to many rats and mice. Gen. Schoepf tried to have them removed, but they were too numerous. He wanted the buildings to be moved out of the fort and rebuilt as part of the Rebel officers' barracks. He needed more space for them and he thought that this would solve his problem. Schoepf received an answer from Col. Hoffman on June 22 telling him that he thought it was a good idea and to start on it right away.[64]

Once he arrived at the fort on June 2, Hoffman decided that he wanted to change a few things on the island. He ordered that sugar and coffee only be issued to the sick.[65] He also wrote to Secretary Stanton on the same day stating that the fort was in satisfactory condition, but he wanted the 5th Maryland to be transferred to another command. Hoffman wanted to have a regiment from a state that was more pro-Union to guard the prisoners. He said he thought that there were too many Rebel sympathizers among the 5th Maryland to guard the 8,124 prisoners on the island.[66] The 5th Maryland was transferred to the front on June 6 and replaced by the 157th Ohio National State Guard, a group of 100-day men. The impression they gave to Private A.J. Hamilton, a member of the Pittsburgh Heavy Artillery who was stationed at Fort Delaware during most of the war, was that they were a very green outfit. Their lack of experience soon showed. Within 24 hours of their arrival at the fort, one of their officers, who was on guard duty, was so drunk that he was relieved of his duties and placed under confinement. [67] When they were guarding the top of the fence and sinks, they rarely spoke to the southern prisoners without cursing them. It appeared that they enjoyed talking that way as if their mission at the fort was to humiliate any available Rebel. When they saw a man with a penknife near the cooking area, they made him come to the base of the fence and surrender the knife to them.[68] The prisoners did not like them because they felt that the 157th Ohio, who did not have any combat experience, treated them in a way that was excessive and unnecessary.[69] Before the guard's 100 days were over, the prisoners would be proven right.

The federal government was not lax in inspecting the conditions at its prison camps. On June 19, 1864, Col. Hoffman ordered Surgeon C.T. Alexander, the acting medical inspector of prisoners of war, to make an inspection into the sanitary conditions at Fort Warren, Fort Lafayette, Fort Delaware, and Point Lookout. Hoffman wanted Alexander to look at the hospitals, barracks, and anywhere else:

> upon which the good health of the command depends and make a detailed report of the conditions of each post. Examine particularly into the management of the hospital post and report how far the regulations issued from this office for the government of hospitals are observed. See that the savings are economically made, that the fund is judiciously expended, and that the hospitals are provided with all necessary clothing for the sick, bedding, and furniture.

Hoffman also informed him that he should begin "such reforms in the administration of the hospital service as you may deem necessary to promote the welfare of the sick." He also wanted Alexander to look over the situation and report to Hoffman for his approval any reforms he felt were needed and how much they would cost.

Nine days later, Surgeon Alexander made his report to Col. Hoffman. He wrote that there were 9,162 prisoners held at Fort Delaware at the time of the visit. They were made up of 1,345 officers, 7,713 enlisted men and 104 political prisoners. There were 556 men in the hospital, 36 officers, and 520 enlisted men. He noted that the hospital was:

> in most excellent condition, under the charge of Asst. Surg. H.R. Stillman, U.S. Army. The last monthly report shows miasmatic disease largely predominate and most fatal. This excess is to be attributed partly to the previous service of the prisoners and in part to the situation of the fort, the prevailing winds blowing from a miasmatic region. The number of deaths has been proportionately large. This is owing probably to nostalgia, as the sick have every attention and comfort. Since the deprivation of tea and coffee disease seems to have increased and the sick not prospered as well. A daily morning issue of coffee to all prisoners at this post I think advisable. A daily morning issue of tea or coffee, as the surgeon in charge may think best, to the sick is a necessity. The hospital fund at the end of May was $2347. Since 1st of June the reduced ration has been issued and is supposed to be sufficient, but whether or not there has been a necessary increase in the purchase of extra articles can only be ascertained at the end of the present month.
>
> The quarters of the prisoners are fairly policed and could be kept in good condition if the inmates were not too lazy to consult even self-interest and comfort. The privies here are a nuisance and source of complaint. They are not set far back enough for the excrescence to be removed by the tide, consequently the odor from it is most foul. It is proposed to remedy this defect by washing out the privies by water from a hose forced up from the ditch by a force pump. I doubt if it will prove a success, and recommend that the privies be placed farther back, in reach of the tide. Upon this subject I have requested Doctor Stillman to make you a special report after the hose has been tried, as pumps for the purpose have been purchased. The men are quite clean in appearance and as a general thing sufficiently well clothed. a large number of cases of itch are reported, but it is now diminishing, as the men are forced to bathe at least once a week. Some tendency to scurvy exists. This is probably owing to there not having been any issue of potatoes or other anti-scorbutic vegetable for three or four weeks. The recent orders have been strictly obeyed in the ration issue. Potatoes of good quality not being procurable nothing has been substituted for them. I would respectfully recommend that the commissary officer here be ordered at once to supply the place of the potatoes with onions or another vegetable in sufficient quantity.
>
> The fund on hand at end of May was $17,087.15. The recent orders in reference to it are understood and obeyed. I inspected the quarters of the troops garrisoning this post. The police is not good, the privies, especially of the troops inside the wall, with one exception, are badly neglected. The One hundred and fifty-seventh Ohio, 100-days' men, form part of this garrison. Nine companies of this regiment are in barracks now, one in tents. The barracks occupied by the nine companies are only sufficient for eight companies. I would respectfully recommend that tents be furnished to one company more of this regiment and they be immediately occupied, relieving the overcrowded state of one set of barracks. This should be done without delay, as most of the sick of this regiment came from this overcrowded set of barracks, and among them are several cases of measles.

Acting on Surgeon Alexander's suggestions, Col. Hoffman suggested to Gen. Schoepf that he should buy more tea and coffee for the prisoners, in contrast to his previous statement of June 2. He also told Schoepf that the commissary-general of subsistence ordered a small supply of "desiccated vegetables" to be sent to him to help with the lack of vegetables at the prison.[70] The term "desiccated vegetables" was used to describe cakes which were made up of dehydrated beans, beets, carrots, onions, turnips, and other assorted vegetables.[71] He also mentioned that he wanted one or two companies of Union soldiers to be placed temporarily in tents until new barracks could be built to hold them. Hoffman was concerned that most of the Union soldiers who were sick were that way because of their overcrowded barracks. He ended his message by asking Gen. Schoepf how many more officers and enlisted men could be detained at the prison.[72]

Gen. Schoepf did not stop there to keep the prisoners as healthy as possible. He also issued orders which said that the prisoners would be sent out of their barracks every day to get air. The barracks would then be cleaned out. He also allowed the prisoners to bathe in the Delaware River twice a week. They were given a regular ration of soap to clean themselves with and a guard would be sent to force some of the prisoners out of the barracks to taking a bath if they were unwilling.[73]

The first week of July 1864 saw a crackdown on the prisoners. The barracks were searched on July 5, after an escape the day before. Everyone was made to come out of his barracks and stand at "the rear" for three hours while the search was conducted.[74] The guards were looking for any items that could be used to help someone escape, such as money, canteens, blue clothing, and sword belts.[75] After the search through the divisions was complete, all the prisoners were marched out through the sally-port and required to give up any gold watches, gold coins, or paper money held on them. Some prisoners tried to hide their valuables under the boardwalk or anywhere else that might be a good hiding place until they could return for them. One prisoner had fifty dollars in gold that he threw away rather than let the guards take it. The Rev. Handy stuck his watch through a hole in the back of his "shebang," or barracks, and picked it up later from someone who took care of it.

On the night of June 6, several Rebel officers attempted to escape by using one of the ditches. A few actually succeeded by crawling the entire length of a division and coming out onto the open island. This put the guards and their officers on edge. All prisoner privileges were revoked. The Rebels were called out the next morning and roll call was done. There were between 75 and 100 extra men than were on the rolls, but some who were listed on the rolls were not in attendance.

During this time, many of the prisoners were suffering from diarrhea and the toilets, or "the rear," were a very popular place.[76] The toilets, also known as the "Retiring Sink," were at the end of a narrow walkway. They were built on posts set in shallow water and could be reached only by crossing a bridge two feet wide and thirty feet long. There was a calcium lantern placed on the flat roof of the sinks that lit up the bridge at night. Besides lighting the way for anyone wanting to use the toilets, the lantern was there to keep the area light enough so that prisoners could not slip through the toilets to escape by swimming to the mainland a mile away.[77] The prisoners' sinks had been moved closer to land by July 1864 because during the previous winter, they had been carried away by the ice in the river. The tide kept the regular sinks clean, but the hospital sinks were taken care of by double force pumps that Gen. Schoepf had ordered for each of the sinks. He believed that they had enough hose and power to keep the hospital sinks clean and healthy. The closeness of the sinks as opposed to their original position allowed greater security and less cost than extending them into the river.[78] Orders were given telling the prisoners to go to the toilets by going up one path and returning by another. Because of the diarrhea, the two lines were in never-ending movement.[79]

On July 7, 1864, Col. Edward Pope Jones of Virginia was returning to his barracks from the sinks at around 9:00 P.M. Jones was a thirty-year-old from Middlesex County, Virginia, who had joined the militia system in 1858, was elected colonel by his 109th Regiment, and was captured in May 1863. Col. Jones had been ill and was walking with the help of crutches. That night, the weather was miserable.[80] The sentry on duty on top of the sinks that night was Bill Douglass, an eighteen-year-old private from Company C, 157th Ohio National State Guard.[81] It was said that he received a visit from an officer soon after he arrived at his post. Whatever was said between the two had an adverse effect on Douglass, because soon after the officer left, he began to yell and berate the prisoners coming to and from the sinks. He swore loudly that he wanted to "shoot one of the d———- Rebels before midnight." He could also be heard from the barracks screaming at the sick prisoners as they walked by him to: "Get along there! Trot, d—n you, trot! Doublequick I say, God d—n you! Doublequick!"[82] Lieut. McHenry Howard of Stuart's Brigade remembered walking back from the sinks that night around 9:00 P.M. and being ordered with a curse to move doublequick. Howard did not do so, but he half expected to be shot. Fortunately, for him, he only had to go a few steps to turn the corner of the dining room. As soon as he returned to his division, he told the other men that he expected the guard to shoot somebody that night.[83] The Rev. Handy also was coming from the sinks at around the same time. He was in a weakened state due to an illness and was walking back slowly when he heard the sentry challenge him. He did not know that he was being addressed until some friends told him. He did not answer, but continued moving. Other prisoners asked about his health, to which he replied, "we have no time to talk; the sentinel is evidently restless or alarmed, and we are in danger."[84] It was not long after that that Howard and Handy were proven correct.

As Col. Jones walked slowly back across the bridge, Douglass took aim at him and bellowed at the same time: "Doublequick, Doublequick, Damn you. Run. Run." Two different stories emerged about what happened next. One story said that Col. Pope was deaf and either did not hear Douglass or did not understand that he was talking to him. Another story said that Jones did hear him, turning toward the sentry and saying: "Sentry, I am lame — I'll go as fast as I can!" Whatever the case, Douglass then fired on Jones. The bullet hit Jones in "the right shoulder, fracturing the humerus about one inch below the shoulder joint; penetrated the chest and made its exit therefrom at the junction of the fifth rib with the sternum of right side,"[85] which sent him off of the bridge and into the slimy water below. As he fell into the water, Jones was heard to say: "Oh, God! Why did you shoot me! I didn't know you spoke to me!" The prisoners already in the shed came running out and pulled Pope out of the water. He was taken to the hospital where he died the next day.

The news of the shooting spread through the prison population and by morning, the guards had been doubled and extra soldiers were placed in the pen. Gen. Schoepf arrived in the pen soon afterward with Capt. Ahl, and the guard Wolf. Some of the Confederate officers wanted to talk with the general about the shooting. The Rev. Handy did get a chance to talk to him. He told Schoepf what he saw and the fear that he felt the night before due to the guard's actions before Col. Jones was shot. As a reply, the commandant mentioned the continuing attempts of the prisoners to escape. He said that he had every intention of putting a stop to the escapes and he defended his guards. He said that the guards "shall shoot down any man who tries to escape."[86] Capt. Ahl then explained that it was he who had spoken to Douglass that night and told him to shoot any prisoner who refused to move doublequick along the plankway. Gen. Schoepf and his men then left and soon there was a rumor that Douglass was seen walking through the gate in a new uniform with new sergeant's chevrons on him. It was then considered among the prisoners that the only thing a guard had to do to get a promotion was to kill a wounded Rebel.

The day after the shooting, Gen. Schoepf did begin an investigation of Col. Jones' death. He created a board of examination to take the testimony of witnesses to find out what happened. Capt. Alexander Smith and Lieut. J. Fletcher Daton of the 157th Ohio State National Guard and Lieut. William Hall of the Pennsylvania Artillery met at the garrison guard-room for a day to listen to Private Douglass and six other men, all Union soldiers, tell what they knew. Douglass stated that while acting as a sentinel at post #20 sometime between 7 and 9 P.M., "a rebel came out of the sink — the officers' sink — and stopped about ten minutes. I told him to 'leave,' think he was twenty or thirty feet from me; went back and turned the light; came back and said, 'Now, you must leave.' Then I said the third time, 'If you don't leave, I'll shoot you.' The man still stood there. I said again, 'Leave.' He muttered something, and then I shot him." The other witnesses called before the board all backed up Private Douglass' story. The final decision was that Private Douglass "was in discharge of his duty as a sentinel" and cleared him of all blame. This information was passed on to Washington and Maj. Gen. E.A. Hitchcock of volunteers stated on July 10 that if "prisoners of war obstinately refuse obedience to the orders of a sentinel, as appears to have been the case in this instance, very unfortunate consequences are to be expected."[88]

In the aftermath of the shooting, orders were posted in the cook house on July 8 stating what the prisoners could expect in the way of treatment if they did not obey an order from a guard. Anyone not obeying an order would be shot.[89] Obviously, there were complaints about this order. One complaint was that some of the guards were not native to the United States and could not speak the language clearly enough to be understood. Another problem was that the wind blew so strongly at times that anything the guards said would be drowned out.

Col. Jones was able to let his dying wish be known. He wanted his body sent back to Virginia for burial. The prisoners got together and collected $100 to cover the expense. They then went to Gen. Schoepf and respectfully requested that he please grant the request. They were quickly refused because he did not wish to make Col. Jones an exception to the rule. Col. Jones was buried, like most of the prisoners who died at Fort Delaware, in the mass gravesite across the river at Finn's Point, New Jersey.[90]

Fort Delaware itself was a contradiction. It was built to keep people out, but was used to keep people in. It was also only supposed to hold prisoners for a short period of time until their exchanges could be worked out, but soon became a full-time prisoner of war camp. Even its commander was a study in contrasts. He was either known as "General Terror" or considered a firm but fair man by both the prisoners and the men under his command. His demands to keep the barracks clean could be considered the actions of either a man satisfying the requirements of the monthly inspections to keep his superiors happy or a man trying to do the best he could with what he had. Whatever the reason for the cleaning, the prisoners benefited from it. The guards themselves disagreed with the way to handle prisoners. Some of them treated their prisoners with respect, while others were drunk on duty or intentionally cruel out of some misplaced sense of patriotism, or just plain meanness. There were prisoners who lived in as much comfort as their money would allow. It would be easy for a visitor, after seeing the way the higher-ranking prisoners lived, to believe that those prisoners who hunted and ate rats did it merely because they liked it and not out of any sense of urgency.

This leads to the biggest contradiction of Fort Delaware. If the conditions were as acceptable as some people claimed, why were there so many deaths among the prison population? The Confederacy blamed it on the overcrowded conditions, the swampy land the prisoners lived on, and the lack of decent food available to the prisoners. The North, on the other hand, blamed the mortality rate on the condition of the men when they arrived and the fact that many of them were not properly vaccinated. The truth is probably somewhere in the middle. So why were there differences of opinion about conditions among the people who visited the island? Maybe they came after the prison was cleaned up for an inspection or they just saw what they wanted to see. The difference also came honestly, as in the case of the man who saw how prisoners like Gen. Thompson lived and found it hard to believe that prisoners were suffering. Notwithstanding these early differences of view, public opinion started to get ugly toward prisoners in the latter part of 1864 because of the conditions at Andersonville and the media attention that was placed on them. This growing hardness toward the prisoners was also due to events which were happening in the South that led to prisoners on both sides being used as weapons of war.

Outside Influences

Toward the end of 1863, the Union forces were pushing close to Richmond. The Confederate government was concerned not only that their capital was going to be captured, but also that the Union prisoners they held at nearby Belle Isle would be rescued. Therefore, to stop that event from happening and to save what food there was for the citizens of Virginia, a new prison was set up in Georgia. Camp Sumter, as it was officially called, was located in Sumter County in the heart of Georgia near the town of Andersonville. The first prisoners were sent there in February 1864. The camp consisted of sixteen acres of open land surrounded by a fifteen foot tall stockade fence. It was designed to hold 10,000 prisoners, but the population ballooned due to captured Federal troops from Sherman's march to the sea as well as prisoners from other battles. The camp was not adequately set up with the proper amount of shelter, clothing, or medical supplies for the number of prisoners they received. The only source of water for these men was Stockade Creek, a sliver of a stream that ran through the prisoner compound to the nearby Sweetwater Creek. This one source of water was anything but sweet. Waste from cooking was dumped into the creek and the sinks were set up in the downstream area. The next few months saw 400 new prisoners a day and by June, the prison had expanded to twenty-six acres. By August, the prison population had grown to 33,000 men who baked in the summer Georgia sun with only the shade they could create from blankets, tent flies, sticks, and anything else they could find. This flat, treeless area created a death toll of a hundred men a day during the summer of 1864. As one prisoner described it:

> The sun was scorching hot, and having nothing to protect us from its burning rays, the whole upper surface of our feet would become blistered, and then would break, leaving the flesh exposed, and having nothing to dress it or protect it in

any way, gangrene would follow, and some would lose their feet, and part of a limb, and death would soon follow. And I have seen others die from want of nourishment. The amputations would average as many as six per day, and I saw not a single instance of a recovery from them. Some became victims of total blindness, occasioned by constant exposure to the heat of the sun and its action on the nervous system.[1]

When word of the conditions at Andersonville began to get out, the press in the Northern cities screamed for revenge. Pictures had been taken of prisoners who had been released on a special exchange and woodcut copies of these pictures were published in Northern newspapers. These graphic images of the mistreatment of the men held at Andersonville and other Confederate prisons enraged the Northern population into demands of revenge against the South. The *New York Times* wrote that the "Confederate authorities and their subordinates have, from the beginning, acted towards our unfortunate men, taken as prisoners of war, as if they were New Zealand savages with a fresh capture of unlucky white men." It also wrote that "the rebel prisoners have better fare than they have been accustomed to for years, cleaner clothing, and a more invigorating climate. No insult or oppression touches them; on the contrary, they receive unbounded sympathy from the thousand half-sympathizers with treason among us. They return invigorated in constitution, and all ready for service again."[2] The paper also reported that the Rebels would continue to be cruel to their prisoners:

> as long as it is in their power to exercise it. The slaveholder is born to tyranny and reared to cruelty, and whether he exercise them, as of old, upon his own slaves, or whether, as a rebel, they lead him to perpetuate such massacres as that at Fort Pillow and those of free laboring blacks upon the Mississippi, or whether they instigate him to such a course as that persistently pursued toward our helpless prisoners—each and all these acts are but manifestations of the same character, inborn or acquired.

The *New York Times* continued on in this vein, reporting on the condition of prisoners returned by the South. They were described as "the most pitiable set of poor wretches ever seen." Another newspaper, the *American*, said that:

> their emaciation was extreme, their feebleness was almost at the last gasp, their dejection was painful to behold, and their squalor was frightful. They were starved to the verge of the grave, and what was left of them was nearly devoured by vermin. Some of them, from hope too long deferred, had fallen into a state of utter listlessness and apathy which bordered upon idiocy. The deepening pallor, the drooping jaw and the glazing eyes told that others had only come to die, and, most to be deplored, too late to die in the arms of the weary watchers and the broken-hearted ones at home, or to wake from their lethargy long enough to know that they were once more under the protecting folds of the Stars and Stripes. Compared with this, the massacre at Fort Pillow was a blessing and a mercy.[3]

Seeing these types of descriptions in the newspapers served to enrage the civilian population against the Confederate prisoners held in Northern prisons. To appease the public, Secretary Stanton agreed in May 1864 to reduce prisoner rations to the same amount that Rebel soldiers received in the field.[4] Confederate soldiers were supposed to receive ¾ lbs. of pork or bacon or 1¼ lbs. of fresh or salt beef, 18 ozs. of bread or flour, and 12 ozs. of hard bread, or 1¼ lbs. of corn meal. However, what Rebel soldiers were supposed to receive for food every day they did not necessarily get.[5] Food was so scarce in the South that the soldiers rarely got their full rations and the prisoners they held received even less.[6] A day's rations for a Rebel soldier consisted of a few black beans, several pieces of sorghum, and six roasted acorns.[7] Therefore, the prisoners the Union held were still eating better than their free comrades.

Even though this imposed shortage of food was not as painful as people in the North wanted it to be, it did show that the attitude of a war-weary public was hardening towards the South. This led to stronger demands for a renewal of the exchange cartel. Soldiers held at Rebel prisons wrote letters to Lincoln begging him to restart the cartel to end their suffering. Conditions at their prisons continued to deteriorate due to the increase in the numbers of prisoners and a decrease in food and other supplies in the South. As the lack of supplies increased, so did the misery in the prisons. The worse the conditions became in the prisons, the stronger the outcry for exchanges from the press, clergymen, and physicians. The more Lincoln turned a deaf ear to their pleas—which he did because he wanted to put pressure on the South to treat African-American prisoners the same as their Caucasian comrades—the more resentment it caused towards the Lincoln administration and the Southern prisoners the North already held.[8]

Prisoners were also used differently as 1864 went on. They began to be used as weapons against the enemy. Major Thomas D. Armesy was arrested on April 18, 1863, behind Union lines and charged with recruiting men for the Confederate army. He was found guilty and confined at Fort Warren, near Boston, and sentenced to 15 years at hard labor on October 14, 1863. The Confederacy did not like this, so on May 3, 1864, Major Nathan Goff, Jr. of the 4th Regiment, West Virginia Cavalry was placed in the basement of Libby Prison in Richmond as a hostage for the release of Maj. Armesy. Maj. Goff had been captured on January 29, 1864, and had been treated as a regular prisoner until May.[9] On June 13, 1864, Gen. Hoffman ordered Gen. Schoepf, by order of Secretary Stanton, to place Maj. W. P. Elliot, commissary of substance of Gen. Morgan's staff, under close confinement in a cell and give him the same treatment as Maj. Goff. Stanton wanted revenge against the South for Maj. Goff's treatment. Maj. Elliot was not allowed to talk with anyone in his cell except on business. He was only allowed to eat what was given to him by his captors and not anything he could get on his own. He could only have two meals a day unless a doctor said otherwise due to illness.

Hoffman also ordered, by order of Stanton, that eight men, Charles F. Fidley, Thomas Edwards, Joseph Rinker, W. S. Prickett, George W. Ryan, Dr. William Cross, E. L. Bentley, and William H. Gray, be transferred from Old Capitol Prison in Washington to Fort Delaware. They were to be held hostage there for eight men who lured two Union soldiers across the Potomac River with a white flag. The soldiers were shot, robbed, and marched through the streets of Leesburg, Va., for the enjoyment of the citizens of the town. The eight hostages were ordered to be held until further notice and if possible, separated from the prison population.[10]

Major Elliot became ill during his imprisonment and it was determined that his confinement had to end for fear of his health. Col. Hoffman then asked Schoepf in a message, "How is Major Mills' health?" Maj. Thomas S. Mills of Chester, South Carolina, who was the assistant adjutant general of Major General Richard Anderson's division in General Lee's army, was also being held at the fort. General Schoepf's orderly was sent to Maj. Mills with the message to ask him about the state of his health. Mills was confused about the intent of the request, but answered by writing on the telegram, "Never was better in my life." The message was taken to Schoepf and soon Mills received a request from the general to pack his things and come to his office. Mills thought he was going to be exchanged. He walked to the office in a happy mood with his head held high, carrying his belongings and letters from other prisoners to be delivered by him to their loved ones in the South. His friends watched with a mixture of happiness and envy as he walked into the office. A little while later, they saw him leave the office, his head hanging down, and march into the dungeon to take the place of Maj. Elliot. When his friends were marched out for their daily walk to the river to swim or bathe, they saw Mills crouching in the doorway of his cell, which was next to the sally port. It appeared to his fellow prisoners that it was a very narrow room, low and dark, and possessing only the small door, which was kept open, for ventilation. They were not allowed to speak to him.[11] Major Mills remained in the dungeon until September 3, 1864, when he was removed due to an order from Washington freeing all prisoners held in close confinement and returning them to the general prison population.

The situation with Majors Armesy and Groff finally ended when Senator P.G. Van Winkle of West Virginia wrote to President Lincoln on August 2, 1864, to request that an exchange between the two prisoners be arranged. On the 18th, Lincoln requested that this be done.[12] That solved their particular situation, but the idea of using non-combatants did not end with merely holding hostages. The Rebels were furious with the North because of the shelling of Charleston, S.C. Attacking the city in this way endangered the lives of women and children and the Confederacy wanted this to end. They felt that the best way to stop the bombardment was to place high-ranking Federal officers in the buildings that were being shelled. That course of action did not sit well with the Union.[13] Maj. Gen. John J. Foster wrote to Maj. Gen. Halleck from Hilton Head, S.C., on June 16, 1864, about this issue and stated:

> I think the cruel determination of the rebels to place our officers in Charleston under our fire is an evidence of their vindictive weakness and of the destruction that the city is sustaining from our fire. This last is not so much from actual demolition as from the depopulation and desolation. Private letters speak of this

and of the grass growing in the streets. I hope the President will decide to retaliate in the manner proposed.[14]

Foster got his wish because Hoffman wrote to Maj. E.N. Strong in Washington on June 23, 1864, to tell him that 50 Rebel officers:

> whom you are to receive to conduct to Major General Foster, at Hilton Head, are at Fort Delaware, and Brigadier General Schoepf, the commanding officer at that post, has been instructed to deliver them to you. You will therefore proceed without delay, in the steamer provided for the purpose by the quartermaster's department, to Fort Delaware, and having received the general and field officers referred to, you will return to Hilton Head and deliver them to Major-General Foster, commanding Department of the South. The guard detailed to accompany you from Fort Delaware is expected to return from Hilton Head with as little delay as possible.[15]

Capt. Ahl went into the officers' barracks on June 24th and announced who would be sent South.[16] Basil Duke was chosen along with four general officers: Maj. Gen. Franklin Gardner of Louisiana, Maj. Gen. Edward Johnson of Virginia, Brig. Gen. George H. Stewart of Maryland, and Brig. Gen. M. Jeff Thompson of Missouri. A number of colonels, majors, and captains filled out the list. All of the men selected considered themselves lucky to have been chosen for several reasons. First, they looked forward to anything to break up the monotony of prison life. Some of them also knew from personal experience that big guns were not always accurate and they thought that they only had a small chance of actually getting hit by a cannonball. The most important reason for their attitude was that they did not believe the stories about how captive Union officers were put into the range of Confederate guns. Therefore, they felt that it would not happen to them and that once the truth was known, a prisoner exchange would occur.[17] Brig. Gen. Thompson did not have any fear of the guns that awaited him because he had "an abiding faith that I was not born to be killed by a big cannon." The fifty men selected all felt that what was happening was unjust, but they would all cheerfully deal with the situation and put their best foot forward about the matter. As it turned out, the prisoners were not far wrong in their belief that they would be exchanged. On July 29, the 50 men were taken to Charleston under a flag of truce and exchanged for the 50 Union men who had been held under fire.[18] General Grant had forbidden prisoner exchanges, but he had made this situation an exception to his rule.[19]

One of the people who did not leave for South Carolina was Gen. Thompson's orderly, Bailey Peyton Key. He had been assigned to Thompson when the general arrived at the prison. Key had the distinction of being one of the youngest prisoners held at Fort Delaware. When he was 12 years old, he enlisted in the 14th Tennessee Cavalry, Co. E, with Gen. John Morgan. A year later, he was captured on May 29, 1863, and sent to Camp Chase, where he was later transferred to Fort Delaware. He was a direct descendant of Francis Scott Key, who wrote the "Star Spangled Banner," and won the respect of his captors with his courage and attitude. After Thompson left, Private Key went on to be an orderly to other Confederate generals at the prison. Throughout his life as a prisoner, he consistently refused to take the Oath of Allegiance. He was exchanged in February 1865 and returned to his old outfit, serving with General Duke's brigade until the end of the war.

Even though Private Key, at the age of 14, was the youngest soldier to be a prisoner at the fort, he was not the youngest person held there. John A. Redd was 9 years old and traveling with his father after the death of his mother. His father belonged to a Virginia regiment and took part in Pickett's Charge at Gettysburg, where he was killed. Redd was captured with other members of his father's company and sent to Fort Delaware.[20] He became the pet of the men held there and was

Bailey Key, at 13, one of the youngest prisoners and a descendant of Francis Scott Key.

happy and content. While there, he learned to play cards, swear, and generally felt as much like a man as the other Rebels. He was considered very stubborn and was the only prisoner who could abuse his captors and get away with it. The guards liked the boy as much as the prisoners and did what they could to help him. They even offered to let him stay with them, but Redd preferred to stay with his own men. He always had plenty to eat and was free to do whatever he liked.[21]

In July 1864, one prisoner who was unable to get out, took matters into his own hands concerning the cut in food rations not only at Fort Delaware, but also in Southern prisons. A Rebel major, James McMichaels, placed an advertisement in the *New York News* requesting money and clothing from the Northern civilians. In return, he stated that he would have his family deliver "provisions, clothing, or Confederate money upon each equitable basis as may be agreed upon" to Union men in Southern prisons. He was able to help some prisoners because he owned a farm near Andersonville, Ga. The major did receive some help, but he was soon transferred to another prison. This was the end of help for both parties.

Another prisoner, Francis Boyle, thought the short rations at the fort were less due to cruelty than to greed. Daily rations were 6 oz. of meat and 4 oz. of bread per man. When the War Department's order to cut rations came, the sutler started "selling us eatables and other contraband articles and charging us extra prices for the risk!!!." Another prisoner learned that his brother had not received several letters which contained requests for a number of items. He believed that the letters were taken so that he would have to buy from the sutler. Whether or not these accusations were true, it confirmed that the sutler was possibly the least popular man on the island.

While the federal government was trying to punish the prisoners, the prisoners were trying to save themselves. In July 1864, the Rebel officers formed a Christian Association. It was open to anyone who declared "a saving faith in Christ." The association was concerned that the prisoners would fall into sloth and immorality because they were away from their families, churches, and government. Its members wanted to minister to the prisoners to give them what support they could. General and Mrs. Robert E. Lee and Mrs. Thomas J. Jackson were made lifetime members, as well as Jefferson Davis.[22] The Rev. Handy and several other ministers held on the island directed "the efforts of the Association, [efforts] that God speedily and abundantly blessed ... with a gracious outpouring of His Spirit, and in the addition of many souls to His Church." As the summer advanced, and the means at its command would permit, the association, besides having the Gospel preached, and holding daily prayer meetings, established a library of religious and miscellaneous reading, and organized classes in the various branches of science and religion; and so wide was the field which was gradually opened to its operations, that it soon became necessary to redraft its constitution. This was done in October, and the new society was named the "Confederate States Christian Association for the Relief of Prisoners," and was designed to "relieve the wants, spiritual, moral, intellectual and physical, of prisoners, whether civil, political, or military, in our own or other lands."[23]

What was happening on the battlefield continued to affect the men in Fort Delaware. Confederate general Jubal Early had been instructed by Robert E. Lee to go north into Maryland and to head for Washington. Lee hoped that having a Rebel force terrorizing the Union's capital would force Grant to remove men from Petersburg to help defend the city. At the very least, this action would take pressure off of the Rebel defenders of Petersburg. If it succeeded, Washington would be held by the Confederacy and the Union would be in disarray. On July 6, Early crossed the Potomac River into Maryland. Grant, realizing where Early was heading, frantically sent men to help in Washington's defense. The extra troops were necessary because Grant had stripped the capital of most of its soldiers and only a force led by Gen. Lew Wallace stood in Early's way. The two sides fought at Monocacy Junction, 40 miles outside of Washington.[24] On July 10, the guards at the fort were read a message stating that Gen. Wallace was defeated at the Battle of Monocacy and the Union forces were falling back to Baltimore.[25] This defeat caused the entire area around Fort Delaware to prepare for the worst. Across the river in Delaware, "the excitement in Wilmington was intense. The people turned out en masse. The bells rang out and the Star Spangled Banner run out, and by night over 600 men had fallen in behind the fife and drum. At Newcastle the people were aroused by telegram, and in an hour afterward sixty men were enrolled, and six hundred dollars contributed to the cause."[26]

The excitement in Delaware spread over onto the island. Guards and prisoners alike were still on edge due to the incident with the shooting of Col. Jones. He had died the night before and the news from Baltimore added to the strain on everyone's nerves.[27] Rules were strictly enforced. Roll call began again for the prisoners. Some of the weaker prisoners found it hard to stand in the hot morning sun as the roll was called. Because of the return of the roll call, the Sunday evening worship service was suspended for that night.[28] The guards were also taken out of their usual routine. All the Delaware soldiers at the fort were ordered to report to Baltimore, due to the invading Rebels.[29] The next day, a detachment of soldiers was assigned to go across the river to Delaware City to guard a sloop which was loaded with guns.

Tension continued to exist in the wake of the Jones shooting. On July 12th, Captain Lewis of the 38th Virginia was walking in the yard when he heard a rumor about Gen. Jubal Early's army crossing the Potomac River. His excitement overrode his sense of self-preservation and he shouted "Hurrah for old Early!" The guard on the wall yelled down to Lewis, interspersed with oaths, "Mark time, d — n you! Mark time." Lewis heard him and, not wanting to risk a repeat of Col. Jones' fate, stood still for more than an hour until the officer of the guard arrived and released him.[30]

The death of Col. Jones did not stop the prisoners from trying to escape. On the 12th, five prisoners were returned to their barracks after an attempt. Col. Cooper, and Captains Allen, Burke, Patton, and Perkins had tried to escape, but had been caught. Two other prisoners were able to make their escape to the Jersey shore by leaving through the ditch.

Early's invasion sparked a great deal of talk, or "grape" among the prisoners. They had heard that the Rebels were successful in a battle that occurred near Havre de Grace and that the Baltimore and Philadelphia Railroad had been cut between Baltimore and Washington.[31] The invasion also gave Lieut. McHenry Howard an idea. The entrance to the fort was a sally port, a covered area that ran from the inner wall for about fifty feet to the outer wall. The muskets of the daily guard, who were about a company of men, were stacked along one wall of the sally port. Howard knew this because every morning, he and some other officers were marched through the entrance by several guards to the river's edge and allowed to go swimming or take a bath. The water was as polluted along the river's edge as the water was below the prison pen, but they still took advantage of the opportunity. He thought that as they were marched through the sally port, a signal could be given and they could seize the weapons. The guards could be overpowered, the gate locked, and they could take possession of the fort. They would then take control of the guns mounted on the walls and force the Union soldiers to release the other prisoners. The prisoners would then go across the river, with the big guns of the fort guarding them from any Union vessels that might try to stop them. From there, they would go cross country until they met with Early and his men. He believed that this idea would work on short notice and decided to keep quiet about it until the time was right. He also read what he could about Early's movements in the newspapers, to look for the right time. One day, another officer, Col. Folk of North Carolina, approached him and told him he had the same plan that Howard was working on. He asked Folk not to tell anyone because he thought the action did not need a great deal of planning and to keep the guards from finding out. Unfortunately for Howard, Col. Folk did not heed his advice and talked about the plan with others. Howard saw him talking about it and decided against trying it. He was probably right that the guards would find out about

Sally port (entrance) of Fort Delaware

the plan, because the daily walk outside the prison was soon cancelled. It was just as well that Howard never tried his idea because he had no way of knowing that his window of opportunity to meet with Early had closed.[32] The Confederacy's chance to take over Washington had disappeared because after the Rebels won at Monocacy, they were so tired that they could not press the advantage of Wallace's retreat. The next day, Federal troops arrived on the scene from Petersburg and Early was forced to leave the area.[33]

On July 22, another incident occurred between the guards and the prisoners. On March 28, 1864, the Coles County, Illinois, riot between Copperheads and furloughed soldiers of the 54th Illinois had left 9 dead and 12 wounded. When it was over, 15 Copperheads were arrested.[34] These political prisoners from Illinois, as well as other Copperheads from various border states, had been sent to the fort. Some of the prisoners suspected that several of these new arrivals were not true Copperheads, but abolitionists spying on the prisoners for the Union. One of the suspected abolitionists was discovered writing a note to Capt. Ahl. When confronted, he declared that he was going to take the oath and leave the pen. Major George M.E. Shearer of the 1st Battalion, Maryland Cavalry, considered by his friends to be impetuous and rough due to his background of gold mining in California in his youth, said, "Let's hang the infernal galvanized Yankee!" At this point, other prisoners brought out a rope and threatened to carry out Shearer's request. The men had no intention of hanging the man, but taking no chances, the accused spy immediately went to alert the guards. Major Shearer and two other prisoners were called out of the pen and roughly used by Ahl and his men. They were then taken to the barracks of the 150 men known as the "Galvanized Yankees." The three men were then each tossed in a blanket. Tossing in a blanket meant that a prisoner was placed in a double blanket. Each corner was held by soldiers and the man would be tossed as high as possible and then dropped. The three men were each tossed by as many of the former Rebels as could hold onto the blanket. The guards laughed and hissed at the prisoners as they were tossed as high as thirty feet in the air. The only way the prisoners could protect themselves was to try to fall in a way so that they would not land on their head or neck. It was hard to tell what hurt more, the physical pain of landing on the ground or the humiliation of being tossed about while one's enemy laughed.[35]

One of the diseases that plagued the prisoners was scurvy. It was created by a lack of vegetables in the diet and caused prisoners to lose their hair and teeth.[36] General Schoepf, knowing that he did not have enough vegetables for the prisoners, took matters into his own hands and contacted many nearby churches to plead for fresh vegetables for his prisoners. The churches in the area, such as the Quakers from across the river in Salem, N.J., had a history of helping the prisoners, by sending food and clothing to the island.[37] Delaware citizens were angered by the conditions at the fort, in particular the Democrats who sympathized with the South. An application to hold a picnic at McCrone's Woods, 6 miles from the prison, on July 28, 1864, for the benefit of the Fort Delaware prisoners was given to the provost marshal.[38] The marshal, who was the chief of the military police and in charge of maintaining security and order,[39] stated that although he did not approve of the picnic party, he "could not condemn it." It was felt that a benefit picnic was safe enough, even though Federal troops had been used in Delaware to disarm members of the secessionist movement.

On the afternoon of the 28th, many of the well-known ladies and gentlemen of the New Castle, Del., area gathered on the hillside of McCrone's Woods for the "Pic Nic Party" to raise money to buy vegetables and other supplies to help the prisoners fight the scurvy that ate up those who were held there too long. At 5:00 P.M., the picnic was suddenly ended when the provost marshal of the New Castle district arrived. He was accompanied by a Union captain and 60 men of the 114th Ohio Regiment. They had arrived by special train from nearby Wilmington, Del. The marshal called for the managers of the picnic and told them that he had to arrest them for having the picnic. He then put 26 men who were "of the highest social standing" on parole and told them to present themselves at headquarters the next day. The picnic quietly folded, except for the arrest of two young men who engaged in heated words with the Federal officers. Those who went to headquarters the next day were locked up for a day and a night in blistering hot conditions. The next day, "not exempt from taunts and insults," they were transported to the railroad station and shipped to Fort McHenry, near Baltimore. They were held there until August 6th, when friends were able to obtain their release. They returned to Wilmington, where the men were greeted by a brass band.[40]

Escape attempts continued into August. On the 2nd, the prisoners were awakened around 11:30 P.M. by the sounds of the guards screaming "Shoot the d — — d

Rebels! They've got no guns! Kill 'em! Kill 'em!" As the prisoners woke up to the sounds of men running in all directions and the rattle of their muskets, the rumor quickly spread that the Rebel privates were rising up against the guards. There had been heightened security by the Union forces with an increase of exterior guards and the guns of the fort turned around to face the barracks. When the guards were heard running to the sound of gunfire, it was believed that the privates had finally had enough and a revolt had begun. However, the truth was far less dramatic. Several prisoners had tried to escape and had reached the water's edge. One man had begun to swim when he suddenly had a cramp. He sank and before he went under, he released a scream that alerted the guards to the others in his party. The guards opened fire on the prisoners and this created a general alarm. On the way back to their barracks, the guards, some of whom were drunk — all were excited — were heard to complain that what happened was not a "row among the Rebels" and that they were "just itching" to take a shot at a prisoner. One of the prisoners who tried to escape was washed ashore the next day. The "canteens [are] still strapped around the waist, [and he] is now lying in the slimy water of the beach near the sinks, tossing and moving as if yet controlled by the brave spirit which dared the triple risk of double guard-lines, the canal and the river — only to succumb miserably at last."

There was another wake up call four nights later when 6 prisoners tried to escape. All of them were shot — one was killed, another lost his arm and the rest were injured. It was believed by the prisoners that the privates were so desperate to escape due to being badly used that they blatantly insulted the guards and rushed past them even though they knew that they would be shot down.[41] The prisoners had picked a bad night to attempt an escape because it was the same night that some of the guards amused themselves by continually shooting at a floating barrel in the river.[42]

Things were getting worse for the prisoners. On the 5th, they did not receive any meat and that lasted for five days. The cooks told the prisoners that they only had a small amount of meat and it had gone bad. For two weeks before that, the meat had been full of worms and it smelled so bad that the prisoners had to hold their noses so that they could eat it.[43] When it was picked up off the table, it fell to pieces because it was so rotten.[44] There had been no rain for some time and the tanks that caught the rain water off of the roofs did not have enough water in them to take care of everyone. The water boat that went up the Brandywine Creek to get water brought back "a brackish briny fluid scarcely one whit better than the water from the Delaware, which oozes through the ditches in the pen." The water that was still in the rain barrels bred "a dense swarm of animalcule[s], and when the hose pipes from the water boats are turned into the tanks the interior sediment is stirred up, and the whole contents become a turgid salty, jellied mass of waggle tails, worms, dead leaves, dead fishes, and other putrescent abominations, most of which is visible to the eye in a cup of it." The heat was so bad that the ground around the prison became "parched and as hard as rock in the long dry season. No shade is there, no elevation, no breeze; only a low, flat, sultry, burning oven! Today the heat is so intense that men by the hundreds are seen sweltering on their backs, fairly gasping for breath, like fish dying on a sand beach."

There was still the dangers of catching smallpox, scurvy, and other illnesses in the prison. The hospital was full and the infected men were only taken out of the barracks if they were either dead or dying. In the first two weeks of August, the prisoners were vaccinated. Many of them were soon suffering in tremendous pain due to the vaccinations. "All round the barracks can be seen men holding their festering limbs in excruciating pain, the flesh livid, the arm swollen, and the sores putrescent — surely not a great deal less torturing than the actual disease." The men who did not survive the diseases soon took their last journey to the Jersey shore. It was said that in one 24 hour period, as many as 40 corpses were taken away. As one prisoner put it:

> Think of eight cart-loads (5 bodies in each cart) of dead men, stiff and stark, uncoffined, unshrouded, unattended; piled like cord wood one upon another — and cast into pits some head foremost, face downward, others rolled in like dumping rubbish; then a thin layer of dirt, and then left until tomorrow, when a new layer of dead will be tumbled upon them! And this is "civilization" as interpreted by the "Best Government the World ever saw." Oh that these daily scenes might be photographed just as they occur and the heartrending picture be scattered far and wide throughout the land.[45]

Things improved on August 9 when a boat load of peaches were sold on the wharf. The guards, who disliked the sutlers as much as the prisoners did because of their high prices, were happy to buy from someone else as the sutlers watched the sight with confusion. One captain bought 25 baskets of peaches. The soldiers all hoped that the monopoly of the sutlers was at an end. They partially got their wish when the sutlers were closed down the next day.

Regardless of the conditions, prisoners continued to be brought to the fort. On the evening of August 12, the steamer *Major Reybold* landed on the island with a cargo of new prisoners. After it had discharged its passengers, it was discovered that some of its prisoners were missing. A gunboat was immediately sent after the steamer and fired four shots at it until it stopped. It was then boarded and searched, but no prisoners were found. As it turned out, the men who escaped that night were not the only ones who were about to leave the prison during the month of August.[46]

The prisoners rarely saw a newspaper. If a letter was sent to a prisoner that had the smallest amount of information about the outside world, unless it was about family matters, it would never be received. However, news about the outside would get inside the prison. This kind of news was called "grape." In August 1864, the word around the camp was that the 50 officers sent in June to Charleston had been exchanged and that the general exchange would begin again and they would soon be free. This was confirmed by the Yankee sergeant who called the prison roll, but he did not know when the exchanges would start. The exchanges then became the topic of conversation and anyone who doubted this "grape" was looked upon as a skeptic to be watched. After days of being discussed, the story died down only to be started up again when a sergeant of the guard told one of the Rebel officers that a new cartel of exchange had been ratified and the exchanges would begin again once the issue of the African-American soldiers being included was settled. A few days later, another "grape" stated that the issue of the African-American soldiers was set aside by both parties and the exchanges would soon begin. The prisoners considered this to be the absolute truth, but it turned out to be nothing but "moonshine".[47]

The reporting of the exchange of the 50 men at Charleston reflected the anger and frustration of the country after 3 years of war. The *New York Times* wrote on the exchange and mentioned how the prisoners were treated. It was stated that the prisoners held by the Union had:

> never been placed under rebel fire, but were kept in the brig Dragon, in Port Royal harbor, till the day they were exchanged. The treatment they have received from Union hands was far better than they deserved. They have been allowed to purchase clothing, to receive contributions, to write to their friends, and have been looked upon and considered as human beings.
>
> In return for this kind treatment, what have our soldiers in their hands been subjected to? A majority of the fifty who were exchanged yesterday have been confined for months and months in prisons from which, on account of the inhuman treatment they received, they never expected to leave alive. On the way to the Charleston prison, the same fifty officers were insulted, maltreated and robbed. The despicable fiends did not even spare the coat buttons of our officers, and when Gen. Seymour was asleep, they actually cut from his coat all but four buttons. For those buttons the rebels received five dollars each in their currency. The officers state that during the first few days of their stay in Charleston, they were subjected to the most barbarous treatment. Dogs, in our section, would receive commiseration if put upon the same footing. Having been in Charleston for a while, the authorities were forced, on humane principles alone, to be more lenient. The rebels allowed them to change their greenbacks for Confederate money, allowing seven and even ten dollars of the latter for one of the former. Whenever our men were allowed the privilege of making purchases, they were charged the most exorbitant prices—such as one dollar for a loaf of bread, five dollars for a common tin plate, ten dollars for a pound of soap, one hundred dollars for a pair of second-hand shoes, and everything else in proportion.
>
> Of what I have to write now I desire the loyal public at the North to take particular notice. Within the past four days 600 Union officers have been placed under fire at Charleston. Had not Stoneman destroyed the railroad in the rear of Macon, the number of prisoners thus placed under fire would be 10,000! It is time for every loyal man to come forward and aid in crushing this rebellion.
>
> If any one who has a relative fighting for the North has the least desire to have our Government deal leniently with rebel prisoners, let him consider the base, inhuman, barbarous treatment to which Union prisoners are exposed, and he will soon change his sentiments. At Charleston, at Macon, at Henderson, the rebels are either starving our men to death, or shooting them outright—and those men are prisoners of war. I appeal to all loyal men at the North, if they will stand still and see our fathers and brothers thus treated. The rebels feed prisoners on an allowance each day of a single rye cake and a small quantity of water. If you do not believe it, ask any of the fifty who go North on the Fulton. Look at the features of some of them, and you will spare questioning.
>
> Our men tell you that forty and fifty Union prisoners die each day at the pen in Henderson. Why is this? They are deprived of food, robbed of clothing, and refused the smallest piece of rag or board for shelter.[48]

The story in the *New York Times* about 600 Union soldiers being held by the Confederacy under fire at Charleston was not quite correct. Gen. Jones, seeing that his actions of placing Union officers under fire created the exchange of 50 Confederate officers, did decide to try it again. He had wanted to increase the number of Union men under fire to 600, but he decided against it because of the transportation problems involved, as the *Times* had stated. However, the Federal government did not know that Jones had given up his idea. That is when the North decided to round up an equal number of prisoners to counter the assumed Rebel action. The decision was made to take the prisoners from Fort Delaware. The orders were then sent to Gen. Schoepf to get 600 men ready to go to Charleston.[49]

At 9:00 A.M. on August 12, life at Fort Delaware changed:

> A strange uproar was heard, such as schoolboys make on being turned out for a holiday; men jumping down from their bunks, hundreds of men running; and a general cry of "Turn out! Turn out!" Looking into the Court I saw the crowd rushing towards the fence, where General Schoepf, Captain Ahl, Lieutenant Woolf, and others were visible on the parapet.
>
> Schoepf with much flourish announced that he had received orders to send six hundred officers down to Hilton Head, S.C., — to be exchanged for an equal number to be sent down from Augusta.

This was the news that the prisoners had waited a long time to hear. A cheer exploded from the Rebels. Captain Ahl then ordered all of the prisoners to get into line near the fence and told each officer who had his name called to step into another line on the left. The prisoners had no idea whose name would be selected, so the "long line of ragged haggard men, with trembling limbs and glistening eyes, standing in an attitude that might be designated as 'all attention' listening to the harsh voice calling the lucky list" waited in an air of excitement, fear, and hope.[50] The roll call began and the prisoners waited in complete silence:

> each man showing on his face the hope of his heart; each asking God, in silent, earnest prayer, that his name would be called. I have looked into the faces of men in line before a battle, when defeat seemed inevitable; I have seen the joy of victory take the place of doubt; but never in all my life did I witness joy so perfect as in the face of the man whose name was called, nor woe so abject as on the face of the men whose names were passed over.[51]

The field officers were called first, followed by the captains and lieutenants. The names were not announced in a regular manner, therefore it made the waiting that much more nerve-racking.[52] Sometimes, a man was so excited when he was chosen, he could not move or speak. Others were not as restricted in the expressions of their feelings. One of the men who was picked, Captain Pinkney, was in his barracks when he heard his name. He was so excited that he did not waste any time running for the door, he simply jumped out of his window and ran for the line. When the selection process was done, some men cried when they were not picked. Other men not called thought that the list was not made by random choice. Some of the men on the list were among the richest prisoners on the island, and that night there were complaints by some of the men not picked that bribes had been used to get certain people onto the list.[53]

Each member of the group picked was given a number when his name was called. This number was his proof that he had actually been chosen. Once each officer received his number, the waiting game began. Every day the men reported for roll call and every day they expected to be told that they were leaving. Instead, they were told to return to their barracks.[54] The officers had what little bit of baggage they owned packed and were ready to leave at a moment's notice. Two large transports were docked at the wharf, waiting to be used, but there was no movement around either ship.[55] Some of the men who were picked called themselves the "600 officers" at first. As the days passed and there was no movement, the "600 officers" were also called "the rumor roll." The names continued to change with every day until the men finally became known as "The Immortal 600."[56]

The guards knew as much about the delay as the prisoners. They too thought that they were going to leave the day after the announcement. They had this belief because on the 14th, 200 soldiers of the 157th Ohio, as well as 125 men from the Pittsburgh Heavy Artillery, were selected to accompany the prisoners to South Carolina.

It rained on the 17th, which cooled off the island and made the weather more comfortable. However, it did not help those waiting to leave.[57] By the 19th, several of the selected prisoners had become sick from the pressure of waiting and wondering when they were going. The anxiety and doubting if they were ever going to leave was beginning to take its toll on the 600.[58] On the other hand, the guards were reacting in the exact opposite manner. General Schoepf and Capt. Ahl had gone to Washington, the guards were relaxed, and Col. McCook, who was in charge while Schoepf was away, was giving out passes to the guards.[59]

It was also a time for the prisoners to witness the arrival of two new inmates. William A. Jones and J. Paul Jones, of the firm J. P. Jones and Co., came to the island on the 16th to begin a one-year sentence. The two Joneses were sutlers of the 16th Reg. Mass. Volunteers and had been found guilty in a special court-martial of unlawfully obtaining and appropriating government property; they had been sentenced to imprisonment for one year or until they paid a $2,500 fine. It seemed ironic that they should be sent to serve their sentence at a prison where the sutlers were accused of profiting from the misfortunes of others.[60]

Most of the prisoners thought that the 600 were part of an exchange of prisoners and they wanted to be a part of it. This led to cases of bribery being used to obtain a way off of the island. Ahl and Woolf were suspected of taking bribes from some of the wealthier prisoners to have their names placed on the list. This led to some men being removed from the list who were originally on it, leaving them bitterly disappointed when they discovered they would now not be going with the others. Other prisoners bribed those on the list directly. Lieut. Mastin of Alabama paid his way on the list with a $300 watch. Capt. Jones of Georgia got on by giving money and ordering a new suit of clothes for one of those selected. Three other men gave watches ranging in worth from $50 to $150 and more than a dozen more paid at least $50 in cash to trade places with those selected.[61] Another prisoner traded his spot because he did not believe that there was really going to be an exchange of prisoners. As it later turned out, he was right.

At 10:00 A.M., Saturday, August 20, the suspense was over.[62] A sergeant walked into the prison compound and announced, "All whose names were down in the six hundred lot be ready to move out at 12 o'clock sharp."[63] The barracks immediately went into a complete state of turmoil. Because of the haphazard way the list of prisoners was made up, many of the messes and divisions were broken apart.[64] The morning was filled with activity. Captain Leon Jastremski of the 10th Louisiana Inf. wrote a quick note to his brother telling him that he was:

> to be sent to Charleston, S.C., for the purpose I believe of being placed under the fire of the Confederate batteries in retaliation for an equal number of Federal officers who have been placed in the city of Charleston, and are said to be exposed to the shelling of their own guns. I am glad of this move as it will be a diversion to the monotonous life led in prison. Little danger is to be appreciated from this movement. Indeed, I am more inclined to think that it will lead to an exchange.[65]

The Rev. Handy held a meeting of the Christian Association so that they could say goodbye to the members who were leaving. In the fort and the divisions, other prisoners were saying their goodbyes. J. Ogden Murray, one of "The Immortal 600," described the scene of friends parting this way:

> We were saying good-bye, telling those we left behind to be of good heart, that it would be but a few days before they would join us in Dixie. We of that six hundred can now look back and laugh at the promises then made, some of them of the most impossible character. I recall one promise made in which we were all in accord. That was, just as soon as we put foot in Richmond we were all to go in a body to President Davis and Congress and demand that our comrades in Fort Delaware should be sent for at once. The fact that it would require the consent of the United States government to carry out this promise never entered our head. Some of the partings between mess-mates and friends, on that August day in the long ago, come back to me most vividly as I write. There were men who had stood together in the line of death, comrades in the army, companions in prison, but now to be separated, perchance forever. I remember now Capt. George W. Kurtz, Company K, 5th Va. Inf., Stonewall Brigade, one of the best and bravest men of that famous old command, coming down the line. As he reached me he said, "Ogden," and the great big tears began to run down his cheeks, "when you get back to the Valley I want you to get Harry Gilmore and a lot of the old brigade; get all you can, go down the Valley, capture Sheridan and hold him until you get me out of this place. If I stay here I will surely die." Of course I promised to comply with his request, and we sealed the compact with a kiss. It strikes me now that Lieutenants Bob Bowie and Pete Akers both promised to join me in the matter. Poor Bowie has passed over the river; Kurtz and Akers are left with myself. During this scene my eyes were not dry nor was my heart joyous in leaving behind me in prison grand old comrades I had learned to love. Poor dear old Pete Akers said to one of his Lynchburg comrades, "You just wait until I get home. Blamed if I don't go out and catch old Grant and half of his army and hold

them until you all get out of this place." Poor dear old Pete, his great heart was always in touch with those in trouble. The Morgan men, the Forrest men, and Wheeler men all made their comrades most extravagant promises. But our dreams of exchange were never to be realized. It was the hope hidden by anticipation that was to make our disappointment acute.

At 3:00 P.M., they were ordered to "Fall into line all you men whose names shall be called and be ready for exchange." "The Immortal 600," 550 healthy men and 50 wounded men got into line and marched by fours through the prison gates to the small gulf steamship *Crescent City*.[66] It took two hours to march the prisoners onto the ship.[67] The Rev. Handy was one of the prisoners who watched the men leave. He had been visited by many of the men during the previous days who wanted to say goodbye to him and he wanted to see them off. He wrote in his diary that as they left, "I stood at the opening of the sally-port, as near by as the guards would allow, and until the very last man disappeared from the enclosure. 'Good-bye! Good-bye!' was uttered, time and again, as the files moved on; and I could do nothing but return farewells, as some one or more in every rank would wave the parting salutation."[68]

The mood changed at Fort Delaware after the 600 left. Sunday services were held as usual, but the attendance was small. The prisoners remaining felt drained physically and emotionally due to the departure of the 600. The excitement of the men leaving also affected the sutler as well. On the 19th, news was sent into the prisoners' quarters that Gen. Schoepf had received orders to shut down the sutler's shop. This brought about a going out of business sale with the sutler so that he would not have a large amount of perishable goods left over. However, due to everyone being more occupied with the preparations for the departure of the 600, the rush to the sutler to buy his goods never happened. So, "to the surprise of all, he opened yesterday morning as if he had forgotten the Sabbath day (he certainly had forgotten to 'keep it holy') and as the prisoners passed the window, he called out, 'Better buy now; I'll close up shop this evening, and your checks won't be worth anything hereafter.'[69] He stayed opened all day on the 21st and he had a crowd in front of his window. He had been ordered to close on Monday and several ministers broke the Sabbath to buy things at the Sutler's before he closed.[70]

The day after the 600 left, Gen. Schoepf wrote to Col. Hoffman about the prisoners' barracks. Schoepf mentioned that one of his surgeons, Dr. Goddard:

> recommends that the prisoner's barracks should undergo a thorough fumigation and cleansing. In order to do that I would respectfully request that 1,000 prisoners be transferred to some other station, in order to have a few empty divisions to begin with. I commence with the officers' barracks to-morrow, but the privates' barracks are full and it cannot be done at present without exposing the prisoners to sleeping out of doors. Small detachments arriving constantly will soon fill the barracks again. I make this request in view of the fact that the smallpox still exists. Seventy-four cases are in hospital at present, and it is of the utmost importance to prevent its spreading as fall approaches.[71]

Before General Schoepf received his reply from Col. Hoffman, he decided to start moving the prisoners around. On Monday morning, the prisoners were told that all the divisions below Number 30 were to be emptied. There were seven divisions affected by this move and the men had to find other places to live.[72] While new living arrangements were being made, Schoepf received his reply. Hoffman wrote back six days later saying that he felt that it was not practical to send 1,000 prisoners away so that the barracks could be cleaned. His major objection was that there was still some smallpox at Fort Delaware and that he did not want to spread it to other camps. He told Schoepf that he should take advantage of the good weather and let a few prisoners sleep outdoors within the enclosure until the cleaning was done.[73]

Instead of getting rid of prisoners as Gen. Schoepf wanted, the fort received more on the 21st. There was a group of political prisoners brought in that day. Dr. Edward Worrell of Delaware City and Dr. William Cross, E.L. Bentley, Charles F. Fadeley, George W. Ryan, William S. Pickett, John L. Rinker, and Thomas W. Edwards of Leesburg were all to be held as hostages for citizens held by the Confederate Col. John Mosby.[74] Holding these men as hostages was part of a Federal strategy to weaken the support Mosby had in northern Virginia. It was a tactic used against Mosby the winter before by the defenders of Washington. They had arrested civilians and held them in prisons to stop Mosby, but it had never worked.[75]

There was a "box call" made on the 22nd which was longer than usual. Prisoners got more boxes from the outside than was the norm because the boat that brought the boxes in from the mainland, the *Osceola*, had been used to tow the water-boat to the island. The towing had created a backlog of merchandise of more than a week.[76] Unfortunately, the ham, turkey, chicken, and vegetables that were part of the delivery were spoiled after having sat on a dock in nearby New Castle, Del.[77] The nonfood items fared better. The Rev. Handy received a box containing books, tea, sugar, and tobacco. He gave away most of the contents of the box to friends. The books were of a religious nature and intended as instructional aids for those men in the prison who were studying for the ministry.[78]

The prisoners were not the only ones on the island who were feeling the effects of the departure of the 600. The guards were on edge a few nights after the prisoners left. Some of them believed that the prisoners would attack them if they were given an opportunity. One such group of guards marched over to the entrance to the pen and refused to enter the prisoners' area. To get them to move, their officer drew his sword and leaped into the pen saying, "Come on boys they are not armed, they cannot hurt us." The soldiers moved into the pen, walking in a hollow square and staying alert for any sign of an attack from the 7,000 remaining prisoners. They waited at the other side of the gate for fifteen minutes. When no attack was forthcoming, a patrol was sent out to check every division. Nothing was found wrong and the guards walked quietly out of the area without most of the prisoners knowing that they had been there.[79]

Besides the removal of the "Immortal 600," there were other changes that occurred as well. New guards came to replace the 157th Ohio on August 24 and the prisoners noticed a difference. The 6th Massachusetts Infantry had been the regiment who had had to fight their way through Baltimore, Md., on April 19, 1861.[80] Some of them were new soldiers, but many had been with the 6th Massachusetts since the beginning of the war and acted like a veteran group. This meant that they treated the prisoners as fellow soldiers and not like the enemy. The new guards did not curse at the prisoners or take personal property from them and openly condemned the actions of their predecessors. As the chaplain of the 6th Massachusetts once stated: "Our boys seemed to cherish not a spark of ill-will toward their captured enemies. The pleasantest relations existed between us, and, so far as the regulations allowed, agreeable intercourse was had." The 6th Massachusetts only stayed until October 19, 1864, when they returned home and were replaced by the 9th Delaware.[81]

The idea of using prisoners to attack the enemy continued to be used. Hoffman also ordered Schoepf on the 27th by order of Secretary Stanton to "please place Capt. W.G. Stewart, Fifth South Carolina Cavalry [Infantry], Company A, in close confinement in a cell, in retaliation for similar confinement of Capt. E. Frey, Eighty-second Illinois, by the rebel authorities at Richmond." He was not allowed to see anyone unless on official business. Schoepf was also instructed to inform Hoffman if Stewart had to be removed due to illness.[82]

The prisoners also received word on the same day that from that point forward, there would be restrictions on the number of letters they would be allowed to write. The prisoners were furious about this order. As one prisoner put it, "Today we are informed that hereafter prisoners will be restricted to two letters a week, ten lines to the letter, or, half a sheet of note paper a week. Here is another needless annoyance. Why should we be restricted to ten lines? or what difference if we wrote a dozen letters a week? No harm can come of it, and the government is gainer by hundreds of dollars worth of postage."[83]

For once, this order to restrict the prisoners did not come from Washington, but from Gen. Schoepf. Col. Hoffman found out about this order after he received many requests to write to the prisoners of Fort Delaware. He then contacted Schoepf to find out about the restrictions. Gen. Schoepf had first put restrictions on prisoner correspondence on August 10th when he issued Special Orders No. 261 which stated that "no letters from prisoners at this post will be forwarded, excepting those written to a father, mother, sister, brother, wife, son, or daughter." Special Orders No. 296, issued two weeks later, stated that "All prisoner-of-war letters must hereafter be limited to ten lines of ordinary letter or note paper; must be legibly written and confined strictly to family matters. All letters exceeding this limit will be destroyed." Schoepf wrote back to Hoffman on September 12 to explain why he overrode the federal government's guidelines concerning Rebel correspondence. It was done merely because Schoepf "found it impossible to permit them to write to everybody as they pleased, for the reason that four clerks in the post-office could not have read 2000 letters a day, which at that time was the general average, and even now there are (with the restrictions in their correspondence) several thousand letters unread." Another reason for the restrictions was that they had found out the names of notorious Rebel sympathizers, to whom hundreds of letters were daily directed asking for assistance. Hoffman was satisfied with the response and allowed the restrictions to continue. However, he did state that if Gen. Schoepf wished to enact further restrictions, he "should report the necessity for the consideration of the Secretary of War."[84]

On August 29, 119 prisoners arrived. The cry of "fresh fish" went out and the old fish ran out to meet them. The prisoners who had been in captivity wanted some news of the war from the new additions. What they saw and heard was a shock to the men hoping to hear some good news. One of the veteran prisoners saw what a:

> pitiable spectacle they presented; these 119 newcomers direct from Dixie! Thin and haggard of face, depressed, dirty and dilapidated; worn out in soul, in body, and in clothes! The shadow of famine stands revealed in their looks; the foreshadowing of failure colors every utterance of their lips! I turned away, sick at heart, after hearing their story of our wretched fortunes, for at last there is open talk of Defeat! and if these men speak the truth the demoralization of our armies must render defeat not only possible, but probable.[85]

Captain Ahl was required to give a weekly report to General Schoepf on the condition of the prisoners. For the week ending September 2, his report stated:

> Conduct — good. Cleanliness — prisoners are required to bathe regularly. Clothing — quality inferior and supply sufficient. Bedding — comfortable, consisting of bunks and blankets. State of quarters — clean and comfortable. State of kitchen — in an excellent condition. Food, quality of — very good. Food, quantity of — sufficient. Sinks — clean and well arranged. Policing of grounds — well conducted. Drainage — good and being further improved. Vigilance of guards — excellent. Security of quarters — very good; no prisoners have escaped during this week. Policing hospital — very well conducted. Attendance of sick (nurses) — every possible attention is paid to the sick. Cleanliness of hospital — could not be better. Hospital diet — very good and sufficient. General health of prisoners — about 15 per cent, sick. Death average — about two daily.[86]

One of the prisoners, Randolph Shotwell, gave a different picture of conditions on September 5 than the somewhat rosy one given by Capt. Ahl. On that day, he said that:

> The Woolf came in, half drunk, as usual, and ordered the sentry on the roof of the shed at the rear where Colonel Jones was shot, to allow no more than four prisoners at a time to come to them. This is shameful cruelty. All night long there are dozens of half-clad, shivering, trembling and debilitated prisoners kept standing along the walks, exposed to cold and rain and excruciating pains. Any one who knows the dreadful effect of the vile stuff given us for food and drink — especially the latter — may be able to comprehend the unnecessary cruelty of such an order.
>   Evening — A terrible storm of rain and sleet is prevailing, so dark is the sky that I can scarcely see to scribble these lines. It seems incredible to our Southern ideas of climate that this is only the fifth of September. Yet I have suffered more than on many a winter day in the army. The barracks are as open as a sawmill; there is no fire; the icy rain and sleet rattles through the broad crevices, and sifts down

through the ventilating holes and we are everyone, chilly, restless, and miserable! If this be September what will November and January be? I doubt if many of us survive in winter.[87]

There was a practice at Fort Delaware to whitewash the prisoners barracks to keep them clean. The prisoners would be taken out of the barracks and left outside while this was taking place. One such time was on September 17, when they stayed outside most of the day. However, this practice was not always appreciated by the prisoners. The Rev. Handy felt that the whitewashing had:

> become quite a nuisance. At proper intervals it would be a healthful, and tolerable change; but it has become so frequent, of late, as to exceed all bounds of utility, or necessity. Were the same labor and expense appropriated towards some more substantial or rational comfort, it would be well. "The outside of the cup and platter" is "the all-important," with our masters. To please the eye of visitors and inspectors, is the great aim; but food and raiment for suffering prisoners, is a matter that impresses itself but little upon their consideration. "The pen" is full of ragged and hungry men. Let them give us pants, and shoes, and better rations, and it would certainly be much more for our comfort, if not for their consciences.[88]

The practice of holding soldiers hostage continued when on September 17, Maj. Gen. Hitchcock reversed the order for all prisoners to be released from close confinement and sent all prisoners back to the dungeons who had been there except Maj. Mills. He was the exception because Maj. Goff had already been exchanged. Three days later, Col. Hoffman informed Schoepf that Secretary Stanton "directs that the twenty-six citizen-prisoners recently sent from this city to Fort Delaware as hostages for a like number of citizens of Pennsylvania now in confinement in Salisbury, N.C., shall be treated and fed as far as practicable in the same manner that the prisoners are for whom they are hostages."

Stanton took a particular interest in this situation because of a letter he received from Mr. James Hamilton, a former prisoner of Salisbury. He had been held as a hostage there for 13 months. In his letter, Mr. Hamilton states that Robert Ould, the Confederate officer for exchange:

> alleges that you hold citizens on insufficient or no charges who are not connected with military organizations. He released us because we promised to try to effect the release of Smithson and Reverend Doctor Handy. We were told that you consent to the release of Handy. Ould proposes to release all civilians and capture no more. He proposes to exchange the soldiers, man for man, and hold the excess, and says you might hold hostages for the negro soldiers if they refuse to exchange them. This much I promised to say. Could you not capture and hold as hostages, say, two or three for one, some prominent citizens of Virginia to procure the release of the seven citizens who are remaining in prison at Salisbury, N.C.? West Virginia did so for some of her citizens, and they were sent North. I received some intimations that such a course would prove successful.
> The treatment of prisoners is severe; food deficient in quantity. Returned prisoners' accounts of treatment are true, Fulton and Ould to the contrary notwith-

standing. Boxes and letters even are not given. I received no letters, nor any one else, for two months previous to my release. The boat that brought me up had boxes on it for rebels in our prisons. Many think that Major Mulford is too kind to them and cares less than he should for our men. The Reverend Doctor Moore, who did much to get us away and contributed largely to our comfort during our imprisonment, has two sons in Northern prisons—one, Lieut. J.B. Moore, at Johnson's Island, and the other, Private J.N. Moore, at Elmira. Could you not make a special exchange for these men, or release them? I think that the son (a lieutenant) of Reverend Doctor Breckinridge would be sent on for Lieutenant Moore. Would you not grant us permits to visit these men and do something for their comfort as an expression of our gratitude for the kindness of their father? Permit me to thank you cordially for your great kindness in making efforts to secure our release. I fear to occupy too much of your time; at any rate, I cannot yet write connectedly, having lost much of healthy mental tone through sufferings experienced in prison. We understood that you had issued an order for the release of Reverend Doctor Handy for the release of Mr. Culbertson. I presume that you know all about the fearful mortality at Andersonville, Ga., and the fiendish treatment that causes it.[89]

This was not the only letter Washington received on this topic. Union soldiers held at Andersonville and other prisons sent petitions to the President asking for the return of the exchange system. Clergymen and doctors also joined in the chorus for renewing the exchange cartel.[90] The Southern press also weighed in on the topic. In the *Richmond Sentinel*, there was a complaint about Secretary Stanton and his handling of the exchange issue. It did not understand why the exchange cartel was not renewed in spite of all of the complaints. It did not:

expect any member of the Lincoln Government to feel sympathy for the cruel sufferings of the gallant Confederates confined in loathsome northern prisons, but we certainly had reason to suppose they would have some tender feeling for their own prisoners languishing in confinement in the South. We frequently see accounts published in Yankee papers of the suffering of Federal prisoners. If Stanton believes those statements to be true, what a fiendish disposition he must have, when he alone has the power to affect [sic] their exchange, and refuses to permit it to be done.[91]

No matter who complained about the prisoners, the President did not reverse his decision. Even the warnings Lincoln received from his own political party telling him that he risked losing the upcoming election if he did not change his mind about exchanges did not deter the President. Lincoln refused to concede on the issue of renewing the cartel at the expense of the African-American soldiers held captive by the South. General Grant was just as determined for that reason, as well as because he believed that holding the Southern prisoners kept them from fighting against the North. Between the two men, there was no chance that the exchange cartel would be restarted unless the South was willing to concede on the issue of exchanging all soldiers equally. If the two sides could not come to an agreement, then the prison camps on both sides would continue to grow.[92]

On the 22nd of September, the Rev. Handy found out about his chances of being exchanged. He was supposed to be exchanged for Mr. Culbertson, but the man had already been exchanged, by mistake, for another man. Handy was also informed that Stanton wanted to know why this had happened and gave a written order to Maj. Gen. Hitchcock to exchange Handy with another prisoner as soon as possible.

Two days later, the heavy guns of Fort Delaware were fired off in honor of Sheridan's victory in the Shenandoah Valley.[93] General Sheridan had been ordered by Grant to chase Early "to the death." He had not only succeeded in defeating the Rebels, but he had also driven them some sixty miles to the south into the Blue Ridge Mountains.[94] The officers got drunk after hearing the news of the Union forces' success. As one prisoner reported, just before the guns went off, Lieut. Woolf called down from the sentinel's platform to a prisoner and said:

> "Colonel! you'll be off tomorrow — Richmond and Petersburg have both gone up!" At that moment, cannon were booming on the other side of the river, and all were anxious to know the cause. Quite an excitement ensued — some imagining sudden bad news — perhaps the very thing that Woolf, though drunk, had just announced; others said it was target firing; or, perhaps, they were trying the guns on the Delaware side. Presently the Inquirer came in, with another flaming head, boasting a second great victory over Gen. Early; and then, in a short time, the roar of the big guns was resumed, and continued at short intervals, until one hundred shots were fired, in honor (as we had by this time learned) of Sheridan's wonderful exploits in the Valley. This is the greatest demonstration we have had during the fourteen months of my imprisonment. I confess that for myself, I did not like to hear it. Others seemed to be but little affected; and we were all sufficiently posted to know, that it constituted one of a series of efforts to help Lincoln, in the approaching election.[95]

The news of Early's defeat also brought home to the prisoners just how bad things were getting in the field. The Union victory:

> slaughtered a host of most steadfast hopes. Great God! What has come over our men? It is heart sickening to read of loss after loss; and then too, how subdued and spiritless are the prisoners, one and all! It is the height of absurdity to fire salutes in honor of Grant and Sheridan as if they were famous generals; whereas they could not well avoid being successful against such crushed-out, half-naked, half starved remnants as we still can muster.[96]

Newspapers and the way they reported the news about the war affected the prisoners. When news of Andersonville reached the North, the newspapers screamed for revenge. Their demand for retribution caused the food cutbacks in May 1864.[97] The papers also created their own vengeance without the help of the government. The prisoners read the newspapers and stories which were written about the war. Sometimes, these stories built up their hopes by accident, hops which were only later dashed to the ground. On September 29, the *Philadelphia Inquirer* printed a telegram that stated that 10,000 prisoners would be released immediately. Normally, this kind of news would be treated as hearsay. However, because of where the news came from, the prisoners thought that it was the truth. The men became excited at the possibility of leaving the island, running about the yard filled with the idea of going home. This excitement did not last long — only until a new group of Rebels captured in the Shenandoah Valley came in on the 30th. The 200 Rebel officers, who were "hard looking, lousy, dirty, and ragged," told the old prisoners that there would not be any exchange. At that, "our exalted hopes take a tumble; an hour later after hearing the tale of the newcomers the air castle is a heap of ruins, and we lie tied hand and foot at its cellar."[98]

Secretary Stanton received some information on the 30th concerning political prisoners. H.L. Bond and John C. King were directed by Special Orders No. 13 and 31 to conduct an investigation into the cases of state prisoners held at Forts McHenry and Delaware. This two-man commission was instructed to look at a list provided by Col. Peter A. Porter and General Schoepf, the commanders of the two installations, of the prisoners of state held in the two forts and determine whether or not they should be released. There were 48 cases they were instructed to look at, 16 from Fort McHenry and 32 from Fort Delaware. They spent 33 days looking at all of the evidence against the men and then sent their recommendations to Stanton. They suggested that the number of men who were "to be handed over to the civil authorities of the United States for trial, 4; to be exchanged as prisoners of war, 4; to be continued in confinement, 8; to be tried by court-martial, 2; to be released on oath not to cross the Potomac, 1; to be released upon taking the oath of allegiance, 18; to be released upon taking the oath of allegiance and parole not to cross the Potomac, 9; to be sent to his regiment for trial as a deserter,1; released by General Lockwood before his case was decided, 1." They felt that the arrests were justified and that they were not done out of malice or revenge. The men had all shown themselves to be sympathetic with the rebellion and were thereby considered "the implacable enemies of the Government."[99]

On October 1, the barracks were whitewashed again. It took the entire day:

> and the square has been covered with baggage, blankets, cooking utensils, and all sorts of extemporaneous [sic] fixtures, and odds and ends, such as prisoners only know anything about. It has been so short a time since this business was attended to before, that it was entirely a redundant work — especially on so unpleasant a day, and with such exposure to the prisoners. A good appearance before the inspectors, who are expected to go around about once a month, seems to be the moving cause. They had much better inspect the quantity and quality of our bread and meat.

Sunday was the day that the "grape" ran free on the island. There was no paper on that day and by nightfall, there were many stories floating around the prison population and no real way of knowing whether or not they were based in reality. On Sunday, October 2, the rumor of a speedy exchange of prisoners once again took flight. Capt. Arnett had been offered a parole of the island for the day and was brought to Gen. Schoepf to receive it. The captain refused the parole because he wanted it to last until he was exchanged. Schoepf replied that that kind of parole would be pointless to ask for because 10,000 prisoners were heading South soon.[100] The story had some basis in the truth. On Oct.1, 1864, General Lee sent a letter to Grant suggesting that an exchange of prisoners occur with "the armies operating in Virginia, man for man, or upon the basis established by the cartel." Grant asked the next day if Lee's suggestion also included African-Americans troops. On the 3rd, Lee replied that he meant all captured soldiers, except for deserters "and negroes belonging to our citizens." Grant sent back his reply on the same day. He refused the offer of the exchange because he felt that the Union was "bound to secure to all persons received into her armies the rights due to soldiers. This being denied by you in the persons of such men as have escaped from Southern masters."

Apparently, the idea of exchanging prisoners was not just on the minds of Lee and Grant. On the same day that Grant refused Lee's offer of exchanges, Hoffman ordered Gen. Schoepf, by way of Secretary Stanton, to "transfer to Point Lookout the invalid rebel officers at Fort Delaware who will not be in a condition to take the field within sixty days, who are not too feeble to be removed and who desire to be exchanged." The same message was also given to the commanders of Camp Chase in Columbus, Ohio, and Johnson's Island at Sandusky, Ohio. Within 48 hours, the prison population in Fort Delaware would have their world affected by the decisions of others far away from the island.[101]

By October 5, the ground in the pen had become ankle deep in mud in many sections because there had been wet weather on the island for several days previously. If it had not been for the board walk, it would have been nearly impossible to walk across the yard. The Sutler was back in business, doing very well. The apples, bread, and other items sold by him were all high-priced. He sold "molasses, $2.40 per gal.; cheese, 60cts. per lb.; butter, 80cts.; coffee, $1.00; tea, $2.25; tobacco, $1.25 per bar, very inferior; sugar, 60cts. per lb.; sweet potatoes, 90 cts. per peck; writing paper, 5 cts. a sheet; envelopes, 2cts. each."

On the same day, there was a baptism of seven Rebel officers. They had been waiting for several weeks so that they could be immersed in water. There were two Baptist ministers in the barracks and since the powers-that-be in the prison did not object, it was decided that the baptism would happen that day. Most of the men considered the Rev. Handy to be their spiritual father, so he went along with them to the ceremony. Drs. Harris and Handy led the men out of the prison, followed by Parson Thomas. They marched to the river with twelve guards, six on either side. When they arrived at the river's edge, they sang a Baptist hymn and read some passages from the Bible. After that, each of the seven men were led to the river and immersed in waist-level water. The ministers did not make any inflammatory remarks and except for some loud talking by several Union officers and young girls who were nearby, it was a quiet and peaceful scene.[102]

It was a busy day at the prison. Dr. Woolsey spent several hours in the afternoon examining Rebel officers to see who among them was sick enough to be a part of the exchange taking place at Point Lookout. The prisoners were examined in order of their divisions, starting with 34 and ending with 27 that day. There had been rumors going around the prison for several days before that the sick and wounded were to be exchanged. When the rumor started, there was a sudden outbreak of lameness among the prisoners. Many prisoners went to Captain Ahl or Lieutenant Woolf and gave them a watch, an expensive ring, or just money to be deemed crippled. A Rebel officer paid out $600 worth of jewelry to be declared sick enough to be exchanged. Another man used a new pair of boots he had just received as payment for his freedom. The Union sergeants were kept busy in the pen taking bribes and arranging for exchanges. However, there were some men who were really sick and put up for exchange. One such man was a Prof. Gounart. He had tried to send letters to Gen. Schoepf through Wolf, but Wolf never got around to passing them on. He finally got to see Schoepf as the general walked through the pen. As it turned out, the two men knew each other and had a quiet conversation. Gounart was given a parole of the island and his name put down for exchange.

There was a high level of excitement throughout the prison as Dr. Woolsey continued his examinations the next day. The devices the men used to get on the list of exchanged prisoners also continued at a brisk pace. One man had a small wound in his leg, so he shaved off the hair around it and applied a mustard plaster to the wound so that it would develop an inflamed look. He was allowed to leave. Another man tied a piece of cord around his leg, which made it look as if it was swollen and varicose. A man from Kentucky even went so far as to take medicine to make himself sick when he first heard the rumor of an exchange. This ploy worked a little too well because he ended up in the hospital for several days before the exchange.[103]

Another prisoner, Lieut. John Blue, tried a tactic along those same lines. Lieut. Blue had been suffering from rheumatism and saw his illness as a way out of the prison. He climbed into his bunk and had a friend plead his case to Dr. Woolsey when he walked into the barracks. His friend then described Blue's condition to the doctor in a way that made it sound much worse than it actually was. When the story was over, the doctor told him that "your friend is in no condition to go on exchange, better send him to the hospital." With that, Woolsey turned and left the room. Blue's friend then looked at him and said, "Jes over done it didn't we?"

Things then picked up for Blue when a Major Chin came to the pen. The major had been chosen for exchange not because of his health, which was good, but because of the one hundred dollar check and a two hundred dollar watch he had given to the right person. He had asked permission to visit the pen to say goodbye to some friends. Since he was due to leave and would no longer need them, Major Chin gave Blue a handful of sutler's checks so that he could buy food or anything else that he might need to make life at the prison a little more bearable. The checks came to about five dollars and it was a present he would not soon forget from a man who was a stranger to him.[104]

The 116 prisoners who were picked on the 6th were paroled according to the cartel of 1862 and ordered to be ready to leave that night or the next day. None of the prisoners expected to leave that soon because of past experience, so it was a great surprise to everyone when the air was pierced with the cry of "Turn out sick and cripples for exchange!" that evening. The men lucky enough or rich enough to be on the list lined up and left the prison. One of the men who left had written out a draft for $200 to be paid by friends from New York and walked out of the prison using a broom handle as a crutch. Some of Morgan's men marched out without even trying to pretend to have any injury. These were some of the more financially well-off prisoners. The other prisoners did not blame those who used bribes to leave the island because if the situation had been different, they would have done the same thing to escape having to endure another winter in there.[105] The prisoners walked out with the departing men and watched them leave. Then:

> slowly and silently returned to their quarters. The weather was quite cool. Many of the prisoners were scantily clad. And especially those from the far South, who [were] now for the first time experiencing the chilling winds of the northern clime, found comfort in wrapping their blankets around them whenever they had occasion to leave their quarters, although the freezing point had scarcely yet been reached.[106]

The weather began to get colder. Those on the island could feel cold, "wintry blasts sweep up the broad river, and across the flat island, with the keenness of an ocean cyclone; roaring round the prison yard, whistling through thousands of crevices in the open barracks with a chill rasping sound that increases the cold by imagination." Dozens of prisoners laid in bed all day, "thinking, thinking, and shivering with intense chilliness; not comfortable a moment of the day!"[107] The prisoners who were not part of the exchange wondered out loud, "How shall we stand it this winter?" The Rev. Handy stayed in his bunk the whole day, "except when at worship. Kept myself covered with my blanket and comforter; but found it almost impossible to read or study." However, later in the day, Dr. Handy finally received the news he had been waiting to hear for fifteen months. He had been requested to go to Gen. Schoepf's office and there found out that there was an order sending him to Fortress Monroe so that he could be exchanged. There was also an order that he should "not be allowed to communicate with any one by the way." The Rev. Handy was concerned that the order could possibly include his family, which would go against a promise made by Secretary Stanton in which he said he would allow Handy's family to accompany him. Handy explained his concern to Schoepf and the General assured him that he would look into the situation. He also permitted Handy to write to his wife to inform her about his release.

Word of his imminent release spread throughout the prison. He was urged to conduct one last service by candlelight that night, to which he reluctantly agreed. The service was to be held at Division 34. That night, the division "was so crowded, when I entered for the evening services, that I was obliged to crawl under the first tier of bunks, over multitudes of legs—so densely packed were even these lower quarters. Every available spot in the division was occupied. All who could do so, stowed themselves away in the several tiers, whilst the benches were filled, and numbers stood, jamming the room to its utmost capacity."

The Rev. Handy was totally unprepared for the depth of emotion his last sermon had on his congregation. He had never:

seen so much feeling in the barracks. Many eyes were suffused with tears. All seemed deeply affected. The effort was wholly impromptu; and I had the consciousness of great leanness in what was said; but the occasion was so overruled of Providence, as to make it effective, independently of any specialty in the matter of my remarks. After the sermon, I found that the adjoining division [33] was also quite well filled with attentive hearers, who had gathered there, hoping to hear, though they could not see.

The Rev. Handy spent the next few days saying goodbye to friends and preparing himself for the trip home. Some of his friends had messages to give him to take with him to Richmond, but "all have desired to have some words of friendship; and my poor heart has been overwhelmed with the astonishing expression of confidence and affection."[108] During his stay at Fort Delaware, he had earned the respect of many of the other prisoners, "even by those whose characters and practices were not in accord with his example and precepts. With untiring energy although almost broken down by his long imprisonment, he established and conducted Sunday schools, Bible classes, religious services, and in every way ministered to his fellow prisoners."[109] He was released on October 13, 1864, and taken over to Delaware where he was met by his wife, seven of their children, and assorted friends.[110]

A week after Dr. Handy left, Lieut. McHenry Howard received a pleasant surprise. His family in Baltimore had been informed that if they came to the island quietly, they would have the chance to visit with him. His parents and two of his sisters arrived and spent the day at General Schoepf's home. They had dinner with the general and he treated them with the utmost courtesy. Before dinner, Howard was brought to his family and spent several hours with them. They gave him some clothes, a ring, a silver watch, and a gold piece. He was taken back to the pen when they sat down for dinner, but the ability to see the family he had not been with for over three years did much to improve his spirits.

That was not the only favor Gen. Schoepf did for Lieut. Howard. In the early part of November, Howard happened to be in the general's office when he asked Howard if he would like to be exchanged. He said that he would not mind just as long as it did not stop anyone who was sick and weak from getting out. Schoepf assured him that it would not. He further made the suggestion that to improve his chances of exchange, Howard should pretend to have an illness. Schoepf asked him, "'What have you got — rheumatism?' I replied, 'No, but I have a slight sore throat.' He said 'Rheumatism is the best thing.'" When Howard had returned to his quarters, he found out that the medical examiner, whose approval was needed for him to be exchanged, had already left. He then sent a letter of false complaint to Schoepf saying that he missed the chance to be exchanged because of his meeting with the general and that he wanted a special examination so that he could be exchanged. He then gave an orderly a bribe so that he would give the letter to Schoepf, instead of Capt. Ahl, because he was afraid that the general would never get the message. At 9:00 the next morning, Howard's name was called at the gate. Before he left, he prepared himself to be examined. He gargled with a mixture of vinegar, red pepper, and salt. This potion caused him to have tears streaming down his face. He then tied a small pillow to his face with a white handkerchief. Howard and a dozen others were standing in a line waiting to be examined when Captain Ahl came up to him and told him that his name had been selected for exchange. He immediately went back to his barracks and began to pack. He put on his gray cloth suit, two sets of underwear, and a gray officer's overcoat. This coat had a cape attached to it that went down to his wrists. He also filled his valise and bundled up the rest of his things to get ready to leave. That afternoon, he and the others who were to be exchanged were called to assemble in front of Gen. Schoepf's office. The general came out and walked among the departing prisoners. He took one look at Howard's padded appearance and pulled him aside. Schoepf told Howard that "there will be no inspection here, but there may be at Point Lookout and half your things may be confiscated. Now there's a fellow"—and he pointed to Capt. Frank Cheatham, a nephew of Confederate major-general B.F. Cheatham —"who has very little. Give the cape of your overcoat to him and scatter your other things among those other fellows to take through for you." Lieut. Howard thought that it was an excellent idea and he did that just before he climbed aboard the boat that would take him to freedom.[111]

Other people were concerned about the welfare of the Rebel prisoners, not only at Fort Delaware, but at all the Northern prison camps. The Confederacy had an idea to help their men in prison camps by selling goods in the North and using the profits to fund sending supplies to their soldiers in prisons across the Union. On October 18, 1864, Gen. Grant wrote to Gen. Lee that he had no objections to letting an agent of the South provide for their men in prison camps, so long as the North could do the same thing. Grant further made the suggestion:

> as a means of satisfying each party that all goods sent reach their proper destination, that a commissioned officer of each party, to be selected from among the prisoners of war, be paroled, to remain within the lines of the party now holding them, whose duty it shall be to receive and receipt for all articles sent for distribution, and who shall see that they are distributed according to the wishes of those sending. Looking entirely to the alleviation of the suffering of those held in captivity. I will not interpose any obstacle to any plan that may be proposed which gives equal privileges to both belligerents.

On October 28, Gov. Zebulon B. Vance of North Carolina wrote to the Confederate commissioner of exchange, Robert Ould, to discuss this idea. Gov. Vance felt that the best man for the job was his brother, Brig. Gen. Robert B. Vance. The Governor felt that his brother's strong character would be an asset in trying to get the needed supplies to the prisoners.[112] Gen. Vance was being held prisoner at Fort Delaware. The Rev. Handy described him as "a very quiet, pleasant man." He was a member of the Methodist Episcopal Church and was a devout Christian. He helped at religious services on the island and occasionally preached. Being a man of such piety in the Confederate army did have its own set of problems. As he confided to Handy, the hardest thing about being a Christian in the army was that very few people respected his determination not to drink any alcoholic beverages. Abstinence did not make the other officers' hearts grow fonder toward him and his stand and they were not above pressuring him to break his vow.[113]

General Grant and Commissioner Ould continued their correspondence on the subject of supplying prisoners with much needed supplies. On November 12, Grant officially agreed to the idea of the South selling goods to pay for the care of their men in prison. On December 6, Brig. Gen. William N. R. Beall was released on parole to receive and sell 1,000 bales of cotton sent to New York from Mobile, Ala.

Other people from Fort Delaware were also getting on boats and leaving to go to the mainland. The election of 1864 was an important one for the nation. It was to decide whether or not the North would continue the war as much as it was to determine who would lead the country. Many of the Federal soldiers had the chance to vote without the necessity of returning to their homes. Nineteen states allowed their soldiers to vote while still in the field.[114] The soldiers at Fort Delaware voted on October 11 and voted for Lincoln. However, some of the soldiers had to return home for a different reason. Members of the 9th Delaware were shipped home on November 5 to help with the elections.[115] Governor Cannon of Delaware had requested the men to help keep order throughout the state because he was concerned that there would be disruptions on election day due to the many Southern sympathizers who lived in Delaware. This request had been made for every election in Delaware during the war.[116] The Southern sympathizers did make their presence known, but in a peaceful manner. Of the three states that did not vote for Lincoln, two of them were New Jersey and Delaware.[117]

Even though the threat of Southern sympathizers voting in the election did not cause the Lincoln Administration much in the way of trouble, it did cause one man a great deal of difficulty. In the fall of 1863, Gen. Schoepf talked with Edward Muhlenbrock, the army engineer assigned to the fort, to make sure that his engineering group voted pro-Union. He told Muhlenbrock that if any of his men did not vote the Union way, they were to be fired. Muhlenbrock refused to do this and sent a letter to his superior officer, Col. Brewerton, in nearby Philadelphia, about the situation. Brewerson then wrote to the chief engineer in Washington, Major Joseph Totten, telling him about the vote tampering accusations. Muhlenbrock also told Schoepf that he had no right to tamper with the vote and that he thought that it was illegal. The matter was dropped for months, but it resurfaced in September 1864. Brig. Gen. Richard Delafield, the chief army engineer, and the former captain of engineers at Fort Delaware during its early construction, received a letter from Col. Brewerton saying that Gen. Schoepf had said to Secretary Stanton that he thought that Mr. Muhlenbrock was disloyal to the Federal government.

Being accused of traitorous actions during the Civil War could destroy a person's entire life. It was hard to prove yourself innocent of a disloyalty charge during this time period. If found guilty, a person could be sentenced to death or a prison sentence. Muhlenbrock saw first hand every day what type of place anyone accused of disloyalty could end up at. That is why he was very concerned about the accusations. Fortunately for him, Mr. Muhlenbrock had the complete faith and support of his superiors. The Corps of Engineers began a formal inquiry into the situation and they sent a letter to Gen. Schoepf asking for any proof of the charges. The general sent no such proof, so Brewerton went to Fort Delaware to find out first hand what was happening. Gen. Schoepf claimed that he did not receive the letter asking about the evidence. The colonel was confused by this statement because Muhlenbrock had received his copy of the letter from the same courier that also carried Schoepf's letter. The general could not come up with any formal charges against Muhlenbrock and told Brewerton that he based his accusation on a statement made by a prisoner, who was supposedly repeating what Muhlenbrock had said. Col. Brewerton then decided to have Muhlenbrock and his family take the Oath of Allegiance in the presence of a judge if Schoepf thought that it was necessary. Schoepf then said that he thought that the accused was a gentleman and his signature would be enough to prove his innocence. Brewerton then reported to Gen. Delafield on October 8th that the situation was over. Even though the matter was resolved, relations between Schoepf and Muhlenbrock were never the same. Schoepf never apologized for the accusations and in turn, Muhlenbrock never gave up an opportunity to make the general look foolish.[118]

Even though President Lincoln was firm on his decision not to resume the exchange cartel, he was not entirely heartless to the plight of Rebel prisoners. On November 11, Lincoln sent word that he wanted Richard Henry Lee, private 1st class, Rebel Maryland Artillery, to be released from Fort Delaware. He was told that Lee, who lived in Division 20, was sick and needed to be released. Lincoln's order was to "Let this man take the oath of Dec. 8 1863, and be discharged."[119]

The reelection of Lincoln did point out several things to the North and South alike. First, that the North had no intention of giving up the fight to preserve the United States. Lincoln was a strong believer in aggressively fighting the war and once it was won, to just as aggressively bringing the country back together. His reelection proved that the North would support Lincoln in his efforts to defeat the South. Lincoln also had generals like Grant and Sherman who believed in the same thing. Their aggressive prosecution of the war left the South reeling and assured both sides that the war would be to the finish. This meant that the war-weary people on both sides would have to continue fighting, whether they liked it or not. This weariness filtered down into every aspect of the war and the prison camps were no exception.[120] The guards were just as unhappy with spending another winter on Pea Patch Island as the prisoners. By November 22, the weather was very cold, everything was frozen solid, and the guards' quarters were no exception. This made one of the guards complain that "money is spent here in fixing up things for officers, sutlers, and prisoners while the men who are on duty more than half of the time are quartered in old shantys with cracks large enough to crawl through."[121]

Things were not any better in the prisoners' quarters. Many of the prisoners were ill prepared to handle a winter on the island, especially those from the Deep South. Most of them did not have underwear and their clothes were of:

Garrison barracks

the merest summer quality, what we wore when we were captured in warm weather — and totally unsuitable as protection against the icy blasts of this latitude.

The most shameful piece of barbarity of recent date was the robbing us of our blankets. No matter how many blankets a man may have brought with him, or purchased from the sutler with his own money, he is striped of all but one single one! altho' it is a well known fact that in these open barracks no man could sleep comfortably under even three blankets, and lying upon as many more. I have never been able to sleep for more than a few minutes at a time since our blankets were stolen from us.

Stoves have been put up, one in each shed, but there is not fuel enough furnished to keep up even a semblance of fire more than half the time, and with a crowd of one hundred and ten shivering men to make a double circle around it, there is not much chance for a diffident person to get anywhere near it.

For three weeks I have not been comfortably warm during the day, nor able to sleep over two hours any night; have not tasted warm food; have not been free from the pangs of actual hunger any moment during the time.[122]

The first of December brought with it another example of prisoners being used to attack the enemy. On December 1, Secretary Stanton authorized the use of Cpl. R.H. Curry, Co. F and Private W.J. Neeley, Co. H, 12th South Carolina Regiment, who were being held at Fort Delaware, as hostages for Cpl. James Pike, Co. A, 4th Ohio Volunteer Cavalry and Private Charles R. Gray, Co. D, 5th Iowa Cavalry. Pike and Gray were scouts sent into Rebel territory when they were captured in May 1864. Stanton ordered Gen. Schoepf to treat Curry and Neeley the same way that Pike and Gray were being treated behind Rebel lines.

When Captain Ahl gave Gen. Schoepf his weekly report for the week ending December 4, 1864, he had written his usual positive stuff stating that everything was running well and that there was nothing wrong. In particular, he noted that: "State of mess-houses — remarkably clean. State of kitchen — excellent. Food, quality of — very good. Food, quantity of — receive full allowance."

The captain may have been pleased with the condition of the camp, but others had a different idea. Brig. Gen. H.W. Wessells, the commissary general of prisoners, had sent a Captain Penrose to the fort to perform an inspection. Unlike previous inspectors, this one was not very happy with what he saw. He gave a list of recommendations to Gen. Wessells, who, in turn, passed them on to General Schoepf. The list gave a clear picture of what some of the problems were with feeding the prisoners at Fort Delaware. The inability to feed the prisoners properly was not always because of a lack of supplies or meanness, but from the operation not being run in an efficient manner. Captain Penrose wrote that:

> First. That a considerable quantity of salt beef is on hand, liable to damage if not issued soon.
> Second. That the component parts of the ration on hand are very unequal in quantity, some being for six weeks and others for only ten days.
> Third. That the bakeries are not kept clean and that the saving arising from the prison bakery is entirely separate from the prison fund.
> Fourth. That the distribution of food to prisoners is not well managed, the meat being unequally divided, the officers getting a larger piece at the expense of the enlisted men.
> Fifth. That instead of pork, the soup is made of bacon and beans, this, with mixed vegetables, being greasy and unpalatable. The officer in charge of the kitchens was absent and his assistant either ignorant or unwilling to give information.
> Sixth. That the assistant in charge of the kitchens stated that there was but little refuse and no more grease than was sufficient to grease their boots, whilst in a mess of some 300 a saving of one barrel of grease, worth $30, had been made in six weeks without much care or attention.
> Seventh. That a considerable quantity of salt and vinegar (the issue being more than sufficient) had been saved, but not turned over to the commissary.
> Eighth. That the commissary is the proper officer to be entrusted with the feeding of the prisoners; that he should have suitable assistants and care be taken that food be distributed equally.[123]

Starting on the 8th, the weather began to get worse. It started out as cold and on the 10th, the first snow storm of the season arrived. Enough wet snow fell that day to make it very hard for people to move around and made the fort look depressing. On the night of the 11th, a strong wind came in from the northwest and froze everything on the island. The force of the wind was so bad that the guards on watch fared no better than the prisoners in their drafty barracks. It was this type of weather that made the guards wish they were anywhere but on a small island in the middle of the Delaware River. One group of guards in particular was anxious to be away from the prison. The Delaware soldiers were concerned that they would miss Christmas with their families. They were 100-day soldiers who should have been mustered out by December 10th but ended up staying at the fort until the January of 1865. On top of having to stay longer than they wanted at the prison, by the end of the month, one of their men became involved in an shooting incident with one of the prisoners.[124]

On December 21, the same day that Gen. Schoepf received a copy of the inspection done by Captain Penrose, Schoepf wrote to Gen. Wessells explaining about an incident that had occurred the day before. Around 7:00 A.M. on the 20th, Private

John Deakyne of the 9th Delaware shot and killed Private John Bibb of the Charlottesville Artillery. General Schoepf had issued Special Orders No. 157 on June 1, 1864, stating that any prisoner who was caught relieving himself near the barracks would be warned to stop three times and if he did not obey the order to stop, would be shot. As Schoepf mentioned in the letter to Gen. Wessells, this problem with the prisoners had begun to be "a very common and annoying custom with them to urinate in a tin cup or bucket and throw it out of their windows, creating a very offensive odor about their barracks. During the last two months two men were shot at, without fatal result, for urinating at their doors, and this has resulted in their using the cups and buckets within their barracks and throwing it out the window." This time, however, the shooting was fatal. Schoepf ordered a court of inquiry to be set up the same day to determine the cause of the shooting. The four men picked to be members of the court questioned eight witnesses, including Private Deakyne, to ascertain what had happened that morning. Two of the witnesses, who were prisoners, testified that someone was throwing liquid out of the barracks, but that Private Bibb was innocent of it because he was sitting nine feet away from the window on his bed. The other witnesses, all of them guards, did not see Private Bibb throw anything out of a window. The last witness to testify was Private Deakyne. He stated that he:

> was stationed on post No. 60, inside the prisoners' enclosure, on the morning of the 20th of December 1864. I went to my post at 7 a.m. The sergeant of the guard instructed me to go around the barracks and see that the prisoners committed no nuisance or did any damage to Government property, wasted the water at the sinks, or threw any filth out of the barracks windows. In case they did, I was to warn them three or four times to cease, and if they still disobeyed I was to fire. While walking my beat I saw filth thrown from several windows. I immediately ordered them to stop. All of them obeyed except two. They continued throwing filth from both windows, notwithstanding I warned them three or four times to stop or I would fire on them. As soon as my back was turned they would throw it out. I am sure they did it three or four times after I ordered them to stop. They could certainly hear me, as I was only about ten feet from the window, and one of them answered that it would be stopped. I turned to move away when the offense was repeated when I again warned them to stop. After I warned them the fourth time and they disobeyed, I fired at the window. I afterward learned that a man was wounded by the shot.

After Private Deakyne finished testifying, the court deliberated and found Private Deakyne innocent of all charges. It was also decided that Private John H. Bibb was innocent of breaking of orders at the time that he was shot. The person who committed the offense in the first place was never discovered.[125]

The holiday season was not very eventful. Christmas Day 1864 was a beautiful day. Some of the guards went on a drunk that lasted into the next day and a good third of them were in the mood to get into trouble. That was evident when one guard got into an argument with the provost marshal and was arrested. This rowdy mood among the guards did not change as the week went on. On New Year's Eve day, the soldiers had a general inspection and were mustered out in spite of a heavy snow storm hitting the island. They did not appreciate having to stand out in the snow and some of them decided to express their displeasure by doing their best to create a disturbance. They first started by trying to blow up a stove. The stove did not cooperate with the guards' efforts to destroy it, but they did succeed in breaking up some gun racks.

Not every guard was bent on getting into some sort of mischief. The Fort Delaware Band performed at a church to bring in the New Year, which was a far cry from the way some of the other Union soldiers stationed at the fort were acting. It was also a time to reflect upon the previous year. One of the guards, A. J. Hamilton, looked back over his year at the fort and did not like what he saw. He felt "that this year has been spent by me without much progress or pleasure. Have neither been useful to myself or country to any extent. Partly my own fault but mostly that of others as I, of course, was subject to their orders. Had not the opportunity of doing anything but guarding prisoners who others had captured and disarmed."[126]

There was some good news for some of the prisoners as the New Year approached. On December 30, Gen. Schoepf was ordered to send all Rebel officers who had been captured at Helena, Ark., on July 4, 1863, and all officers captured by Maj. Gen. Steele in the Dept. of Arkansas prior to July 28, 1864, to Johnson's Island. He was also ordered to send all officers captured at Fort Butler in Donaldsonville, La., in June 1863 to New Orleans for exchange.[127]

The prisoners who were not leaving to be exchanged did not look forward to staying the winter in prison. One in particular who definitely did not want to be on the island was Sam W. Hardinge. He was a political prisoner and husband of Belle Boyd, the most famous spy for the Confederacy. He was transferred from the Old Carroll Prison to Pea Patch Island at the end of the year. When he arrived at the island, he was registered and, because it was after 10:00 P.M. when this was done, he and his fellow prisoners were placed in the privates' barracks in the Virginia section, where there were about thirteen hundred privates living in:

> a place that a gentleman-farmer in this country would not have permitted his pigs to live in, much less human beings.
> As we entered the doorway, yells and shouts from every side greeted us, of "Fresh fish! fresh fish!" Men and boys crowded around us to find out from "whence we came," "what we were held for," "who we were"; and last, but not least, "had they gone through us," in other words, and more plainly speaking, "had the sentries outside searched us."
> To this last inquiry I assured my questioners that the Yankees outside had done so most effectively.
> Several of them proposed "tossing us in a blanket," by way of diversion to the rest, and many were evidently in favor of it, when suddenly Sergeant B———, of the division, sprang forward, and shouted at the top of his voice —
> "By Jove, boys! this gentleman is Miss Belle Boyd's husband; you wouldn't wound her feelings by insulting him, would you?"

Armed with that knowledge, the prisoners gave Hardinge a heartwarming cheer and accepted him happily among them. The reception he received was the only thing about Fort Delaware that was warm. He spent New Year's Eve huddled in front of a fire trying to stay warm. He tried to sleep, but once again he slept on the floor, "and I sleep as the dogs sleep — half waking, half sleeping."[128]

January 1, 1865, was ushered in for the prisoners with the sound of:

> the clattering windows and fierce howling of the wind [which] kept me in a con-dition of "half asleep half awake"; until near daybreak when a perfect calm fell upon the earth, the stamping of the half frozen sentries ceased, the rattling sub-sided, and the atmosphere grew warm enough for me to fall into real sleep for perhaps an hour. Dawn brought a resumption of the noises, for the garrison was well supplied with liquor, and ushered in the New Year with a general drunk. Looking out, I perceived the cause of the calm; the weather having moderated brought down nearly a foot of snow, which as it lay unbroken over the surface of all the island was undoubtedly the ... purest, whitest element thereon, and one might imagine it had been sent during the dark hours of the early morning to gently mantle all the filth, the black sand, the greenish water, the dingy buildings with a white robe appropriate to New Year.[129]

Those on the island endured the storm and the sun came out. Private Hamil-ton looked out upon 1865 as something to look forward to. The reason for his joy was that August 22, 1865, would be his last day of being a soldier. On that day, he would "(if living) have fulfilled my oath to my country and will be no longer the slave to a set of debauchees wearing shoulder straps."[130] Mr. Hardinge also saw some good in the new year. On New Year's Day, he went to visit Gen. Vance and his staff and soon became friends. New friends appeared the next day when one prisoner gave him a blanket and another an overcoat. These acts of kindness from strangers helped him deal not only with the cold, but also the idea of being imprisoned far from home.[131]

Fortunately for Hardinge, he received his gifts just in time because on the 3rd, there was a heavy snow storm that hit the island. Once again, the guards were as uncomfortable as the prisoners because of the bad weather. Standing guard over prisoners on an island in the middle of a snowstorm was bad enough, but the guards soon had other concerns. The next day, five men escaped. The prisoners, who were all heavily ironed in their cell, cut a bar out of a window and made their escape by going across the river. A search party went after them, but no sign of the prisoners could be found.[132] This type of escape was possible because the weather was so cold that the Delaware River was frozen solid and anyone could walk to the mainland. That was the good part of the weather. The bad news was that because it was so cold, the water in the ditches and the drinking water in the collection tanks was also frozen solid. The prisoners had to melt water for washing and drinking, which they did as soon as they were able to create enough fire to do so.[133]

On the same day as the escape, Hardinge wrote a letter to Capt. Ahl to make a request. He stated that while he was at the Old Carroll Prison, his mother had writ-ten to him to inform him that she was sending two blankets and a trunk filled with clothes and toiletry items to him. Before he received it, he was transferred to Fort

Delaware. Hardinge wanted Ahl's permission to have these things sent to him. He waited for an answer from Capt. Ahl for five days. When Hardinge did not receive an answer, a fellow prisoner suggested that he write another letter, this time addressed to Gen. Schoepf, to request the articles from the Old Carroll Prison. The next day, Hardinge received a letter from the general stating that everything he had requested would be arriving shortly.

Regardless of the time of year, the prisoners barracks were whitewashed on a regular basis to keep them clean. Hardinge's division was whitewashed on the 11th. He and the other prisoners stood outside in the snow under guard while this was being done. They decided to pass the time by throwing snowballs at each other. This bit of recreation almost ended tragically when one of the snowballs landed near a guard. The soldier reacted by raising his weapon and firing upon the prisoners. The bullet kicked up some snow near one of the prisoners, but no one was hurt.[134]

On January 16, 1865, eighty officers and a group of civilians were brought in as prisoners. It was a double blow to the prisoners to see the new arrivals. The sight of prisoners walking into the pen destroyed any hope that the rumors of a partial exchange, which had spread throughout the prison, were actually true.[135] The other shock was to see the men being brought in as political prisoners. The four men, "old and decrepit, one of them tottering on the entrance to the valley of shadows, men whose gray beards and venerable aspects ought to have commanded at least sympathy from the presiding powers at Washington, were brought in as prisoners." None of them was less than fifty and one of them had only one leg. They had been captured the previous August in Georgia by a captain of the Union navy, who was on a raiding party on shore, and held in the hold of a Union ship for five months until being transferred to Pea Patch Island. The men, Wm. James Cannon, Charles Lingoaut, Wm. Rily Townsend, and Wm. Somerlin, maintained that they were not a part of the Confederate war effort in any way. They looked so bad and their story was so sad that even Capt. Ahl took pity on them. He suggested that if they were willing to take the oath and write a petition to Secretary Stanton, he would personally send it to the proper authorities. The four men received the help of other prisoners in drafting the petition and the letter was sent.[136]

On the 17th, Robert Ould wrote to Gen. Grant to tell him that Gen. Vance or anybody else that Gen. Beall chose to help him with distributing supplies to prisoners was fine with him. Gov. Vance continued to show his support for this project by writing a letter on the same day to the Confederate Secretary of War, James Seddon, to inform him that the General Assembly of North Carolina approved a motion to purchase $200,000 worth of cotton or tobacco. These goods would be added to the merchandise the Confederacy was going to send to New York to sell to raise money for the prisoners.[137]

For all the activity going on about the supplies for the prisoners in the North, the supplies were not being shipped very quickly. General Schoepf wrote a letter to Brig. Gen. H.W. Wessells on the 23rd requesting 2,000 blankets for the prisoners. Schoepf did this because after looking at the letters written between Generals Vance and Beall, he felt that the idea of them supplying their own men in Northern prisons would take too long. He thought that the prisoners would suffer unless the North supplied them with blankets.

This concern about the prisoners suffering from the Delaware winter had begun a month before. Capt. Ahl mentioned on December 19, in his weekly report to General Schoepf on the state of the fort, that the prisoners had requested clothes from Gen. Beall. Nine days later, Ahl again reported to Schoepf that "some of the prisoners are needy, and, as the weather is very cold, the deficiencies should be promptly supplied by General Beall." At the end of the report, Ahl wrote under "Remarks and Suggestions" that "A requisition for such clothing as is really needed (and for, in fact, much more than is necessary) has been made on General Beall by the prisoners some time ago, but has not been filled, hence the increase in sickness and deaths." Captain Ahl continued to mention the clothing needs of the prisoners to Schoepf even after the general wrote to Gen. Wessells. On the 29th, Ahl again stated that "Some are too thinly clad for such exceedingly cold weather."[138] This exposed the fatal flaw in the idea of the Confederacy taking care of their own men. The time it took to get the supplies to the camps was too long to be effective for the men who were in need.

On the 24th, Gen. Vance, Colonels Dick and Charlton Morgan, Major Mills, and Captain Kilgore were removed from the pen and placed inside the fort. The rooms they were moving to were more comfortable than in the officers' barracks and the other prisoners were somewhat envious of them.[139] They wished that their lot in life would improve as it did for the five officers. Their wish was about to be granted.

The Confederate Government was overrun with problems in the first month of 1865. One of the more pressing problems was the lack of soldiers to continue the war. In 1863, Gen. Pat Cleburne had suggested to the general officers of the Army of Tennessee that the South should free some of its slaves and put them into the army to fight. A few of them agreed with Cleburne, but most of them were horrified by the thought and the idea was quickly buried. However, in 1865, the idea did not seem so outrageous.[140] If the South was willing to consider using slaves as soldiers, then it also opened the door for exchanging African-American Union soldiers on an equal basis with their Caucasian brothers in arms. If the South was willing to bend on this issue, then they could not only have the thousands of Rebel soldiers languishing in Federal prisons back on the battlefield, but also the possibility of slaves swelling the dwindling ranks of their armies. Therefore, on January 24, the Confederate Congress offered to do exchanges that also included African-American soldiers. Gen. Grant agreed and the exchanges that all the prisoners hoped for soon began.[141] For once, the outside influence on Fort Delaware was a positive one and it heralded the beginning of the end for all of the prisoner of war camps.

9

The End of the Line

Sam Hardinge's days as a political prisoner ended on February 3, 1865, when he was summoned to General's Schoepf's office. It was a cold afternoon and Hardinge wrapped his blanket around him to protect him from the weather as he walked to present himself to the general. When he arrived at the office, he was handed a message from the War Department stating that he was a free man. Schoepf told him that "you have now our permission to leave the island. Will you go to-night or to-morrow morning? Do you go to Baltimore or New York City?" Hardinge told him that he would go to "New York; and I thank God I am free! Rest assured that I shall not trouble the Government by remaining longer than I can help. Good afternoon, sir."

He quickly packed his few things and said his goodbyes. His friends gathered around him, shaking his hand, and "wishing me a 'God speed you, Hardinge!' 'God bless you, my boy!' 'Hope to see you in Dixie soon,' 'Write to me,' etc." His clothes and suitcase were inspected and then he boarded "a small steam-tug which lay at the wharf. This in a few moments cast off from the Chateau d'If of America, daintily picking our way through the miniature bergs that impeded our progress to the mainland."[1]

While Hardinge was leaving, another prisoner arrived. Capt. Lucien Bean of the 17th Miss. had been captured on December 10, 1864, near Richmond. He had been held at the Capitol building at Washington, D.C., until February 1865, when he was transferred to Fort Delaware. Bean and other prisoners were placed on a train and taken from Washington to Middletown, Del. They were then marched from the train station to a ship waiting on the Appoquinimink Creek near Odessa, Del., which would take them to Fort Delaware. As they marched, the prisoners were cheered by the citizens of the town to the annoyance of the guards. Middletown was filled with South-

133

ern supporters and the women of Middletown and the surrounding area brought food and clothing to the prisoners at Fort Delaware. One of the people who stood and watched the shivering prisoners go past that day was Annie Foard. She lived in nearby St. Augustine, Md., and she felt sorry for Capt. Bean as he marched by. She then took off her shawl and gave it to Bean. What she gave the captain that day was something more than a shawl. To a man who was far from home and friends and heading towards one of the most dreaded prison camps in the North, having a total stranger give him a gift gave him the strength to deal with an uncertain future. He never forgot her kind gesture and promised himself that when the war was over, he would come to see her and thank her for her kindness. Bean lived up to his promise and on June 19, 1865, he called on the stranger who had given him a shawl and hope. He never left the area because he eventually married Miss Foard and lived in St. Augustine for the rest of his life.[2]

Things were beginning to change for the prisoners. On February 9, 1865, rumors were circulating throughout the prison that exchanges were going to begin. The story had it that 10,000 men were going to head South in several days. The consensus was that the story was too good to be true. On the 10th, General Vance was freed on parole to go to New York to help General Beall buy blankets for the prisoners. They were not very impressed with Gen. Beall's skills in obtaining help for them. As one prisoner stated: "The Lord grant he may show more activity and zeal in our behalf than Beall has! The cotton sent by our government to pay for this clothing has been in New York for weeks; but not a blanket nor pair of shoes has come hither, altho' we suffer as no words will describe!"[3]

Even though the prisoners had a hard time believing that Gen. Beall would be able to help them, in February, the long hoped for supplies began to appear. On February 8, Gen. Beall sent 984 blankets and 1,000 socks to Fort Delaware. He shipped 848 drawers and 156 socks on February 11 by express from Baltimore. He then followed up on the 14th by sending 1,340 shirts, 600 drawers, and 500 socks by the U.S. quartermaster.[4]

There were improvements at the prison. But the suffering of the prisoners continued with the news from the battlefields. On the 13th, the prisoners heard that Sherman had joined Grant and was marching towards Columbia, S.C. The idea that Northern forces could march through the South without much resistance spoke of the terrible state the Confederacy was in. Sherman had burned Atlanta, captured Savannah, and was heading toward South Carolina.[5] February 22 was Washington's birthday and a 39 gun salute was fired at noon in his honor. The salute was also fired for the capture of Wilmington, N.C., and Charleston. The cannons firing to celebrate Union victories demoralized the prisoners at Fort Delaware. The handwriting was on the wall and even the most ardent Rebel knew that it was only a matter of time before the Confederacy fell.[6]

The exchanges of prisoners were being worked on throughout the month of February. The federal government wanted to know how many prisoners they had in the prisons. There were 82 civilians, 1,260 officers, and 5,642 privates being held at

Fort Delaware as of February 3, 1865. On the 7th, Col. Hoffman informed General Grant that there were 1,000 prisoners at Fort Delaware who were ready to be exchanged. Hoffman was not sure if he should send them to City Point, Va., to be processed or how many officers Grant wanted sent for exchange. Grant informed him that the prisoners should be sent to City Point and that he did not care what percentage of exchanged prisoners were officers. Once he knew what to do with the prisoners, Hoffman then contacted Bvt. Major General M.C. Meigs, the quartermaster general of the army. He told Meigs that he had Gen. Grant's permission to send out prisoners from Fort Delaware to City Point for exchange and that he needed a ship big enough to carry 1,000 prisoners with a 200 man guard. On the 17th, Hoffman informed General Schoepf that prisoner exchanges were being resumed and that the prisoners at Fort Delaware would be sent to City Point for exchange "from time to time as transportation can be provided. None will be included who do not wish to be exchanged, and none against whom there are any special charges or who are held as guerrillas unless specially ordered."[7]

The rumors of exchange came true on February 27 when the steamboat *Cassandra* came to the wharf around 8:00 A.M. to take prisoners to Aiken's Landing to be exchanged. There were 30 Union soldiers, one officer, one doctor, and one hospital steward to accompany 1,018 Rebel prisoners. They left the island around 2:00 P.M. and arrived on March 1. Due to a problem that the Confederacy had with getting enough transportation for the prisoners, they had to wait another day to be freed. The transportation problems had not been corrected the next day, so 500 healthy prisoners were dropped off on shore to make their own way back to Dixie. The remaining Rebels were transferred from the *Cassandra* to the *State of New York*, so that the guards from Fort Delaware could be returned to the prison. The Union guards arrived back on the island on the 6th.[8]

Plenty of things happened while the guards were away. On the 1st of March, it was requested that General Robert B. Vance be given a release as soon as possible. The petition for his release stated that Gen. Vance had saved the lives and property of hundreds of Union citizens in Carter County, Tenn., in 1861 by protecting them from Rebel horsemen. It was requested that due to the protection he offered to the people of Carter County that he be given his freedom. Five days later, Vance was ordered to be exchanged with the next group of prisoners.[9]

In March 1865, the weather was bad and all of the prisoners had colds. They shivered from head to toe, day and night. If a prisoner only had a cold, he could consider himself lucky. Dysentery was a common occurrence at that time. There was very little salt in the meat they ate and the soup was no help. Hundreds of men, weakened by illness, went through the wind and snow to the sinks, some of them walking 700 yards, at all hours. Many of them slipped on the ice in the pen and added injuries to their list of suffering. In many cases, colds turned into something worse and they died. After they finished their business at the sinks, they would return to their barracks so thoroughly cold that they were unable to get warm again for the rest of the night. All of this caused a hardening of the heart toward their captors that was difficult to erase.

The prisoners were usually glad to see new prisoners come to the island because they would pump them for information about what was going on in the outside world. In 1865, the arrival of "fresh fish" did not excite the men already in captivity. To see their proud comrades walking into the prison yard dejected with nothing but bad news from the front depressed them even more than they were already. General Richard L. Page, the commander of Mobile, Ala., arrived on March 12 with 50 other officers after Page had surrendered to Farragut. Once again, to see the man in charge of the defenses of a large city deep in the Confederacy brought in as a prisoner brought home to the Rebels how low their fortunes had fallen. Reality became even more painful for the prisoners to see when the remaining members of the Immortal 600 returned to Fort Delaware on March 15. It was "a saddening spectacle to see these wretched victims of Lincolnite barbarity tottering back to the places they had left six months before, full of bright hopes and spirits! It will be remembered that General Schoepf, Ahl, Wolfe and the other understrappers gave out false impressions and then cleaned out the pocket of every prisoner who could afford to buy himself free."[10]

The men had barely arrived back at the fort when the other prisoners asked them what had happened to them. The returning prisoners said that when the 600 were placed on the *Crescent*, they had discovered that there were four rows of bunks built between decks for them. Each of the rows contained:

> three tiers, and it was calculated that all of us were to stay between decks except at limited times, when a few were allowed to go on deck and get a little air. Between decks there were ports fore and aft on each side, and little air-holes every ten feet, from stem to stern. The bunks and machinery occupied all the room except two passages of three feet. The distance from each bunk to the one above it was about twenty-seven inches, and the bunk in which I stayed with a friend was about three feet wide. The majority of the bunks were as dark as night, and those near the machinery were above fever heat at all times. Of course there was no place to sit down or to stand up and, therefore, we laid in our bunks day and night. A few, rendered desperate by the heat, would night and day block up the ports, and thus the little air we might otherwise have had was excluded. Some, who could get no bunks, slept in piles under the steps of the gangway and between the ports. So soon as we were taken aboard a few men, who were favorites of General Schoepf, were taken to the cabin and there slept in beds and ate with the Yankee officers. The wounded and sick, of whom there were about forty, were allowed to sit and sleep on deck around the forecastle gangway, where they were exposed to the sun and rains during the whole trip.[11]

Their destination was not a place where they would be exchanged, but Morris Island, S.C. They were to be placed under fire in a stockade on the beach halfway between Fort Wagner and Fort Gregg.[12] This is where their true suffering began. Capt. Leon Jastremski described to his brother what happened next. The Northern guards:

> almost made us die of hunger. We received only four hardtack biscuits per day and four ounces of meat and a half pint of bean soup, and all full of revolting

worms. At that time we were under the fire of our forts which in returning constant cannonades of the Yankees on Charleston, constantly dropped bombs among our tents which were entirely unprotected. It happened to me often at night to be awakened by the noise of bombs among our tents. By the dictates of divine providence none of us was hit by these bombs during the six weeks of this very miserable existence.

Finally when we all began to succumb to this treatment, on October 20th they told us that the retaliation was finished and they were going to send us to Fort Pulaski where we would be well treated. In fact, we went to this fort and until January, 1865, all went well, but from that day on by an order from General Foster, they started torture in the following manner: For forty days we received as ration only ten ounces of corn meal full of worms and four ounces of bread and a half pint of cornichons per day. Not a bit of meat or anything else.

On the 10th day, after having eaten all the cats that we could catch in the fort, about 200 of us had an attack of scurvy.

To make matters worse, we were not allowed to receive anything from outside, but we were allowed to buy from the sutler. It is this that saved us. By a miracle the sutler was a humane man and took pity on us. He gave us food on credit on our drafts, without knowing if he would ever be paid. In accordance with this and pushed by hunger I gave him a draft on Messrs. Mioton in New Orleans for $60.00, asking them to send it to you. In this way I saved myself from the scurvy and perhaps certain death.

At that time I had dysentery which was wasting my constitution. Finally, that stopped when the Yankees saw they were going to kill us all. They gave us good rations and on March 4th they sent us, as they said, to be exchanged at Monroe Fortress.

The prisoners were being removed from Fort Pulaski because the Union needed the fort to hold spies, deserters, and other undesirables that General Sherman was sending there. It was decided to send the 600 officers back to Fort Delaware. A two-masted square rigger named the *Ashland* picked up the 313 Rebel officers who were kept at Fort Pulaski and crossed the harbor to pick up the remaining 182 members of the 600, who had been sent to Hilton Head Island, S.C., on November 19.[13] Once the *Ashland* landed at Hilton Head, the officers of the 157th New York Volunteers, who were guarding the prisoners, complained that the ship was too small and too crowded to head out to sea. They switched over to a large ocean streamer, the *Illinois*, and began their journey. The guards were combat veterans, therefore they treated the prisoners well. They allowed them the run of the ship and permission to stay in the staterooms if they had the money to pay for them. The prisoners were also given decent food while they were out at sea. The guards told the prisoners that the ship was headed to Fortress Monroe, where they would be exchanged. It was certainly good news to hear, but most of the men were in such bad condition that they did not really care if it was true or not.[14]

The prisoners were under the impression that they were going to be exchanged. That impression did not last very long. On the morning of March 8, a gunboat moored at Hampton Roads, Va., hailed the *Illinois* and called, "Where are you bound?" The captain of the *Illinois* answered by saying: "Fort Delaware." As Capt. William H. Morgan, one of the 600, put it: "Oh, horror of horrors! our hearts sank within us; visions of exchange, of home and friends, vanished in a twinkling. Doomed to further incarceration in a detestable Yankee prison when we had expected in a few short hours to be free and with friends!" All of the prisoners were depressed when they heard the news of their fate. Three officers died on the way to Fort Delaware and were buried at sea. When they landed at the fort, 75 sick prisoners were taken to the hospital. Many others were barely able to walk.[15] Fortunately for the returning prisoners, their comrades gave them food and spare clothing to replace the ragged uniforms they came in with. The feeling among the returning prisoners was that it was a pity that the Northern newspapers did not take any pictures of them when they returned to Fort Delaware. As one prisoner put it:

> What a grand chance the United States Sanitary Commission missed in not having a photograph made of the survivors of Secretary Stanton's brutality. What a grand contrast our photo would have made with those photos alleged to have been made at Andersonville and other Southern prisons after the surrender. It is a pity, indeed, those loyal souls who were ever anxious to stir the northern heart did not have taken, for distribution in the North, our photos. Our condition would have brought the blush of shame to every northern cheek, and made even Edwin M. Stanton turn pale at the sight of the victims of his brutality.

Not all of the prisoners that left the South arrived at the fort. Several of the prisoners escaped on the voyage. Capt. Leon Jastremski of the 10th Louisiana Infantry, Capt. Thomas F. Perkins of the 11th Tenn. Cavalry, Capt. Emmett E. DePriest, 23rd Virginia Infantry, and Lieut. Cicero M. Allen, 2nd Ark. Cavalry were given information from a member of the crew, who was a Southern sympathizer, on how to escape. He suggested that the prisoners hide in the forepart of the hold, where the anchor, ropes, etc. were stored and wait there until the ship landed in New York City. Once there, they could head back South or anyplace else they wanted to go. After they reached the hold, Capt. Perkins began having severe pain in his bowels. He did not want to give the others away but decided not to go back. The others became more worried about his condition as it worsened to the point where they were afraid for his life. They finally convinced him to leave the hiding place and find a doctor to take care of him. They helped Capt. Perkins find a doctor to treat him and then the remaining three resumed their hiding place. The guards never knew that they were gone because they had friends impersonate them during roll call. The trio were successful in not being noticed and they left the ship in New York City.[16]

Soon after the Immortal 600 returned to the island, Rebel officers at the fort came up with a plan to help them get back on their feet. They decided to hold a benefit minstrel show for them to raise money so that they could buy food and clothing. The show was such a success that the prisoners continued to hold them to help any destitute prisoners, not just the Immortal 600. Originally, the prisoners were the only ones who came to the shows. When the Union officers heard about how much the prisoners enjoyed them, they bought reserved seats and came to see the shows as well.[17] Even Gen. Schoepf and his staff came to the shows to see, among other things, Lieut. Peter B. Aker on the tambourine, Major J. Ogden Murray on the bones and Capt. Edward Chambers as the manager.[18]

The minstrel show was a popular form of entertainment that had its start in the colonial era. These shows consisted of music, comedy, and dance. They were performed by Caucasians who painted their faces to look like African-American men and tried to sing and sound like them as well. A master of ceremonies, also known as an interlocutor, ran the show. The show was made up of three parts. The first part consisted of the entire troupe sitting on a stage in a semicircle singing popular songs and telling jokes. The second part, which was called the olio, was the variety portion of the program in which the members of the troop performed solo. The final part was a sketch that blended comedy and music together to perform a satire on current events.[19]

The shows at Fort Delaware charged 25 cents for general admission and 50 cents for reserved seating. They were held at the mess hall of the prisoners' barracks. The doors opened at "Early candlelight" and continued until late into the night. One such show started with songs and dances from the officers. They sang "In the Prison at Fort Delaware" and "Over on Pea Patch Island." The lyrics of "Pea Patch Island," sung to the tune of "King of the Solomon Island," went as follows:

> Oh, have you heard the news of late,
> Of a grand Hotel of State
> To board the rebels small and great,
> Over on Pea Patch Island.
>
> They call the place Fort Delaware
> Just what they call it we don't care
> We'd rather be — I won't say where —
> Than over on Pea Patch Island.

The second part of the show had solos performed on cornet, guitar, violin, and banjo. The show continued with a comedy sketch called "Man-Monkey," featuring three characters: Mr. Van Willikins, Mrs. Van Willikins, and the "Man-Monkey." This was followed by a lecture on phrenology. The talk on the study of the human skull was given by Professor Julius Caesar Hannibal Turner. The program then stated that the show would "be concluded with the laughable farce of the Southern Negro Regiment." The topic came from the news that the South had recently agreed to start bringing African-American men into the Rebel army. The Confederate officers held on the island were completely against the idea, and it was a perfect subject to be satirized in the show.[20]

Supplies coming into the prison from people other than the federal government continued on March 21. Brig. Gen. Richard L. Page and Lieut. Anderson handed out shoes, blankets, and clothing that were bought from the cotton sent to New York. The next day, Private Henry Robinson Berkeley was told by Beverly B. Turner of Fouquier County, Virginia, by a note that if he ever needed clothing, shoes, etc. that he should contact Mrs. S. Dickinson of Philadelphia. She was the head of an organization that helped Rebel prisoners of war. Turner's uncle, Henry Turner, and other supporters gave Mrs. Dickinson the money she needed to carry on her work.[21]

The prisoners also did their best to look out for themselves. One day, Lieut. John Blue was walking in the prison yard when Lieut. Luther Ashby, a friend of Blue's, came up to him and asked to borrow a fifty cent check. He wanted the money "to fight the tiger," meaning to gamble. Blue was reluctant to give it to him since he only had two checks left, but in the end, he gave him one because Ashby had done several favors for him in the past. That night, Ashby returned and told Blue that he had won. The money was split evenly between the two men. Blue spent several hours that night trying to think of a way to buy some food and not spend the capital. He came up with the idea of creating a beer stand. There were several in the pen and he thought that they must make a considerable profit since they sold their beer at five cents for a half pint mug. He took in two partners and started his business. Unfortunately, the business never took off because the other beer stands had loyal customers and they could not lure them away to buy their goods.[22]

As the war was drawing to a conclusion, the prisoners continued to amuse themselves the best way they could. One prisoner went to visit a friend and have a glass of port with him at Division 22. He stayed to listen to the Debating Club and its question for the evening. It was: "What gives the greatest pleasure, the pursuit or the possession of an object?" At first, the visiting prisoner thought that it was an odd way for Confederate officers to spend their time. By the end of the evening, the prisoner was wondering about the question himself. The president of the club ruled that the possession of the object was the correct answer.[23]

April 3, 1865, was a study in contrasts for the guards. The shortage of vegetables throughout the previous winter showed itself when many of the guards came down with scurvy. Dr. Nugent reported the problem to Gen. Schoepf to see if there was anything he could do to bring some relief to the soldiers. That problem was overshadowed that evening when word came to Fort Delaware that Richmond and Petersburg had both fallen to the Union. When that happened, one guard described it by writing that he had "never before heard such a shout of joy as was sent up from these old walls and never before a lot of men so perfectly happy." He also noted that the Fort Delaware Band "honored us with some of their finest music while three sets of cotillions enlivened the scene. At the close of each strain the boys raised a shout of joy which made the old vaults ring." The celebration continued when the hospital gave out as much whiskey as the soldiers could drink. The next day, General Schoepf ordered the sutlers to stop selling whiskey to the officers and soldiers. It did not do any good and the drinking continued until the 7th.[24]

While the news from the front became worse with every day, the prisoners tried to continue on with their daily lives. One way they did that was to publish a newspaper. In April 1865, the *Stonewall Register* was released. It contained sections very much like other newspapers and gave out information on what was going on in the prison. It started with an editorial and continued with a letter to the editor, news, and classified ads. The editorial of the first paper stated that "the most cruel persecution of the prisoners is monotony." It suggested that "constant employment of the mind" was their only escape. Whether that "employment" was through games of skill and chance, working on a trinket, music, poetry, or the study, not just the reading, of instructional books that improve the mind. The paper stated that if they could "persuade any one to act upon our suggestion we will be more than paid for any trouble in writing these lines."

The paper contained news on where to buy services in the prison. There were advertisements for bowls at Division 31, engraving by W.B. White at Division 24, jewelry by Whilton and Neighbors at 24, smoking tobacco by Lieut. Roos at 22 at the Sign of the Elephant, and the latest designs by Lieut. W.B. Cartwright at 24. It also advertised violin lessons, a saloon and restaurant open every evening at Division 28, and Roberts and Bucks, Jewelers at 26. Another establishment offered washing and ironing that could be done on short notice, as well as putting buttons on. The advertisement also stated that "'Fresh Fish'" will do well to patronize." There was also clear starching, washing, and ironing every day except Sundays at Division 26 and haircutting, shaving, and shampoo at 24. There was also a listing for the roll of the Stonewall Chess Club. The members were broken down into groups and the rules were listed as well.[25]

As much as the prisoners tried to carry on with their everyday routine, a general depression hung over the island. The news of the fall of Richmond hit the prisoners hard. A 100 gun salute to honor the Union victory and a new group of prisoners arriving from Petersburg on the 4th did nothing to help their mood. The rumors continued to circulate about the fate of the Southern forces.[26] Finally, on April 10, 1865, the rumors came true. That morning, a Union corporal read a report stating that Lee had surrendered to Grant. The Union soldiers let out a cheer and there were the sounds of joy everywhere. Secretary Stanton had ordered "a salute of two hundred guns be fired at the headquarters of every army and department, and at every post and arsenal in the United States," to celebrate the surrender.[27] At noon, Lieut. Herr commanded a 225 gun salute. Many of the officers and men began drinking in celebration; that, as well as "dancing and singing[,] became the order of the evening."[28] On the Jersey side of the river, the citizens of Salem were surprised and then happy when a frightening roar came from the cannons of Fort Delaware. Salem responded by ringing the church bells all day in celebration.[29] Wilmington, on the Delaware side of the river, was "in an uproar and blaze of glory, rejoicing over the greatest of victories yet achieved by our arms. Guns are firing, bells are ringing, and a large procession is proceeding through the streets."[30]

The feelings of the Rebel prisoners were somewhat different at the news of the surrender. Lieut. Blue was in his quarters with several friends when Lieut. Ashby ran in, his hat in his hand. "'Boys,' exclaimed he, 'She is gone up, and so are we.'" What had gone up came from different directions. "The Confederacy, Old Uncle Bob, has surrendered everything, his whole army, Richmond, Petersburg, everything every Confederate soldier to be banished. If they ever return the penalty will be death. Every man who can swim must take water to night or it will be too late."

Some one said how about those who can't swim. "Get a board," said Ashby and dashed out to spread the news.[31]

Private Berkeley wrote in his diary that he thought April 10 had:

> been a day of the most intense mental anxiety I have ever experienced. Thousands of thoughts have passed through my mind as to what fate awaits my country, my family, my neighbors, my friends and myself. May God who has cared for, and protected them during the last four bloody years of war and destruction, continue his fatherly care and protection over them is my most earnest prayer. Lee has certainly surrendered. The Yanks are firing four hundred guns in honor of Lee's surrender. The firing of these guns makes my heart sink within me. To think that all the blood and treasure, which the South has so unsparingly poured on the alter [sic] of our country, should have been shed in vain. Oh! How many unhappy mothers are now mourning throughout the South for the useless slaughter of their sons.[32]

The Virginia officers in the prison held a meeting to decide what course of action to take. They felt that they could either give up, take the oath and get out of prison, or wait and see what would happen. Gen. Joseph Johnson in North Carolina and Gen. Kirby Smith in Texas still had troops in the field. Several officers spoke during the meeting, among them Capt. Don P. Halsey of Lynchburg. He ended his speech by suggesting the motion: "That the meeting take no action at present." Capt. William Morgan seconded the motion and the vote was unanimous.[33]

The next day was very quiet.[34] The rumors started to make their rounds on the 12th on the fate of the prisoners. Two days later, many of the prisoners began to ask to take the Oath of Allegiance on the condition that they could go home once they signed it. Nothing much happened at the prison until Saturday, April 15, 1865, the day after Good Friday. It was then that the prisoners heard that President Lincoln had been shot and killed by John Wilkes Booth. Some of the prisoners thought that the assassination "will make the Yanks hard on us. I don't see why they should take revenge on us. We certainly could not possibly have had a hand in it. He ought to have been at church instead of at the theater as it was Good Friday." Lieut. Ditz, the Yankee commandant of the barracks, went into the prisoners' barracks drunk about 5:00 P.M. He had in his hand a club about five feet long; and whenever he saw a group of two or more prisoners talking together, he would rush them and try to hit them. Several men were severely hurt, but most of the men stayed out of his way.[35]

The attitude that Lieut. Ditz had toward the prisoners after the death of Lincoln was not an unusual one during this time. After the surrender of Lee, the guards became friendlier. The death of Lincoln changed that at once. Guards and prisoners alike were in a state of great excitement. The guard was doubled and the Union soldiers looked angry. The prisoners were worried about retribution from the guards and the North. They feared banishment to the Dry Tortugas or worse. They thought they would have to cast lots to see who would be their victims. While everyone was talking seriously about this topic, Lieut. Peter Akers, the wit of Fort Delaware, broke the tension by saying: "It was hard on old Abe to go through the war and then get bushwhacked in a theatre."[36] The sutler closed his window on the prisoners' side and did not open again for three days. The Rebels were not allowed to be together in groups or talk in groups outside of their barracks. It was not safe for a prisoner to talk above a whisper for a few days after the assassination for fear of being shot.[37]

The prisoners were right in fearing for their safety in the first few days after Lincoln's death. The day the assassination was announced, an employee of the *Osceola*, a boat used by the fort, said that Lincoln "was a G-d D — — d old Nigger loving Son of a B — — and ought to have been killed long ago." The man was immediately arrested and brought before Gen. Schoepf. The general was furious with the man. Schoepf slapped him across the face and had him hung by his hands for an hour. He then had the man's head shaved and he was whipped off the island by an African-American at 5:00 P.M. Private Hamilton wrote in his diary that the night before, he had been filled with joy. The next day, he was completely the opposite. He wondered what if anything was ever "so Horrible? Last night in my joy, I could have forgiven all of those wretches of Rebels tonight in my grief (I'll confess the truth) and my rage I would crush them as I would a serpent. The wretch who could devise and execute so cruel and wicked an action is deserving of the Deepest and Hottest Hell."[38]

The guards were not the only ones who did not approve of the assassination. Captain William Morgan thought that Booth was "a scatter-brained actor" who "did the South no good."[39] Ben Crampton, another prisoner, did not meet any officers in the barracks who were in favor of John Wilkes Booth's actions. Crampton said that "For my part, I think it is a most unfortunate affair, particularly at this time." He also said that "If the worst comes," he would prefer Lincoln to Andrew Johnson.[40]

The anger the Union troops felt towards the prisoners soon lessened. One guard told Lieut. Blue that he thought Gen. Schoepf was being too hard on the Rebels and that "I know it was none of you kill Mr. Lincoln just soon as I heard it."[41] Another guard, Sgt. E. Cox, told Frank Kinckle that mail would be given out regularly again on the 22nd. He said that Secretary Stanton had forbidden the prisoners from receiving any mail since Lincoln's death. By the 29th, the "Yanks have somewhat gotten over Old Abe's murder, and are not quite as mean about it."[42] This may have been helped along by the news that Gen. Johnson had surrendered.[43] This news took the heart out of many of the prisoners. As Randolph Shotwell put it:

> About 10 A.M., Ape Ahl, or All Ape, came upon the parapet, together with a gang of flunkeys, and ordered the prisoners to form in double ranks at about fifty feet from the fence.
> He then began a false, and foully conceived harangue about the triumph of Liberty and Freedom, the rout and capture of Lee, the flight of Jeff Davis, etc., etc.! In short, the Rebellion having been crushed the loyal bosom of the Government yearned to welcome the well thrashed prodigal; or at any rate, would give each prisoner below the rank of a field officer, a chance to foreswear his evil practices, repent and confess his crimes, and escape the punishment, or expatriation that awaits those who should prove obdurate, and refuse to bow the knee to Bael! It therefore behooved every man of wisdom and prudence to step forth ten paces, in public acknowledgment of his willingness to foreswear his country!
> Result! Nearly nine hundred officers, many of them among the most intelligent

and comfortably situated in all the prison, stepped forth and announced their desire to swear allegiance to Yankeedom!

The event has crushed the spirit out of every man in the pen. Tonight we are like two hostile camps; the oath-takers as subdued and embarrassed as if they had really "swallowed the little yellow dog."[44]

Most of the prisoners agreed to take the oath if they could go home. Four years of fighting had taken its toll on soldiers on both sides and they just wanted to go home. The *Richmond Whig* newspaper arrived at Fort Delaware, and it contained a long list of names of prominent men in Richmond and the South who had taken the Oath of Allegiance. Once the prisoners saw the list, they had no objections to taking the oath. If a person did not take the oath, he could not engage in any type of trade or business. If it was not taken in prison, it would have to be taken at home.[45]

On May 2, 1865, General Schoepf entered the prisoners' pen with (Jack) Ahl, Wolfe, Fox, and the other bluecoated brutes to insult us in the hour of our deep humiliation and despondency, by tender of the "Yellow dog" to those who gagged and refused to swallow it last week. Schoepf's speech was exceedingly offensive to every prisoner who has a particle of self-respect. "Your Confederacy"—this Dutchman prefaced—"is gone up and busted! De bottom it did fall de pot, an' you's better get out from under de rubbish. Dat's what I tink; Git out, an' take allegiance to de pest government vat ever vas"—etc., etc. He added that this was the last chance, that the Yankees had now offered two chances for "you Rebels" to come back, confess and repent, and say "I'm sorry, don't skin me alive!" So we might understand those who refused this would never have another. They might be sent into exile; imprisoned for life, or hanged for their crimes. I do not quote his words exactly—but that was the general understanding of the spirit of the harangues.[46]

The next day, the prisoners received visitors. Crowds of people from Philadelphia and other places came to Fort Delaware. They walked on the platforms, looking at the prisoners as if they were animals in a zoo. This made the prisoners angry and gave them a poor opinion of the men and women who were looking at them. They did not blame the children that came, since they thought that it was the parents' fault for bringing them. Private Berkeley went to his barracks when the visitors came so that they could not spy on him. Some of the male visitors went down among the prisoners so that they could buy toothpicks and other items that the prisoners had made.[47] There were also fears that the Mexican army was sending agents to recruit soldiers to fight against Emperor Maximillian. Rumor had it that they were offering men $3,000 in gold to go into Mexico to fight.[48]

On May 10, 1865, the guards informed the prisoners that Jefferson Davis had been captured in Georgia with several members of his cabinet. The news made the guards happy, since it meant that they could all go home soon. However, on the 18th, the guards heard something that did not make them happy. A Rebel officer from Division 16 was walking in the yard when a guard asked him if he had heard that Lincoln had been assassinated. The officer replied: "Good! You don't say so? Hurrah for that!" The guards heard his statement, seized him, marched him out of the pen, where he was thrown in a blanket until he was covered with bruises and his clothes were torn off.[49]

Several members of Davis's staff, including Lieut. Gen. Joseph Wheeler, were sent to Fort Delaware and arrived on May 22. Gen. Schoepf was under orders to keep them away from the prison population and allow them to talk to no one. They did not stay very long, because they were all released, except Burton Harrison, two months later.[50]

Prisoners were being sent out of Fort Delaware on a regular basis once they took the Oath of Allegiance. There were 120 prisoners released in April 1865, 1,071 in May, and 6,997 in June.[51] The huge increase in the number of men being released in June was caused by the federal government beginning to process the prisoners more quickly. On the first of June, the Oath of Allegiance was administered to all of the remaining prisoners in alphabetical order.[52]

June 13 saw a great deal of activity at the fort. Battery G of the Pittsburgh Heavy Artillery was mustered out. They were awakened early, "had a hearty breakfast, fell into line, stacked arms and started for the boat. At about 7:30 we started for the wharf, followed by the whole of the garrison. At the wharf we cheered for our devoted officers and friends. Was responded to by General Schoepf who wished us all the good things we could think of."[53]

> It was also the same day that six hundred Rebel officers were sent home. Such a large number of prisoners leaving at the same time brought about a sudden change in the atmosphere at the prison. Lieut. Shotwell noted in his diary that:
> 	The vacancy would be very enjoyable were it not for the suggestiveness of the deserted bunks. Gone home! not back to comrades at the front; not to resume the Rebel grey, nor even pause on the old camping and campaigning ground; but to stagger wearily back down through war worn Virginia, seeking out the ruins of what were once their happy homes.
> 	How strange the thought that there is not anywhere today a single Southern soldier under arms, a single flag flying, a single representative of the Confederacy in existence![54]

There may have not been any more Rebels fighting in the field, but that did not stop them from continuing to fight for what they believed in. At the end of June, there were still 109 prisoners. The delay in processing them came from the prisoners themselves. Out of the 109 Rebels, 82 of them refused outright to sign the oath and leave the prison. Their refusal lay in the wording of the oath, which stated that the oath was taken "freely and voluntarily." They would not sign the oath unless that statement was removed. General Schoepf called a meeting to try to change their minds. It was held at the mess hall and attended by the entire garrison and their wives. The latest threat from the government was that if they did not sign the oath, they would be hung. Col. John R. Fellows denounced the hard line actions with verses that said:

> They threatened to hang us, unless we add perjury to perfidy,
> 	if they will, let them hang, and the moment they do it the
> 	gallows will become next to holiness to the Cross.

The mess hall exploded as the women in the audience waived their handkerchiefs and the Union soldiers showed their support. One soldier said that "If you hang these men you'll have to get another garrison." The prisoners were not punished for their stand. Instead, they were given the run of the island. The offending phrase was removed and the 83 gladly signed the oath and were soon home.[55]

As most of the former Rebels were leaving, there were a few who were coming into the barracks. Henry Kyd Douglas, a member of Stonewall Jackson's staff, was arrested and tried on three counts on May 8, 1865. His offense was that he posed for a picture in his Confederate uniform at the request of a young lady. He carried the uniform coat on his arm so as not to attract attention while they went to the photographer. This happened while he was on parole after surrendering to the Yankees after Appomattox. He was found innocent of treason and violation of parole, but guilty of a violation of military orders and sentenced to two months at Fort Delaware. He did not arrive until July because he was held in Washington as a witness for the Lincoln assassination trial.

When he arrived, there was only Col. Burton H. Harrison, President Davis' private secretary, beside himself being held on the island. They were well taken care of, but they were not permitted to communicate with each other. General Schoepf treated Douglas well and allowed him all the freedom he wanted. He visited Schoepf and his family and vice versa, drove with the general's family around the island, taught Schoepf how to handle the reins of his new horse, and had access to the fort's library. On August 23, 1865, the general issued Special Order #328 to release Douglas. Schoepf and his family took him to Wilmington on his boat to have dinner before he left.[56]

The next day, Col. Hoffman wrote to Gen. Townsend concerning Fort Delaware. Townsend had ordered Hoffman to inspect the prison and let him know its condition. He informed Townsend that all the Rebel prisoners were gone except two men captured with Jefferson Davis who were awaiting trial. The barracks for the prisoners and the guards and the prison hospital were empty. Hoffman recommended that the barracks be torn down by the 60 Union convicts being held on the island. The barracks were filled with rats and they went to every house looking for food. He wanted them torn down so that the rats would no longer have a home. He also suggested that the wood from the barracks be separated. The good lumber could be sold and the bad lumber be used for fuel.[57]

The barracks that had held so many men and had seen much in the way of suffering and despair was soon taken down. Burton Harrison had the distinction of being the very last prisoner to be released. His last day on the island was January 1, 1866, which ironically, was also the last day that Gen. Schoepf served at Fort Delaware. The convicts had already been transferred to other prisons and as Harrison and Schoepf left, so ended the mission of Fort Delaware. The fort was manned sporadically until the 1940s, but it never again attained the prominence that it had during the Civil War years.[58] It had been built to be the greatest defensive outpost in the United States, a place to be feared by its nation's enemies. Fort Delaware became a place to be feared, but not in the way its architects intended it to be. Like the nation it was created to defend, the fort was shaped by the Civil War into something that it was never designed to be, and in being so shaped, secured for itself a place in American history.

Appendix: Regulations for Union War Prisons

I. Circular sent from Colonel William Hoffman, Commissary General of Prisoners, to all Northern prisoner of war camps dated July 7, 1862. From the Official Records of the Civil War, Series II, Vol.4, pp. 152–153.

The following regulations will be observed at all stations where prisoners of war are held:

1. The commanding officer at each station is held accountable for the discipline and good order of his command and for the security of the prisoners, and will take such measures as will best secure these results. He will divide the prisoners into companies and will cause written reports to be made to him of their condition every morning showing the changes made during the preceding twenty-four hours, giving the names of the "joined," "transferred," "deaths," &c. At the end of every month commanders will send to the commissary general of prisoners a return of prisoners, giving names and details to explain alterations. Where rolls of "joined" or "transferred" have been forwarded during the month it will be sufficient to refer to them on the return.

2. On the arrival of prisoners at any station a careful comparison of them with the rolls that accompany them will be made and all errors on the rolls will be corrected. When no roll accompanies the prisoners one will be immediately made out containing all the information required as correct as can be from the statements of the prisoners themselves. When the prisoners are citizens the town, county, and State from which they come will be given on the rolls under the heads, rank, regiment, and company. At the same time they will be required to give up all arms and weapons of every description and all moneys which they have in their possession, for which the commanding officer will give receipts.

149

3. The hospital will be under the immediate charge of the senior surgeon who will be held responsible to the commanding officer for its good order and the condition of the sick. "The fund" of this hospital will be kept separate from the fund of the hospital for the troops and will be disbursed for the sole benefit of the sick prisoners on the requisition of the surgeon approved by the commanding officer. When the fund is sufficiently large there will be bought with it besides the articles usually purchased all articles of table furniture, kitchen utensils, articles for policing, shirts and drawers for the sick, the expense of washing, and all articles that may be indispensably necessary to promote the sanitary condition of the hospital.

4. The commanding officer will cause requisitions to be made by his quartermaster on the nearest depot for such clothing as may be absolutely necessary for the prisoners, which requisition will be approved by him after a careful inquiry as to the necessity and submitted for the approval of the commissary-general of prisoners. The clothing will be issued by the quartermaster to the prisoners with the assistance and under the supervision of an officer detailed for the purpose, whose certificate that the issue has been made in his presence will be the quartermaster's voucher for the clothing issued. From the 30th of April to the 1st of October neither drawers nor socks will be allowed except to the sick.

5. A general fund for the benefit of the prisoners will be made by withholding from their rations all that can be spared without inconvenience to them, and selling this surplus under existing regulations to the commissary, who will hold the funds in his hands and be accountable for them subject to the commanding officer's order to cover purchases. The purchases with the fund will be made by or through the quartermaster with the approval or order of the commanding officer, the bills being paid by the commissary, who will keep an account book in which will be carefully entered all receipts and payments with the vouchers, and he will keep the commanding officer advised from time to time of the amount of the fund. At the end of the month, he will furnish the commanding officer with an account of the fund for the month showing the receipts and disbursements, which account will be forwarded to the commissary-general of prisoners with the remarks of the commanding officer. With this fund will be purchased all such articles as may be necessary for the health and comfort of the prisoners and which would otherwise have to be purchased by the Government. Among these articles are all table furniture and cooking utensils, articles for policing purposes, bedticks and straw, the means of improving or enlarging the barrack accommodations, extra pay to clerks who have charge of the camp post-office, and who keep the accounts of moneys deposited with the commanding officer, &c., &c.

6. The sutler is entirely under the control of the commanding officer who will see that he furnishes proper articles, and at reasonable rates. For the privilege the sutler will be taxed a small amount by the commanding officer according to the amount of his trade, which tax will make a part of the general fund.

7. Prisoners will not be permitted to hold or receive money. All moneys in possession or received will be taken charge of by the commanding officer who will give receipts for it to those to whom it belongs. They will purchase from the sutler such articles as they may wish, which are not prohibited, and on the bill of the articles they will give an order on the commanding officer for the amount, and this will be kept as a voucher with the individual's account. The commanding officer will keep a book in which the accounts of all those who have money

deposited with him will be kept, and this book with the vouchers must be always ready for the inspection of the commissary-general of prisoners.

8. All articles contributed by friends for the prisoners in whatever shape they come if proper to be received will be carefully distributed as the doners [sic] may request; such articles as are intended for the sick passing through the hands of the surgeon who will be responsible for their proper use. Contributions must be received by an officer who must be held responsible that they are delivered to the persons for whom they are intended.

9. Visitors to these stations out of mere curiosity will in no case be permitted. Persons having business with the commanding officer or quartermaster may with the permission of the commanding officer enter the camp to remain only long enough to transact their business. When prisoners are seriously ill their nearest relatives, parents, wives, brothers or sisters if they are loyal people may be permitted to make them short visits; but under no other circumstances will visitors be allowed to see them without the approval of the commissary-general of prisoners.

10. Prisoners will not be permitted to write letters of more than one page of common letter paper, the matter to be strickly [sic] of a private nature, or the letter must be destroyed.

11. Prisoners will be paroled or released only by the authority of the War Department, or by direction of the commissary-general of prisoners.

II. Rules posted at Fort Delaware on the day after the death of Col. Edward Pope Jones. Taken from the Personal Reminiscences of the War of 1861–65 by William H. Morgan, p. 230.

Headquarters, Fort Delaware, Del., July 8, 1864.

I. Roll call at reveille and retreat.

II. Police call at 7 A.M. and 4 P.M.

III. Breakfast at 8 A.M. Dinner at 4 P.M.

IV. Sergeants in charge of prisoners will exact from them strict compliance with the above calls, which will be regularly enforced, and must promptly report to the officer in charge the number present and absent, sick, etc., and any who are guilty of insubordination or any violation of the Rules of Prison. They must also notify their men that if they do not promptly obey any order given them by a sentinel, officer or man in charge of them, they will be shot.

V. Sergeants in charge will be held responsible for the due execution of these Rules, and for the regular accounting for the full number of their men.

III. Preamble and Constitution of the Christian Association at Fort Delaware as taken from United States Bonds by the Rev. I.W.K. Handy, pp. 625–628.

We, the undersigned, members of the different branches of the Christian Church, impressed with the importance of association in our efforts to promote the cause of Christian benevolence in the relief of the wants, spiritual, moral, intellectual and physical, of prisoners, whether civil, political or military in our own or other lands, in humble reliance upon the Divine blessing for success, do agree to and adopt the following Constitution:

Art. I. This society shall be known as the "Confederate States Christian Association for the Relief of Prisoners."

Art. II. In the event of the subsequent formation of a National Association with the same objects, this Association shall be subordinate thereto.

Art. III. The objects of the Association shall be to alleviate the sufferings and supply the wants of Prisoners, military or political, whether in the "United States," "Confederate," or other national prisons, and of civil prisoners wherever confined.

Art. IV. The officers of this Association shall be a President, three Vice Presidents, Corresponding Secretary, Recording Secretary, Treasurer, and Librarian, who shall be elected by ballot at the last regular meeting in March, June, September, and December, a majority of the votes cast being necessary for a choice. They shall hold office for three months.

Art. V. It shall be the duty of the President to preside at all meetings of the Association, and to enforce all parliamentary rules and usage observed by deliberative bodies, so far as applicable to our present organization.

Art. VI. The Senior Vice-President present, shall, in the absence, removal, or death of the president, be the presiding officer. All vacancies other than the Presidency and Vice-Presidency, shall be filled by appointment of the presiding officer.

Art. VII. All standing committees shall be appointed by the President, and shall act as such during the term in which they are appointed. The following standing committees of seven (7) each shall be appointed at the first regular meeting of each term, viz: "Divine Worship," "Sick and destitute," "Procuring and Distributing Religious Reading," "Order and Arrangement," "Education," "State of the Church," "Finance," and "Introduction."

Art. VIII. It shall be the duty of the Recording Secretary to enroll the names of the members, keep a correct minute of all the transactions of the Society, and to receive all literary contributions, and with the approval of the Committee on Education, read them at the ensuing meeting.

Art. IX. It shall be the duty of the Treasurer to receive all moneys, and disburse them only upon the order of the Finance Committee.

Art. X. It shall be the duty of the Finance Committee to examine all bills and requisitions for money for the purchase of articles for the use of the Society; and it shall be the further duty of said Committee to collect all contributions and hand them over to the Treasurer.

Art. XI. There shall be an active membership during imprisonment, associate, life, and honorary membership of this Society. The profession of a saving grace in Christ shall be the only condition of active membership — any person of good moral character, desirous of using his influence on the side of religion and morality, may become an associate member — any member of the Evangelical Church may become a life member upon the payment of $2.00 in coin, or its equivalent in currency. Honorary members shall be elected by the Association, not exceeding two (2) at any meeting.

Art. XII. Any active member of this Association shall be eligible to any office of the Association, but no person shall be elected to fill the office of President for two consecutive terms. The honorary and associate members shall not be eligible to any office of the Association; nor shall they be entitled to vote upon any subject. They may address the Association upon any subject before the body for deliberation.

Art. XIII. There shall be constituted a Board of Directors, consisting of Quarterly, Annual and Life Directors.

> Sec. 1. Any person professing a saving faith in Christ may be constituted a Quarterly Director upon payment of $1.00 in coin, or its equivalent in currency; an Annual Director upon payment of $2.00; and a Life Director upon the payment of $10.00 in coin, or its equivalent in currency.

> Sec. 2. The President of the Association shall be "ex-off." Chairman of the Board of Directors; and may convene them whenever in his judgment the interests of the Association demand it.

> Sec. 3. The Directors (five to constitute a quorum) shall constitute a Board of Publication, to whom shall be referred all articles or works for the Press.

Art. XIV. Life Directors and Life Members in the several States shall be authorized, in the absence of any State organizations in their respective States, to receive contributions, make collections, and in every way promote the general welfare of the Association; the sums so collected to be paid over to the Treasurer selected from their own body — the Treasurer to receipt for such moneys and to pay them over to the Treasurer of the Association or disburse them at its order; or to organize Associations, State or National, for the promotion of the objects of this Society, in which event the moneys collected shall be employed for the benefit thereof.

Art. XV. No member shall be allowed to speak more than twice upon the same subject without the permission of the presiding officer, nor more than three times without the consent of a majority of the Association present.

Art. XVI. Any one member may demand the ayes and noes upon any question before the Society; and upon such demand each member shall vote "aye" or "no" as his name is called by the Secretary.

IV. Excerpts from General Orders No. 100 — Instructions for the government of armies of the United States in the field. Dated April 24, 1863, by order of the Secretary of War and approved by President Lincoln. From the Official Records of the Civil War, Series II, Vol. 5, pp. 674–680.

Section III.—Prisoners of War

49. A prisoner of war is a public enemy armed or attached to the hostile army for active aid who has fallen into the hands of the captor either fighting or wounded on

the field or in the hospital by individual surrender or by capitulation. All soldiers of whatever species of arms; all men who belong to the rising en masse of the hostile country; all those who are attached to the army for its efficiency and promote directly the object of the war except such as are hereinafter provided for; all disabled men or officers on the field or elsewhere if captured; all enemies who have thrown away their arms and ask for quarter are prisoners of war and as such exposed to the inconveniences as well as entitled to the privileges of a prisoner of war.

50. Moreover citizens who accompany as army for whatever purpose, such as sutlers, editors or reporters of journals or contractors, if captured may be made prisoners of war and detained as such. The monarch and members of the hostile reigning family, male or female, the chief and chief officers of the hostile Government, its diplomatic agents and all persons who are of particular and singular use and benefit to the hostile army or its Government are if captured on belligerent ground and if unprovided with a safe-conduct granted by the captor's Government prisoners of war.

53. The enemy's chaplains, officers of the medical staff, apothecaries, hospital nurses and servants if they fall into the hands of the American Army are not prisoners of war unless the commander has reasons to retain them. In this latter case or if at their own desire they are allowed to remain with their captured companions they are treated as prisoners of war and may be exchanged if the commander sees fit.

56. A prisoner of war is subject to no punishment for being a public enemy nor is any revenge wreaked upon him by the intentional infliction of any suffering or disgrace, by cruel imprisonment, want of food, by mutilation, death or any other barbarity.

57. So soon as a man is armed by a sovereign Government and takes the soldier's oath of fidelity he is a belligerent; his killing, wounding or other warlike acts are no individual crimes or offenses. No belligerent has a right to declare that enemies of a certain class, color or condition when properly organized as soldiers will not be treated by him as public enemies.

59. A prisoner of war remains answerable for his crimes committed against the captor's army or people committed before he was captured and for which he has not been punished by his own authorities. All prisoners of war are liable to the infliction of retaliatory measures.

72. Money and other valuables on the person of a prisoner, such as watches or jewelry as well as extra clothing, are regarded by the American Army as the private property of the prisoner and the appropriation of such valuables or money is considered dishonorable and is prohibited. Nevertheless if large sums are found upon the persons of prisoners or in their possession they shall be taken from them and the surplus after providing for their own support appropriated for the use of the army under the direction of the commander, unless otherwise ordered by the Government. Nor can prisoners claim as private property large sums found and captured in their train although they had been placed in the private luggage of the prisoners.

73. All officers when captured must surrender their side-arms to the captors. They

may be restored to the prisoner in marked cases by the commander to signalize admiration of his distinguished bravery or approbation of his humane treatment of prisoners before his capture. The captured officer to whom they may be restored cannot wear them during captivity.

74. A prisoner of war being a public enemy is the prisoner of the Government and not of the captor. No ransom can be paid by a prisoner of war to his individual captor or to any officer in command. The Government alone releases captives according to rules prescribed by itself.

75. Prisoners of war are subject to confinement or imprisonment such as may be deemed necessary on account of safety, but they are to be subjected to no other intentional suffering or indignity. The confinement and mode of treating a prisoner may be varied during his captivity, according to the demands of safety.

76. Prisoners of war shall be fed upon plain and wholesome food whenever practicable and treated with humanity. They may be required to work for the benefit of the captor's government according to their rank and condition.

77. A prisoner of war who escapes may be shot or otherwise killed in his flight; but neither death nor any other punishment shall be inflicted upon him simply for his attempt to escape which the law of war does not consider a crime. Stricter means of security shall be used after an unsuccessful attempt at escape.

78. If prisoners of war having given no pledge nor made any promise on their honor forcibly or otherwise escape and are captured again in battle after [having] rejoined their own army they shall not be punished for their escape, but shall be treated as simple prisoners of war although they will be subjected to stricter confinement.

79. Every captured wounded enemy shall be medically treated according to the ability of the medical staff.

80. Honorable men when captured will abstain from giving to the enemy information concerning their own army, and the modern law of war permits no longer the use of any violence against prisoners in order to extort the desired information or to punish them for having given false information.

SECTION VI. EXCHANGE OF PRISONERS—FLAGS OF TRUCE—FLAGS OF PROTECTION.

105. Exchanges of prisoners take place number for number, rank for rank, wounded for wounded, with added condition for added condition such for instance as not to serve for a certain period.

106. In exchanging prisoners of war such numbers of persons of inferior rank may be substituted as an equivalent for one of superior rank as may be agreed upon by cartel, which requires the sanctions of the Government or of the commander of the army in the field.

108. A prisoner of war is in honor bound truly to state to the captor his rank, and he is not to assume a lower rank than belongs to him in order to cause a more

advantageous exchange nor a higher rank for the purpose of obtaining better treatment. Offenses to the contrary have been justly punished by the commanders of released prisoners and may be good cause for refusing to release such prisoners.

109. The exc,hange of prisoners of war is an act of convenience to both belligerents. If no general cartel has been concluded it cannot be demanded by either of them. No belligerent is obliged to exchange prisoners of war. A cartel is voidable so soon as either party has violated it.

Section VII. The Parole

119. Prisoners of war may be released from captivity by exchange and under certain circumstances also by parole.

120. The term parole designates the pledge of individual good faith and honor to do or to omit doing certain acts after he who gives his parole shall have been dismissed wholly or partially from the power of the captor.

121. The pledge of the parole is always an individual but not a private act.

122. The parole applies chiefly to prisoners of war whom the captor allows to return to their country or to live in greater freedom within the captor's country or territory on conditions stated in the parole.

123. Release of prisoners of war by exchange is the general rule; release by parole is the exception.

124. Breaking the parole is punished with death when the person breaking the parole is captured again. Accurate lists, therefore, of the paroled persons must be kept by the belligerents.

125. When paroles are given and received there must be an exchange of two written documents in which the name and rank of the paroled individuals are accurately and truthfully stated.

126. Commissioned officers only are allowed to give their parole and they can give it only with the permission of their superior as long as a superior in rank is within reach.

127. No non-commissioned officer or private can give their parole except through an officer. Individual paroles not given through an officer are not only void but subject the individual giving them to the punishment of death as deserters. The only admissible exception is where individuals properly separated from their commands have suffered long confinement without the possibility of being paroled through an officer.

128. No paroling on the battle-field; no paroling of entire bodies of troops after a battle; and no dismissal of large numbers of prisoners with a general declaration that they are paroled is permitted or of any value.

129. In capitualtions for the surrender of strong places or fortified camps the com-

manding officer in cases of urgent necessity may agree that the troops under his command shall not fight again during the war unless exchanged.

130. The usual pledge given in the parole is not to serve during the existing war unless exchanged. This pledge refers only to the active service in the field against the paroling belligerent or his allies actively engaged in the same war. These cases of breaking the parole are patent acts and can be visited with the punishment of death; but the pledge does not refer to internal service such as recruiting or drilling the recruits, fortifying places not besieged, quelling civil commotions, fighting against belligerents unconnected with the paroling belligerents or to civil or diplomatic service for which the paroled officer may be employed.

131. If the Government does not approve of the parole the paroled officer must return into captivity, and should the enemy refuse to receive him he is free of his parole.

132. A belligerent Government may declare by a general order whether it will allow paroling and on what conditions it will allow it. Such order is communicated to the enemy.

133. No prisoner of war can be forced by the hostile Government to parole himself, and no Government is obliged to parole prisoners of war or to parole all captured officers if it paroles any. As the pledging of the parole is an individual act so is paroling on the other hand an act of choice on the part of the belligerent.

134. The commander of an occupying army may require of the civil officers of the enemy and of its citizens any pledge he may consider necessary for the safety or security of his army and upon their failure to give it he may arrest, confine or detain them.

V. General Orders No.11, dated July 10, 1863, concerning clothing for the prisoners. From the Official Records, Series II, Vol. 6, p. 98.

Issues of clothing to prisoners of war by the quartermaster at stations where they are confined will be made with the assistance and under the supervision of an officer detailed for the purpose, whose certificate that the issue was made in his presence will be the quartermaster's voucher for the clothing issued. From the 30th of April to the 1st of October neither drawers nor socks will be issued to prisoners of war, except to the sick. (General Orders, War Department, June 17, 1862, and circular of Commissary-General of Prisoners, July 7, 1863.)

Issues of clothing to prisoners of war will be made only at stations where such prisoners are held, unless specially ordered by the general commanding an army in the field, in which case the provisions of the foregoing paragraph must be complied with.

VI. Special Orders No.165, dated September 3, 1863, concerning visitors to Fort Delaware. From the Official Records, Series II, Vol. 6, p. 291.

I. Visiting this post out of curiosity is strictly prohibited. Relatives of prisoners seriously ill will be allowed to make them short visits on written application, accompanied with satisfactory proof of their loyalty to the United States Government, to

Brigadier-General Schoepf, commanding post. Under no circumstances will any person be allowed to visit the prisoners without special permission from the Secretary of War or Commissary-General of Prisoners.

II. All contributions to prisoners must be forwarded to this post by express, and plainly directed, giving name, rank, and regiment, in care of Capt. G.W. Ahl, commissary of prisoners. Coats and pants of a gray, drab, or blue color will not be given to prisoners.

Notes

1. Construction of Fort Delaware

1. Reginald Horsman, *The Causes of the War of 1812* (New York: Octagon Books, 1962), pp. 16–20.

2. Ruthanna Hindes, ed., *Fort Delaware Notes*, extracts from a manuscript by Alexander B. Cooper (Wilmington: Fort Delaware Society, 1958), p. 1.

3. W. Emerson Wilson, *Fort Delaware* (Newark: University of Delaware Press, 1957), p. 6.

4. The Federal Writers' Project of the W.P.A., *Stories of New Jersey: A Confederate Shrine in New Jersey* (1937), p. 1.

5. *Salem Sunbeam*, Vol. #2, no.11, p. 1.

6. Surgeon W.C. Spencer, *U.S. Army, Circular #4* (U.S.A.: Surgeon General's Office, 1870), p. 1.

7. *Coast Defense Study Group Journal* (November 1995), p. 33.

8. Wilson, *Fort Delaware*, p. 6.

9. *Coast Study*, p. 33, *Philadelphia Forum* (October 1950), p. 8.

10. *Coast Study*, pp. 35–36.

11. J.C.A. Stagg, *Mr. Madison's War: Politics, Diplomacy, and Warfare in the Early American Republic, 1783–1830* (Princeton: Princeton University Press, 1983), p. 410–411, 424–425.

12. *Coast Study*, pp. 36–37.

13. Wilson, *Fort Delaware*, p. 6.

14. Phyllis O. Whitten, ed., *Samuel Fogg 1628–1672: His Ancestors and Decendants*, Vol. 2, Appendix R (Columbia Planograph Co., 1976), p. 1.

15. Frank E. Snyder and Brian H. Guss, *The District: A History of the Philadelphia District U.S. Army Corps of Engineers 1866–1971* (Philadelphia: U.S. Army Engineer District, 1974), p. 46.

16. Ashley Halsey, Jr., *Who Fired the First Shot? And Other Untold Stories of the Civil War* (New York: Hawthorn Books, 1963), p. 144.

17. Wilson, *Fort Delaware*, p. 6.

18. Hindes, p. 1.

19. Snyder and Guss, p. 46.

20. Opinion of Garret D. Wall, *Brief of title: Pea Patch Island*, copy in Fort Delaware Society Library, p. 7.

21. *Ibid.*, p. 15.

22. Snyder and Guss, p. 46.

23. W. Emerson Wilson, *The Story of Fort Delaware*, ed. by William P. Frank, (Wilmington: Wilmington Printing Co., 1955), p. 1.

24. Snyder and Guss, p. 47.

25. James St. Clair Morton, *Memoir of the Life and Service of Captain and Brevet Major John Sanders of the Corps of Engineers, U.S. Army* (U.S.A.: W.S. Haven, 1861), p. 7.

26. Snyder and Guss, p. 47.

27. Wilson, *The Story of Fort Delaware*, p. 1.

28. Snyder and Guss, pp. 47–48.

29. Morton, p. 43.

30. Snyder and Guss, p. 48–49.

31. *Today's Sunbeam*, April 23, 1989, p. A-1.

32. Snyder and Guss, pp. 51–52.

33. *Fort Delaware Notes*, extracts from John Sanders' memoirs (Wilmington: Fort Delaware Society, January 1962), p. 1.

34. Stephen W. Sears, *George B. McClellan: The Young Napoleon* (New York: Ticknor and Fields, 1988), p. 32.

35. Snyder and Guss, p. 54.

36. Wilson, *Fort Delaware*, p. 8.

37. Snyder and Guss, p. 54.

38. Michael J. Varhola, *Everyday Life during the Civil War* (Cincinnati: Writer's Digest Books, 1999), p. 42.

39. Snyder and Guss, pp. 54–55.

40. Wilson, *Fort Delaware*, p. 8.

41. Snyder and Guss, p. 57.

42. Wilson, *Fort Delaware*, p. 8; Edward Pinkowski, *Pills, Pen, and Politics: The Story of General Leon Jastremski, 1843–1907* (Wilmington: Captain Stanislaus Mlotkowski Memorial Brigade Society, 1974), pp. 49–50.

43. *Today's Sunbeam*, Sunday, April 23, 1989, p. A-8.

2. From One Extreme to Another

1. W. Emerson Wilson, *Fort Delaware Notes* (Wilmington: Fort Delaware Society, January 1961), p. 1; James M. McPherson, *Battle Cry of Freedom* (New York: Oxford University Press, 1988), p. 264.

2. Russell A. Alger, Secretary of War and Director of Book Written by Col. Fred C. Ainsworth U.S.A., Leslie J. Perry, and Joseph W. Kirkley (Civilian Experts), *The War of the Rebellion: A Compilation of the Official Records of the Union and Confederate Armies*, Series I, Vol. 1 (Washington, D.C.: Government Printing Office, 1899), p. 225. (Known hereafter as "*O.R.*")

3. Wilson, *Fort Delaware Notes*, January 1961, p. 1; McPherson, p. 264.

4. Harold Bell Hancock, *Delaware During the Civil War: A Political History* (Wilmington: The Historical Society of Delaware, 1961), pp. 18, 50–51, 56–57.

5. Pinkowski, p. 50.

6. McPherson, p. 274.

7. *Ibid.*, p. 276.

8. J.G. Randall and David Donald, *The Civil War and Reconstruction* (Lexington: D.C. Heath and Co., 1969), pp. 233–234.

9. Snyder and Guss, p. 59.

10. *Today's Sunbeam*, July 24, 1986, p. A-3.

11. Wilson, *Fort Delaware*, p. 9.

12. Snyder and Guss, p. 59–60.

13. Marc McCutcheon, *The Writer's Guide to Everyday Life in the 1800's* (Cincinnati: Writer's Digest Books, 1993), p. 227.

14. Snyder and Guss, p. 59–60.

15. *Sampler*, Wednesday, April 2, 1986.

16. Wilson, *Fort Delaware*, p. 9.

17. Pinkowski, p. 50.

18. *Wilmington* [Del.] *Morning News*, Thursday, May 31, 1956, p. 6.

19. *O.R.*, Series I, Vol. 9, pp. 19–20.

20. McPherson, p. 425.

21. *Today's Sunbeam*, Sunday, April 23, 1989, p. A-8.

22. *Today's Sunbeam*, Tuesday, June 4, 1985, p. A-3.

23. Robert E. Denny, *Civil War Prisons and Escapes: A Day by Day Chronicle* (New York: Sterling Pub. Co., 1993), pp. 378–379.

24. *Ibid.*, p. 380.

25. *Ibid.*, pp. 375–376.

26. Kenneth C. Davis, *Don't Know Much About the Civil War* (New York: W. Morrow and Co., 1996), p. 348.

27. Wilson, *The Story of Fort Delaware*, p. 2.

28. *Courier Post*, Sunday, September 25, 1988, p. 1.

29. *Salem Sunbeam*, Friday, October 2, 1925, p. 1.

30. *O.R.*, Series II, Vol. 3 pp. 384–385.

31. *Ibid.*, p. 417.

32. *Ibid.*, pp. 449, 458.

33. *Ibid.*, p. 677.

34. *Wilmington Morning News*, Thursday, May 31, 1956, p. 6.

35. *O.R.*, Series II, Vol. 4, p. 23.

36. Copy of a letter to President Lincoln, June 23, 1862, at Fort Delaware Society.

37. *O.R.*, Series II, Vol. 4, p. 120.

38. Pinkowski, p. 51.

39. *O.R.*, Series II, Vol.4, pp. 152–153.

40. *Ibid.*, pp. 225–227, 237.

41. *Wilmington Morning News*, Thursday, May 31, 1956, p. 6.

42. *O.R.*, Series II, Vol. 4, pp. 292–294, 302–303.

43. A.J. Hamilton, *A Fort Delaware Journal: The Diary of a Yankee Private 1862–65*, ed. by W. Emerson Wilson (Wilmington: Fort Delaware Society, 1981), p. 8.

44. *O.R.*, Series II, Vol. 4, p. 365.

45. *Wilmington Morning News*, Thursday, May 31, 1956, p. 6.

46. Hamilton, p. 9; *O.R.*, Series II, Vol. 4, pp. 502.

47. Hamilton, p. 9.

48. *O.R.*, Series II, Vol. 4, p. 365.

49. *Wilmington Morning News*, Thursday, May 31, 1956, p. 6.

3. Exchanges and the Writ of Habeas Corpus

1. *O.R.*, Series II, Vol. 4, p. 567.
2. Davis, pp. 180–181.
3. McPherson, p. 288.
4. E.B. Long with Barbara Long, *The Civil War Day by Day: An Almanac 1861–1865* (Garden City: Doubleday and Co., 1971), pp. 79, 90, 127.
5. Benjamin P. Thomas and Harold M. Hyman, *Stanton: The Life and Times of Lincoln's Secretary of War* (New York: Alfred A. Knoff, 1962), pp. 157–158.
6. John J. Marshall, *American Bastille: A History of the Illegal Arrests and Imprisonment of American Citizens during the Late Civil War* (1869; reprint, New York: Da Capo Press, 1970), pp. 428–429.
7. *Ibid.*, pp. 207–209.
8. *O.R.*, Series II, Vol. 4, p. 566.
9. Marshall, p. 210.
10. *O.R.*, Series II, Vol. 4, p. 662.
11. Marshall, pp. 211, 439.
12. *Ibid.*, pp. 509, 526, 528.
13. *Ibid.*, pp. 168–172.
14. William B. Vanneman, "Golden Days," clipping from the Salem County Historical Society, p. 4.
15. Marshall, p. 211.
16. Isaac W.K. Handy, D.D., *United States Bonds; or Duress by Federal Authority: A Journal of Current Events During an Imprisonment of Fifteen Months, At Fort Delaware* (Baltimore: Turnbull Bros., 1874,) pp. 1–17.
17. Handy, pp. 625, 631; Henry C. Dickinson, *The Diary of Henry C. Dickinson C.S.A.*, copy at Fort Delaware Society, pp. 48–49.
18. Hancock, p. 132.
19. Matthew Page Andrews, ed., *The Women of the South in War Times* (Baltimore: The Norman Remington Co., 1920), pp. 40–41, 43–44, 47–49, 52.
20. William Best Hesseltine, *Civil War Prisons: A Study in War Psychlogy* (New York: Frederick Ungar Pub. Co., 1930), pp. 76–81.
21. McPherson, p. 792.
22. *Ulysses S. Grant: Memoirs and Selected Letters*, ed. by Mary and William McFeely, (New York: The Library of America, 1990), pp. 1048–1049.
23. *Ibid.*, p. 1066.

4. The Growth of the Prison Population

1. Hamilton, p. 15.
2. George Baylor, *Bull Run to Bull Run or Four Years in the Army of Northern Virginia (Containing a Detailed Account of the Career and Adventures of the Baylor Light Horse, Co. B, 12th Virginia Cavalry, C.S.A., with Leaves from My Scrapbook)* (1900; reprint, Washington, D.C.: Zenger Pub., Co., 1983), p. 104.
3. Hamilton, p. 16.
4. *O.R.*, Series II, Vol. 5, pp. 216–217.
5. *Ibid.* pp. 220–221.
6. Wilson, *Fort Delaware*, p. 14.
7. Hamilton, p. 21.
8. *O.R.*, Series II, Vol. 5, p. 421.
9. Baylor, pp. 100–102, 114, 408.
10. *O.R.*, Series II, Vol. 5, p. 421.
11. *Ibid*, pp. 422, 425.
12. Hamilton, pp. 25–26.
13. *O.R.*, Series II, Vol. 5, pp. 425–426.
14. Hamilton, p. 25.
15. Nancy Scott Anderson and Dwight Anderson, *The Generals: Ulysses S. Grant and Robert E. Lee* (New York: Alfred A. Knopf, 1988), pp. 121–122.
16. *O.R.*, Series II, Vol. 5, p. 457.
17. *Ibid.* pp. 467, 492–493.
18. *Ibid.* pp. 465.
19. *Ibid.* pp. 477–478.
20. *Ibid.* p. 487.
21. Decimus et Ultimus Bargiza, *The Adventures of a Prisoner of War 1863–1864*, ed. by R. Henderson Shuffler (Austin: University of Texas Press, 1988), p. 88.
22. Charles Chaille-Long, *My Life in Four Continents*, pp. 9–10.
23. Bargiza, p. 88.
24. Chaille-Long, p. 10.
25. Bargiza, p. 88.
26. *O.R.*, Series II, Vol. 5, p. 538.
27. *Ibid.* p. 484.
28. *Ibid.* pp. 501–502.
29. *Ibid.* p. 618.
30. Hamilton, p. 28; *O.R.*, Series II, Vol. 5, p. 688.
31. *O.R.*, Series II, Vol. 5, p. 760.
32. *Ibid.* p. 767.
33. Hamilton, p. 31; *O.R.*, Series II, Vol. 5, p. 771.
34. *O.R.*, Series II, Vol. 6, p. 20.
35. Hamilton, p. 31.
36. Hamilton, p. 29; *O.R.*, Series II, Vol. 6, p. 116.
37. Hamilton, pp. 31–33.
38. *O.R.*, Series II, Vol. 6, pp. 80–81.
39. *O.R.*, Series II, Vol. 6, p. 104; Spencer, p. 2.
40. *O.R.*, Series II, Vol. 6, p. 92.
41. Hamilton, pp. 33–34.
42. Hancock, pp. 134–135.
43. Hamilton, p. 34.
44. *O.R.*, Series II, Vol. 6, pp. 88, 105–106.
45. *Ibid.* p. 181.

46. *Ibid.* pp. 215–216.
47. *Ibid.* p. 228.
48. *Ibid.* p. 235.

5. Life on the Devil's Half Acre

1. Randolph Shotwell, *The Papers of Randolph Abbott Shotwell*, Vol. II, ed. by J.E. DeRoulhas Hamilton and Rebecca Cameron (Raleigh: The North Carolina Historical Commission, 1931), pp. 131–132.

2. Henry C. Dickinson, *The Diary of Capt. Henry C. Dickinson, C.S.A.*, copy at Fort Delaware Society Library, p. 43.

3. Shotwell, p. 132.
4. Dickinson, p. 44.
5. Shotwell, p. 133.

6. Capt. James N. Bosang, *Memoirs of a Pulaski Veteran of the Stonewall Brigade, 1861–1865* (Pulaski: 1912), p. 19.

7. Shotwell, pp. 132–135.
8. Pinkowski, p. 58.
9. Dickinson, p. 38.
10. Shotwell, pp. 134–135.
11. Dickinson, pp. 44–45.
12. Shotwell, pp. 135, 138.
13. Rivenbark, p. 726.
14. Shotwell, pp. 138–139.

15. J. Ogden Murray, *The Immortal Six Hundred: A Story of Cruelty to Confederate Prisoners of War* (Winchester, Va.: The Eddy Press Corp., 1905), p. 56.

16. Rivenbark, p. 727.

17. William H. Morgan, *Personal Reminiscences of the War of 1861–5* (1911; reprint, Freeport: Books for Libraries Press, 1971), p. 226.

18. Dickinson, p. 41.
19. Shotwell, p. 140.
20. Pinkowski, p. 58.
21. Dickinson, p. 42.
22. Shotwell, pp. 177–179.
23. *Ibid.* p. 141.
24. *Ibid.* p. 136.
25. *Ibid.* p. 160.
26. *Ibid.* pp. 137–138.
27. Rivenbark, p. 725.
28. *O.R.*, Series II, Vol. 6, pp. 235–236.
29. *Ibid.* pp. 244–245.
30. *Ibid.* p. 281.
31. *Ibid.* pp. 290–291.
32. Dickinson, pp. 45–46.
33. *O.R.*, Series II, Vol. 6, pp. 291–292.
34. *Ibid.* pp. 309–310.
35. *Ibid.* p. 359.

36. Stewart Brooks, *Civil War Medicine* (Springfield: Charles C. Thomas Pub., 1966), p. 120.

37. *O.R.*, Series II, Vol. 6, p. 422.
38. *Ibid.* pp. 435, 440.
39. *Ibid.* pp. 476–477.
40. *Ibid.* p. 494.
41. *Ibid.* pp. 516–518.

6. Hope and Survival on the Devil's Half Acre

1. Handy, pp. 443, 457.
2. Hamilton, p. 39.
3. Shotwell, pp. 149–150.
4. Rivenbark, p. 728.
5. Hamilton, p. 39.
6. Shotwell, p. 142.
7. Dickinson, p. 50.

8. Yankee Rebel: *The Civil War Journal of Edmund De Witt Patterson*, ed. by John G. Barrett (Chapel Hill: The University of North Carolina Press, 1966), p. 121.

9. Handy, p. 440.
10. Dickinson, pp. 49–50.
11. Shotwell, pp. 142–143.
12. Hamilton, pp. 40–41.
13. Rivenbark, p. 731.

14. C. Jeanenne Bell, G.G., *The Antique and Collectable Jewelry Video Series* [Vol.1] *Victorian Jewelry Circa 1837–1901* (Antique Images, Inc., 1994).

15. Dickinson, p. 49.
16. Shotwell, p. 143.

17. James L. McCown, *Memoirs of James L. McCown, Co. K, 5th Virginia Infantry, Stonewall Brigade, April 2, 1864–August 4, 1864*, copy at Fort Delaware Society, p. 4.

18. Howard, p. 330.

19. Letter from Sidney Wailes, Sept. 20, 1863, p. 2, copy at Fort Delaware Society.

20. Bosang, pp. 20–21.

21. Laura Virginia Hale, *Four Valiant Years in the Lower Shenandoah Valley 1861–1865* (Strasburg, Va. Shenandoah Pub. House, 1968), p. 311.

22. Shotwell, p. 141; Michael J. Varola, *Everyday Life During the Civil War* (Cincinnati: Writer's Digest Books, 1999), p. 98.

23. *M. Jeff Thompson in Fort Delaware*, ed. by W. Emerson Wilson (Wilmington: Fort Delaware Society, 1972), pp. 8–10.

24. Howard, pp. 306–307.

25. C. Brian Kelly and Ingrid Sayer-Kelly, *Best Little Stories from the Civil War* (Nashville: Cumberland House, 1994), p. 17.

26. Shotwell, p. 143.

27. T.H. Bowen, *The Way It Used to Be*, Vol. 3 (Salem: Salem County Cultural and Heritage Commission, 1977) p. 36.

28. Basil Duke, *Reminiscences of Gen. Basil W. Duke, C.S.A.* (1911; reprint, Freeport: Books for Libraries Press, 1969), p. 370.

29. *Salem Sampler*, April 2, 1986, p. 27; Handy, p. 482.

30. J. Stephen Lang, *The Complete Book of Confederate Trivia* (U.S.A.: Burd Street Press, 1996), p. 349.

31. Handy, pp. 148, 446.

32. Howard, p. 316.

33. *The Collected Works of Abraham Lincoln*, Vol. VI, ed. by Roy P. Basler (New Brunswick: Rutgers University Press, 1955), pp. 422, 452.

34. *Ibid.* Vol. VII, pp. 89, 309.

35. Seth Hinshaw, *Mary Barker Hinshaw, Quaker*, copy at Fort Delaware Society Library, pp. 81–89.

36. Shotwell, p. 145.

37. Dickinson, p. 52.

38. The Diagram Group, *The Little Giant Encyclopedia of Card Games* (New York: Sterling Pub. Co., 1995), p. 164.

39. Dickinson, p. 52.

40. Shotwell, p. 144.

41. Dickinson, p. 52.

42. Bell Irwin Wiley, *The Life of Johnny Reb: The Common Soldier of the Confederacy* (New York: The Bobbs-Merrill Co., Pub., 1943), pp. 36–37.

43. Varhola, p. 98.

44. Wiley, p. 17.

45. Duke, p. 371.

46. Shotwell, p. 144.

47. Dickinson, pp. 51–52.

48. Shotwell, p. 144.

49. Handy, p. 439.

50. Duke, pp. 372–374.

51. Handy, pp. 14–15.

52. Howard, p. 329.

53. Handy, pp. 149–150.

54. Shotwell, pp. 152–154.

55. Handy, pp. 448–449, 457–459.

56. Shotwell, p. 154.

57. Handy, p. 467.

58. McCown, p. 5.

59. Dickinson, p. 45.

60. Murray, p. 59.

61. Varhola, p. 100.

62. Handy, pp. 350–351.

63. Pinkowski, pp. 54, 58.

64. *Salem Sunbeam*, Friday, Oct. 2, 1925, Vol. 82, No. 11, p. 1.

65. Pinkowski, p. 55.

66. Dickinson, pp. 53–54, 57.

67. Halsey, pp. 144–145.

68. Dickinson, pp. 54–56.

69. Rivenbark, pp. 729–730.

70. *Fort Delaware Notes*, December 1954, pp. 1, 3.

71. Hamilton, pp. 36–37.

72. *Salem Standard and Jerseyman*, Thurs., June 25, 1953, p. 2.

73. Spencer, p. 3.

74. *Standard and Jerseyman*, p. 2.

75. Alden T. Cottrell, April 12, 1964, newspaper clipping from the Salem County Historical Society.

76. Rivenbark, p. 730.

77. Bowen, p. 36.

78. *Salem Sunbeam*, Oct. 2, 1925, p. 1.

79. *Standard and Jerseyman*, p. 2.

80. Rivenbark, p. 730.

81. Hamilton, p. 42.

82. Rivenbark, p. 729.

83. Dickinson, p. 56, 58.

84. *O.R.*, Series II, Vol. 6, p. 292.

85. Baylor, pp. 98–100, 104–106.

86. Handy, pp. 348, 354.

87. Sally Salem, *Sunbeam*, June 2, 1977, clipping from the Salem County Historical Society.

88. Handy, p. 435; Capt. J.R. McMichael, *Diary 1864–65*, unpublished manuscript from Fort Delaware Society Library, p. 2.

89. Bosang, pp. 10–11, 13.

90. *O.R.*, Series II, Vol. 6, p. 291.

91. Howard, p. 316.

92. Handy, pp. 18, 438.

93. McCown, p. 5.

94. Handy, pp. 447–448, 462.

7. Difference of Opinion — The Other Side of the Dead

1. *O.R.*, Series II, Vol. 6, pp. 651–653.

2. Handy, p. 18.

3. Shotwell, p. 136.

4. Handy, pp. 151–152.

5. *O.R.*, Series II, Vol. 6, pp. 703, 706, 716, 825, 1000–1001.

6. Letter in Fort Delaware Society, August 24, 1863.

7. Chaille-Long, pp. 11–12.

8. Norman B. Wilkinson, *The Brandywine Home Front During the Civil War 1861–1865* (Wilmington, Del.: Kaumagraph Co., 1966), p. 95.

9. Hamilton, pp. 33, 36.

10. Handy, pp. 149–150.

11. Lang, pp. 353–354.

12. Howard, p. 449.

13. Dickinson, p. 16.

14. *Lincoln*, Vol. VIII, p. 325.

15. Henry Hall Brogden, *An Account of His Experiences During the War*, copy at Salem County Historical Society, pp. 1–5.

16. *Lincoln*, Vol. VIII, p. 325.

17. Brogden, pp. 6–7.

18. Howard, p. 308.
19. Handy, p. 364.
20. Howard, p. 309.
21. Handy, p. 366.
22. Howard, p. 309.
23. Hamilton, p. 83.
24. Howard, p. 450.
25. Shotwell, p. 169.
26. *Ibid.* p. 193.
27. Howard, p. 450.
28. Murray, p. 58.
29. Dickinson, p. 47.
30. Murray, p. 59.
31. Dickinson, p. 39.
32. Shotwell, p. 159.
33. Riverbark, p. 727.
34. Dickinson, p. 47.
35. Rivenbark, pp. 728–729.
36. Shotwell, pp. 149–151.
37. Lang, pp. 345–346.
38. Pinkowski, p. 59.
39. Dickinson, p. 58.
40. Baylor, pp. 109–110.
41. Pinkowski, p. 55.
42. Howard, p. 317.
43. Hamilton, pp. 37, 43, 45.
44. Handy, pp. 349–350, 359–360, 372.
45. *O.R.*, Series II, Vol. 6, p. 954.
46. *Thompson in Fort Delaware*, pp. 6, 8–9.
47. Howard, p. 308.
48. *Fort Delaware Notes* (Wilmington: Fort Delaware Society, Dec. 1958), p. 2.
49. *O.R.*, Series II, Vol. 6, pp. 1014–1015.
50. *Ibid.* pp. 1039–1041.
51. Howard, p. 349.
52. Hamilton, pp. 50, 52.
53. Handy, p. 355.
54. *O.R.*, Series II, Vol. 6, pp. 1033, 1073, 1076, 1079.
55. Handy, pp. 356–357, 361–362, 368.
56. Hamilton, p. 53.
57. Handy, p. 368.
58. *O.R.*, Series II, Vol. 7, pp. 90, 92–93.
59. Howard, pp. 316–317, 319.
60. Hamilton, p. 55.
61. McCown, p. 4.
62. Rivenbark, p. 727.
63. U.S. Sanitary Commission, *A Narrative of Privations and Sufferings of the U.S. Officers and Soldiers While Prisoners of War in the South and the Treatment of Rebel Prisoners in the North* (1864), pp. 215–216.
64. *O.R.*, Series II, Vol. 7, pp. 187, 394.
65. Handy, pp. 435–436.
66. *O.R.*, Series II, Vol. 7, p. 187.
67. Hamilton, p. 54.
68. Howard, p. 318.
69. Hamilton, p. 54.
70. *O.R.*, Series II, Vol. 7, pp. 379, 421–422, 439.

71. Varhola, p. 100.
72. *O.R.*, Series II, Vol. 7, p. 439.
73. U.S. Sanitary Com., p. 214.
74. Handy, pp. 470–471.
75. Pinkowski, p. 55.
76. Handy, pp. 471–473.
77. Shotwell, p. 145.
78. *O.R.*, Series II, Vol. 5, p. 446.
79. Handy, p. 473.
80. Shotwell, p. 145.
81. Handy, p. 475; *O.R.*, Series II, Vol. 7, p. 453.
82. Shotwell, p. 145.
83. Howard, p. 38.
84. Handy, p. 473.
85. *O.R.*, Series II, Vol. 7, p. 453.
86. Handy, p. 475.
87. Hamilton, p. 147.
88. *O.R.* Series II, Vol. 7, pp. 452–454.
89. Dickinson, p. 64.
90. Shotwell, pp. 146–148.

8. Outside Influences

1. Davis, p. 352.
2. *New York Times*, Thursday, March 31, 1864, p. 4.
3. *New York Times*, Friday, April 22, 1864, p. 4.
4. McPherson, pp. 795–796.
5. Halsey, p. 155.
6. McPherson, p. 797.
7. Burke Davis, *The Civil War: Strange and Fascinating Facts* (New York: The Fairfox Press, 1982), p. 124.
8. McPherson, pp. 795–799.
9. *O.R.*, Series II, Vol. 7, pp. 84, 148–149.
10. *Ibid.* pp. 368–369.
11. Howard, pp. 320–322, 451.
12. *O.R.*, Series II, Vol. 7, pp. 522, 833.
13. Hamilton, p. 55.
14. *O.R.*, Series II, Vol. 7, p. 371.
15. *O.R.*, Series I, Vol. 35, p. 147.
16. Handy, pp. 454–455.
17. Duke, pp. 374–375.
18. Wilson, *Thompson in Fort Delaware*, pp. 11–12.
19. Webb Garrison, *Civil War Curiosities* (Nashville: Rutledge Hill Press, 1994), p. 64.
20. Jocelyn P. Jamison, *Fort Delaware Notes*, Vol. VLVI (Wilmington: Fort Delaware Society, Feb. 1996), pp. 23–24.
21. McCown, p. 16.
22. Reid Mitchell, *Civil War Soldiers* (New York: Penguin Books, 1988), pp. 46, 50–53.
23. Handy, p. 629.
24. Thomas B. Buell, *The Warrior Generals:*

Combat Leadership in the Civil War, (New York: Crown Pub., 1997), pp. 338–339.
25. Hamilton, p. 56.
26. *New York Times*, Tuesday, July 12, 1864, p. 1.
27. Hamilton, p. 56.
28. Handy, p. 480.
29. Hamilton, p. 56.
30. Shotwell, pp. 150–151.
31. Handy, p. 480.
32. Howard, pp. 322–324.
33. Buell, p. 340.
34. Shotwell, p. 154; Basler, Vol. 7, p. 422.
35. Shotwell, pp. 154–156.
36. Lang, p. 354.
37. Sally Salem, *Sunbeam*, June 2, 1977 (clipping from the Salem County Historical Society).
38. Federal Writers Project of the Works Progress Administration, *Delaware: A Guide to the First State* (1938), p. 330.
39. Alan Axelrod, *The Complete Idiot's Guide to the Civil War* (New York: Alpha Books, 1988), p. 253.
40. W.P.A., pp. 330–331.
41. Shotwell, pp. 157–159.
42. Hamilton, p. 57.
43. Shotwell, p. 159.
44. McCown, p. 6.
45. Shotwell, pp. 159–162.
46. Hamilton, p. 57.
47. Murray, pp. 59–61.
48. *New York Times*, Wednesday, August 10, 1864, p. 1.
49. Garrison, p. 64.
50. Shotwell, p. 164.
51. Murray, pp. 62–63.
52. Handy, p. 505.
53. Shotwell, pp. 164; Pinkowski, p. 59.
54. Pinkowski, p. 60.
55. Shotwell, p. 165.
56. Pinkowski, p. 60.
57. Hamilton, p. 57.
58. Shotwell, p. 165.
59. Hamilton, p. 58.
60. *New York Times*, Thursday, Aug. 17, 1864, p. 1.
61. Shotwell, pp. 166–167.
62. Pinkowski, pp. 60, 62.
63. *Hanging Rock Rebel*, ed. by Dan Oates (Shippenburg: Bund St. Press, 1994), p. 299.
64. Shotwell, p. 166.
65. Pinkowski, pp. 62–63.
66. Murray, pp. 64–68.
67. Hamilton, p. 58.
68. Handy, pp. 507, 515.
69. Shotwell, pp. 166–168.
70. Handy, pp. 516–517.
71. *O.R.*, Series II, Vol. 7, p. 665.
72. Handy, p. 517.
73. *O.R.*, Series II, Vol. 7, p. 686.
74. Handy, p. 517.
75. Jeffry D. Wert, *Mosby's Rangers* (New York: Simon and Schuster, 1990), pp. 197–198.
76. Handy, p. 517.
77. Oates, p. 298.
78. Handy, p. 517.
79. Oates, pp. 299–300.
80. Howard, p. 326; McPherson, p. 285.
81. Howard, pp. 326–327, 452.
82. *O.R.*, Series II, Vol. 7, p. 687.
83. Shotwell, p. 171.
84. *O.R.*, Series II, Vol. 7, pp. 809–811.
85. Shotwell, p. 171.
86. *O.R.*, Series II, Vol. 7, p. 766.
87. Shotwell, p. 173.
88. Handy, p. 560.
89. *O.R.*, Series II, Vol. 7, pp. 834, 849–850.
90. McPherson, p. 798.
91. *New York Times*, Monday, August 14, 1864, p. 1.
92. McPherson, pp. 798–799.
93. Handy, pp. 564, 574.
94. McPherson, p. 777.
95. Shotwell, p. 175; Handy, pp. 574–575.
96. Shotwell, p. 175.
97. McPherson, pp. 798–799.
98. Shotwell, pp. 175–176; Hamilton, p. 63.
99. *O.R.*, Series II, Vol. 7, p. 898.
100. Handy, pp. 584–586.
101. *O.R.*, Series II, Vol. 7, pp. 906–907, 909–910, 914–915.
102. Handy, pp. 589–591; Oates, p. 303.
103. Handy, pp. 581, 590–593; Shotwell, p. 178.
104. Oates, p. 303.
105. Shotwell, pp. 177–178; Handy, p. 591.
106. Oates, p. 303.
107. Shotwell, pp. 180–181.
108. Handy, pp. 597–599.
109. Howard, p. 329.
110. Handy, pp. 602–606.
111. Howard, pp. 328, 332–334.
112. *O.R.*, Series II, Vol. 7, p. 1058.
113. Handy, p. 358.
114. McPherson, pp. 803–804.
115. Hamilton, pp. 63–65.
116. Lee Jennings, *Fort Delaware Notes: Fort Delaware Engineer Disloyal?* (Wilmington: Fort Delaware Society, 1997), p. 18.
117. McPherson, p. 805.
118. Jennings, pp. 18–19.
119. Basler, p. 103.
120. McPherson, pp. 792–809.
121. Hamilton, p. 66.
122. Shotwell, pp. 181–182.
123. *O.R.*, Series II, Vol. 7, pp. 1174, 1187.
124. Hamilton, p. 66; Jamison, p. 27.
125. *O.R.*, Series II, Vol. 7, pp. 1252–1256.
126. Hamilton, p. 67.
127. *O.R.*, Series II, Vol. 7, p. 1297.
128. Curtis Carroll Davis, ed., *Belle Boyd in*

Camp and Prison (U.S.A.: Thomas Yoseloff Ltd., 1968), pp. 324–325.

129. Shotwell, p. 183.
130. Hamilton, p. 69.
131. Davis, pp. 325–326.
132. Hamilton, pp. 67–69.
133. Shotwell, p. 184.
134. Davis, pp. 327, 346–348.
135. Shotwell, p. 184.
136. Davis, pp. 331–334.
137. *O.R.*, Series II, Vol. 8, pp. 83–85.
138. *O.R.*, Series II, Vol. 7, pp. 1244, 1284, 1301; Vol. 8, pp. 40, 80, 114, 143.
139. Shotwell, p. 185.
140. Bruce Catton, *Never Call Retreat* (Garden City, N.Y.: Doubleday and Co., 1965), pp. 424–426.
141. Long, p. 628.

9. The End of the Line

1. Davis, pp. 349–351.
2. *South County Courier*, Dec. 1, 1988, p. 1, 3, copy at Fort Delaware Society Library.
3. Shotwell, p. 186.
4. *O.R.*, Series II, Vol. 8, p. 318.
5. Shotwell, p. 187.
6. Hamilton, p. 73.
7. *O.R.*, Series II, Vol. 8, pp. 173, 191–192, 243.
8. Hamilton, pp. 73–74.
9. *O.R.*, Series II, Vol. 8, pp. 32, 322, 369.
10. Shotwell, pp. 188–189.
11. Dickinson, pp. 62–63.
12. Shotwell, p. 192.
13. Pinkowski, pp. 74, 78.
14. Murray, pp. 182–183.
15. Morgan, pp. 251–254.
16. Murray, pp. 187, 221, 223–225.
17. W. Emerson Wilson, unpublished article at the Fort Delaware Society, pp. 1–2.
18. Murray, p. 188.
19. Varhola, p. 101.
20. Wilson (unpublished article), pp. 1–3.
21. William H. Runge, ed., *Four Years in the Confederate Artillery, The Diary of Private Henry Robinson Berkeley* (Chapel Hill: The University of North Carolina Press, 1961), p. 130.
22. Oates, p. 310.
23. *Stonewall Register*, April 1, 1865, p. 2, copy at the Fort Delaware Society Library.
24. Hamilton, pp. 76–77.
25. *Stonewall Register*, pp. 1, 3–4.
26. Berkeley, p. 132.
27. *New York Times*, April 10, 1865, p. 1.
28. Hamilton, p. 77.
29. Thomas H. Bowen, *Today's Sunbeam*, Thursday, Sept. 7, 1989, p. A-3.
30. *New York Times*, April 10, 1865, p. 1.
31. Oates, pp. 310–311.
32. Berkeley, p. 133.
33. Morgan, p. 266.
34. Hamilton, p. 78.
35. Berkeley, pp. 133–134.
36. Morgan, p. 267.
37. Oates, p. 331.
38. Hamilton, pp. 78–79.
39. Morgan, p. 268.
40. Allan Nevins, *The War for the Union* [Vol. 4] *The Organized War to Victory 1864–1865* (New York: Charles Scribner and Sons, 1971), pp. 337–338.
41. Oates, p. 311.
42. Berkeley, p. 134.
43. Hamilton, p. 80.
44. Shotwell, pp. 193–194.
45. Berkeley, p. 136.
46. Shotwell, p. 195.
47. Berkeley, p. 136.
48. Hamilton, pp. 80–81.
49. Shotwell, pp. 195–197.
50. Hamilton, p. 81; *O.R.*, Series II, Vol. 8, p. 569.
51. Dan M. Byrd, Jr., unpublished manuscript at Fort Delaware Society Library, p. 405.
52. Jack Lewis, *Bay and River Delaware* (Bridgeview: Jack Lewis, 1980), p. 119.
53. Hamilton, p. 82.
54. Shotwell, pp. 200–201.
55. Byrd, p. 2.
56. Henry Kyd Douglas, *I Rode with Stonewall* (Chapel Hill: University of North Carolina Press, 1940), pp. 348–349.
57. *O.R.*, Series II, Vol. 8, p. 727.
58. Wilson, *Fort Delaware*, pp. 27–30.

Bibliography

Books

Anderson, Dwight, and Nancy Scott. *The Generals: Ulysses S. Grant and Robert E. Lee.* New York: Alfred A. Knopf, 1988.

Andrews, Matthew Page, ed. *The Women of the South in War Times.* Baltimore: The Norman, Remington Co., 1920.

Axelrod, Alan. *The Complete Idiot's Guide to the Civil War.* New York: Alpha Books, 1998.

Barrett, John G., ed. *Yankee Rebel: The Civil War Journal of Edmund De Witt Patterson.* Chapel Hill: University of North Carolina Press, 1966.

Barzina, Decimus et Ultimus. *The Adventures of a Prisoner of War 1863–1864.* Ed. by R. Henderson Shuffer. Austin: University of Texas Press, 1964.

Basler, Roy P., ed. *The Collected Works of Abraham Lincoln.* New Brunswick, N.J.: Rutgers University Press, 1955.

Baylor, George. *Bull Run to Bull Run or Four Years in the Army of Northern Virginia (Containing a Detailed Account of the Career and Adventures of the Baylor Light Horse, Co. B, 12th Virginia Cavalry, C.S.A., with Leaves from My Scrapbook).* Washington, D.C.: Zenger Pub. Co., 1900; reprint, 1983.

Bosang, James N. *Memoirs of a Pulaski Veteran of the Stonewall Brigade, 1861–1865.* Pulaski, Va.: 1912.

Bowen, T.H. *The Way It Used to Be.* Vol. 3, Salem: Salem County Cultural and Heritage Commission, 1977.

Brogden, Henry Hall. *An Account of His Experiences During the War.* Copy at Salem County Historical Society.

Brooks, Stewart. *Civil War Medicine.* Springfield: Charles C. Thomas Pub., 1966.

Buell, Thomas B. *The Warrior Generals: Combat Leadership in the Civil War.* New York: Crown Pub., 1997.

Burr, Anna Robeson, ed. *Weir Mitchell: His Life and Letters.* New York: Duffield and Co., 1929.

Byrd, Dan M., Jr. Manuscript in Fort Delaware Society Library.

Catton, Bruce. *Never Call Retreat.* Garden City, N.Y.: Doubleday and Co., 1965.

Chaille-Long, Charles. *My Life in Four Continents.* 1912.

Davis, Burke. *The Civil War: Strange and Fascinating Facts.* New York: The Fairfox Press, 1982.

Davis, Curtis Carroll, ed. *Belle Boyd in Camp and Prison.* Thomas Yoseloff, 1968.

Davis, Kenneth C. *Don't Know Much About the Civil War.* New York: W. Morrow and Co., 1996.

Denney, Robert E. *Civil War Prisons and Escapes: A Day by Day Chronicle.* New York: Stirling Pub. Co., 1993.

The Diagram Group. *The Little Giant Encyclopedia of Card Games.* New York: Sterling Pub. Co., 1995.

Dickinson, Henry C. *Diary of Capt. Henry C. Dickinson, C.S.A.* Copy at Fort Delaware Society Library.

Douglas, Henry Kyd. *I Rode with Stonewall*. Chapel Hill: University of North Carolina Press, 1940.

Duke, Basil. *Reminiscences of Gen. Basil W. Duke, C.S.A.* 1911; reprint, Freeport, N.Y.: Books for Libraries Press, 1969.

Fort Delaware Notes. Wilmington, December 1954.

Fort Delaware Notes. Wilmington, December 1958.

Fort Delaware Notes. Wilmington, January 1962.

Garrison, Webb. *Civil War Curiosities*. Nashville: Rutledge Hill Press, 1994.

Hale, Laura Virginia. *Four Valiant Years in the Lower Shenandoah Valley 1861–1865*. Strasburg, Va.: Shenandoah Pub. House, 1968.

Halsey, Arthur Jr. *Who Fired the First Shot? and other untold stories of the Civil War*. New York: Hawthorn Books, 1963.

Hamilton, J.C., and Rebecca Cameron, eds. *The Papers of Randolph Abbott Shotwell*. Vol. II. Raleigh: North Carolina Historical Commission, 1931.

Hancock, Harold Bell. *Delaware During the Civil War: A Political History*. Wilmington: The Historical Society of Delaware, 1961.

Handy, Isaac W.K., D.D. *United States Bonds; or Duress by Federal Authority: A Journal of Current Events During an Imprisonment of Fifteen Months, at Fort Delaware*. Baltimore: Turnbull Bros, 1874.

Hesseltine, William Best. *Civil War Prisons: A Study in War Psychology*. New York: Frederick Ungar Pub. Co., 1930.

Hindes, Ruthanna, ed. *Fort Delaware Notes*. Wilmington, February 1958.

Horsman, Reginald. *The Causes of the War of 1812*. New York: Octagon Books, Div. of Farrar, Straus, and Giroux Inc., 1962.

Howard, McHenry. *Recollections of a Maryland Confederate Soldier and Staff Officer under Johnson, Jackson, and Lee* (Introduction, Corrections, and Notes by James I. Robertson, Jr.) Dayton, O.: Press of Morningside Bookshop, 1975. Original printing Williams and Wilkins Co., Baltimore, 1914.

Jamison, Jocelyn. *Fort Delaware Notes*. February 1996.

Kelly, C. Brian, and Ingrid Sayer-Kelly. *Best Little Stories from the Civil War*. Nashville: Cumberland House, 1994.

Lang, J. Stephen. *The Complete Book of Confederate Trivia*. U.S.A.: Bund Street Press, 1996.

Lewis, Jack. *Bay and River Delaware*. Bridgeville, Del.: Jack Lewis, 1980.

Long, E.B., with Barbara Long. *The Civil War Day by Day: An Almanac 1861–1865*. Garden City, N.Y.: Doubleday and Co., 1971.

Marshall, John A. *American Bastille: A History of the Illegal Arrests and Imprisonment of American Citizens during the Late Civil War*. Philadelphia: Thomas W. Hartley, 1869; reprint, 1970.

McCown, James L. *Memoirs of James L. McCown, Co. K, 5th Virginia Infantry, Stonewall Brigade, April 2, 1864–August 4, 1864*. Copy at Fort Delaware Society.

McCutcheon, Marc. *The Writer's Guide to Everyday Life in the 1800's*. Cincinnati: Writer's Digest Books, 1993.

McFeely, Mary Drake, and William S. McFeely, eds. *Ulysses S. Grant: Memoirs and Selected Letters*. New York: The Library of America, 1990.

McMichael, Capt. J.R. *Diary 1864–65*. Unpublished manuscript in the Fort Delaware Society Library.

McPherson, James M. *Battle Cry of Freedom*. New York: Oxford University Press, 1988.

Mitchell, Reid. *Civil War Soldiers*. New York: Penguin Books, 1988.

Morgan, William H. *Personal Reminiscences of the War of 1861–65*. Freeport, N.Y.: Books for Libraries Press, 1911; reprint 1971.

Morton, James St. Clair. *Memoir of the Life and Services of Captain and Brevet Major John Sanders of the Corps of Engineers*. Pittsburgh: W.S. Haven, 1861.

Murray, J. Ogden. *The Immortal Six Hundred: A Story of Cruelty to Confederate Prisoners of War*. Winchester, Va.: Eddy Press Corp., 1905.

Nevins, Allan. *The War for the Union* [Vol. IV] *The Organized War to Victory 1864–1865*. New York: Charles Scribner's Sons, 1971.

Oates, Dan, ed. *Hanging Rock Rebel*. Shippenburg: Burd St. Press, 1994.

Petition to President Lincoln, copy of. June 23, 1862. Fort Delaware Society Library.

Pinkowski, Edward. *Pills, Pen, and Politics: The Story of Gen. Leon Jastremski 1843–1907*. Wilmington: Capt. Stanislaus Mlotkowski Memorial Brigade Society, 1974.

Randall, J.G., and David Donald. *The Civil War and Reconstruction*. Lexington: D.C. Heath and Co., 1969.

Rivenbark, Sgt. Charles W. *Two Years at Fort Delaware (North Carolina Troops 1861–1865)*. Charlotte, N.C.: April 9, 1901.

Runge, William H., ed. *Four Years in the Confederate Artillery, The Diary of Private Henry Robinson Berkeley*. Chapel Hill: University of North Carolina Press, 1961.

Sears, Stephen W. *George B. McClellan: The Young Napoleon*. New York: Ticknor and Fields, 1988.

Stagg, J.C.A. *Mr. Madison's War: Politics, Diplomacy, and Warfare in the Early American Republic, 1783–1832*. Princeton, N.J.: Princeton University Press, 1983.

Thomas, Benjamin P., and Harold M. Hyman. *Stanton: The Life and Times of Lincoln's Secretary of War*. New York: Alfred A. Knoff, 1962.

Varhola, Michael J. *Everyday Life During the Civil War*. Cincinnati: Writer's Digest Books, 1999.

Wailes, Sidney, letter from, copy of. August 24, 1863. Fort Delaware Society Library.

Wailes, Sidney, letter from, copy of. September 20, 1863. Fort Delaware Society Library.

Wert, Jeffry D. *Mosby's Rangers.* New York: Simon and Schuster, 1990.

Wiley, Bell Irwin. *The Life of Johnny Reb: The Common Soldier of the Confederacy.* New York: The Bobbs-Merrill Co. Pub., 1943.

Wilkinson, Norman B. *The Brandywine Home Front During the Civil War 1861–1965.* Wilmington: Kaumagraph Co., 1966.

Whitten, Phyllis O., comp. *Samuel Fogg 1625–1672 — His Ancestors and Descendants, Vol. 2., Appendix R.* Washington, D.C.: Columbia Planograph Co., 1976.

Wilson, W. Emerson, ed. *A Fort Delaware Journal: The Diary of a Yankee Private A.J. Hamilton 1862–65.* Wilmington: Fort Delaware Society, 1981.

_____. *Fort Delaware.* Newark, Del.: University of Delaware Press, 1957.

_____. *General M. Jeff Thompson in Fort Delaware.* Wilmington: The Fort Delaware Society, 1972.

_____. *The Story of Fort Delaware.* Ed. William P. Frank. Wilmington, Del.: Wilmington Printing Co., 1955.

Government Publications

Alger, Russell A., Secretary of War and Director of Book. Written by Col. Fred E. Ainsworth U.S.A., Leslie J. Perry and Joseph W. Kirkley (Civilian Experts). *The War of the Rebellion: A Compilation of the Official Records of the Union and Confederate Armies.* Washington, D.C.: Government Printing Office, 1899.

The Coast Defense Study Groups Journal. November 1995.

Federal Writers Project of the Works Progress Administration. *Delaware: A Guide to the First State.* Copy in the Fort Delaware Society Library, 1938.

_____. "Stories of New Jersey: A Confederate Shrine in New Jersey." *School Bulletin # 22,* Newark, N.J., April 1937.

Snyder, Frank E., and Brian H. Guss. *The District: A History of the Philadelphia District U.S. Army Corps of Engineers 1866–1971.* U.S. Army Engineer District Philadelphia, January 1974.

Spencer, Surgeon W.C. *U.S. Army, Circular #4, Surgeon General's Office.* December 1870. Copy at Salem County Historical Society Library.

U.S. Sanitary Commission. *A Narrative of Privations and Sufferings of U.S. Officers and Soldiers While Prisoners of War in the South and the Treatment of Rebel Prisoners in the North.* 1864.

Wall, Garrett D., opinion of. *Brief of Title: Pea Patch Island.* Fort Delaware Society Library.

Newspapers

Cottrell, Alden T. Newspaper clipping from April 12, 1964 at the Salem County Historical Society Library.

Courier Post. Sunday, September 25, 1988.

New York Times, Thursday, March 31, 1864.

_____. Tuesday, July 12, 1864.

_____. Wednesday, August 10, 1864.

_____. Monday, August 14, 1864.

_____. Wednesday, August 17, 1864.

_____. Monday April 10, 1865.

Philadelphia Forum. October 1950.

Salem Standard and Jerseyman. June 25, 1953.

Salem Sunbeam. Friday, October 2, 1925.

Sampler. Wednesday, April 2, 1986.

Stonewall Register. April 1, 1865. Handwritten copy at the Fort Delaware Society Library.

Sunbeam. June 2, 1977.

Today's Sunbeam. June 4, 1985.

_____. July 24, 1986.

_____. Sunday, April 3, 1989.

_____. September 7, 1989.

_____. Unpublished article in the Fort Delaware Society Library.

Vanneman, William B. "Golden Days." Newspaper clipping from the Salem County Historical Society Library.

Wilmington Morning News. May 31, 1956.

Videos

Bell, C. Jeanenne G.G. *The Antique and Collectable Jewelry Video Series* [Vol. 1] *Victorian Jewelry Circa 1837–1901.* Pittsburgh: Antique Images Inc., 1994.

Index